Jeep Wrangler

MW00333903
629.2222 ACK
Ackerson, Robert C.
Jeep Wrangler /
NO LONGER THE PROPERTY OF
LONGMONT PUBLIC LIBRARY
39.95

SpeedPro Series
4-Cylinder Engine - How to Blueprint & Build a Short Block for High Performance by Des Hammill
Alfa Romeo DOHC High-performance Manual (SpeedPro) by Jim Kartalamakis
Alfa Romeo Twin Cam Engines - How to Power Tune by Jim Kartalamakis
Alfa Romeo V6 Engine High-perfomance Manual (SpeedPro) by Jim Kartalamakis
BMC 998cc A-Series Engine - How to Power Tune by Des Hammill
The 1275cc A-Series High performance Manual (SpeedPro) by Des Hammill
Camshafts - How to Choose & Time them for Maximum Power by Des Hammill
Cylinder Heads - How to Build, Modify & Power Tune Updated & Revised Edition by Peter Burgess
Distributor-type Ignition Systems - How to Build & Power Tune by Des Hammill
Fast Road Car - How to Plan and Build New Edition by Daniel Stapleton
Ford SOHC 'Pinto' & Sierra Cosworth DOHC Engines - How to Power Tune Updated & Enlarged Edition by Des Hammill
Ford V8 - How to Power Tune Small Block Engines by Des Hammill
Harley-Davidson Evolution Engines - How to Build & Power Tune by Des Hammill
Holley Carburetors - How to Build & Power Tune New Edition by Des Hammill
Jaguar XK Engines - How to Power Tune New Edition by Des Hammill
MG Midget & Austin-Healey Sprite - How to Power Tune Updated Edition by Daniel Stapleton
MGB 4-Cylinder Engine - How to Power Tune by Peter Burgess
MGB V8 Power - Third Edition by Roger Williams
MGB, MGC & MGB V8 - How to Improve by Roger Williams
Mini Engines - How to Power Tune on a Small Budget 2nd Edition by Des Hammill
Motorsport - Getting Started in by SS Collins
Nitrous Oxide by Trevor Langfield
Rover V8 Engines - How to Power Tune by Des Hammill
Sportscar/Kitcar Suspension & Brakes - How to Build & Modify Enlarged & Updated 2nd Edition by Des Hammill
SU Carburettors - How to Build & Modify for High Performance by Des Hammill
Suzuki 4WD by John Richardson
Tiger Avon Sportscar - How to Build Your Own Updated & Revised 2nd Edition by Jim Dudley
TR2, 3 & TR4 - How to Improve by Roger Williams
TR5, 250 & TR6 - How to Improve by Roger Williams
V8 Engine - How to Build a Short Block for High Performance by Des Hammill
Volkswagen Beetle Suspension, Brakes & Chassis - How to Modify for High Performance by James Hale
Volkswagen Bus Suspension, Brakes & Chassis - How to Modify for High Performance by James Hale
Weber DCOE & Dellorto DHLA Carburetors - How to Build & Power Tune 3rd Edition by Des Hammill

Those were the days ... Series
Alpine Rallies by Martin Pfundner
Austerity Motoring by Malcolm Bobbitt
Brighton National Speed Trials by Tony Gardiner
British Police Cars by Nick Walker
Crystal Palace by SS Collins
Dune Buggy Phenomenon by James Hale
Dune Buggy Phenomenon Volume 2 by James Hale
Motor Racing at Brands Hatch in the Seventies by Chas Parker
Motor Racing at Goodwood in the Sixties by Tony Gardiner
Three Wheelers by Malcolm Bobbitt

Enthusiast's Restoration Manual Series
Citroën 2CV, How to Restore by Lindsay Porter
Classic Car Body Work, How to Restore by Martin Thaddeus
Classic Cars, How to Paint by Martin Thaddeus
Reliant Regal, How to Restore by Elvis Payne
Triumph TR2/3/3A, How to Restore by Roger Williams
Triumph TR4/4A, How to Restore by Roger Williams
Triumph TR5/250 & 6, How to Restore by Roger Williams
Triumph TR7/8, How to Restore by Roger Williams
Volkswagen Beetle, How to Restore by Jim Tyler
Yamaha FS1-E, How to Restore by John Watts

Essential Buyer's Guide Series
Alfa GT Buyer's Guide by Keith Booker
Alfa Romeo Spider by Keith Booker & Jim Talbott
VW Bus Buyer's Guide by Richard Copping and Ken Cservenka
Jaguar E-Type Essential Buyer's Guide
MGB Essential Buyer's Guide
Porsche 928 Buyer's Guide by David Hemmings
Triumph TR6 Essential Buyer's Guide
VW Beetle Buyer's Guide by Ken Cservenka & Richard Copping

Auto-Graphics Series
Fiat & Abarth by Andrea & David Sparrow
Jaguar MkII by Andrea & David Sparrow
Lambretta LI by Andrea & David Sparrow

General
1½-litre GP Racing 1961-1965 by MJP Whitelock
AC Two-litre Saloons & Buckland Sportscars by Leo Archibald
Alfa Romeo Giulia Coupé GT & GTA by John Tipler
Alfa Tipo 33 by Ed McDonough & Peter Collins
American Ford in Miniature by Randall Olson
Anatomy of the Works Minis by Brian Moylan
Armstrong-Siddeley by Bill Smith
Autodrome by SS Collins & Gavin Ireland
Automotive A-Z, Lane's Dictionary of Automotive Terms by Keith Lane
Automotive Mascots by David Kay & Lynda Springate
Bahamas Speed Weeks, The by Terry O'Neil
Bentley Continental, Corniche and Azure by Martin Bennett
BMCs Competitions Department Secrets by Stuart Turner, Marcus Chambers & Peter Browning
BMW 5-Series by Marc Cranswick
BMW Z-Cars by James Taylor
British 250cc Racing Motorcycles by Chris Pereira
British Cars, The Complete Catalogue of, 1895-1975 by David Culshaw & Peter Horrobin
Bugatti Type 40 by Barrie Price
Bugatti 46/50 Updated Edition by Barrie Price
Bugatti 57 2nd Edition by Barrie Price
Building a Dune Buggy - The Essential Manual by Paul Shakespeare
Caravans, The Illustrated History 1919-1959 by Andrew Jenkinson
Caravans, The Illustrated History from 1960 by Andrew Jenkinson
Chrysler 300 - America's Most Powerful Car 2nd Edition by Robert Ackerson
Citroën DS by Malcolm Bobbitt
Cobra - The Real Thing! by Trevor Legate
Cortina - Ford's Bestseller by Graham Robson
Coventry Climax Racing Engines by Des Hammill
Daimler SP250 'Dart' by Brian Long
Datsun Fairlady Roadster to 280ZX - The Z-car Story by Brian Long
Ducati 750 Bible, The by Ian Falloon
Dune Buggy Files by James Hale
Dune Buggy Handbook by James Hale
Ferrari Dino - The V6 Ferrari by Brian Long
Fiat & Abarth 124 Spider & Coupé by John Tipler
Fiat & Abarth 500 & 600 2nd edition by Malcolm Bobbitt
Ford F100/F150 Pick-up 1948-1996 by Robert Ackerson
Ford F150 1997-2005 by Robert Ackerson
Ford GT40 by Trevor Legate
Ford Model Y by Sam Roberts
Ford Thunderbird by Brian Long
Funky Mopeds by Richard Skelton
Honda NSX by Brian Long
Jaguar, The Rise of by Barrie Price
Jaguar XJ-S by Brian Long
Jeep CJ by Robert Ackerson
Jeep Wrangler by Robert Ackerson
Karmann-Ghia Coupé & Convertible by Malcolm Bobbitt
Land Rover, The Half-Ton Military by Mark Cook
Lea-Francis Story, The by Barrie Price
Lexus Story, The by Brian Long
Lola - The Illustrated History (1957-1977) by John Starkey
Lola - All The Sports Racing & Single-Seater Racing Cars 1978-1997 by John Starkey
Lola T70 - The Racing History & Individual Chassis Record 3rd Edition by John Starkey
Lotus 49 by Michael Oliver
Marketingmobiles, The Wonderful Wacky World of by James Hale
Mazda MX-5/Miata 1.6 Enthusiast's Workshop Manual by Rod Grainger & Pete Shoemark
Mazda MX-5/Miata 1.8 Enthusiast's Workshop Manual by Rod Grainger & Pete Shoemark
Mazda MX-5 (& Eunos Roadster) - The World's Favourite Sportscar by Brian Long
Mazda MX-5 Miata Roadster by Brian Long
MGA by John Price Williams
MGB & MGB GT - Expert Guide (Auto-Doc Series) by Roger Williams
Micro Caravans by Andrew Jenkinson
Mini Cooper - The Real Thing! by John Tipler
Mitsubishi Lancer Evo by Brian Long
Motor Racing Reflections by Anthony Carter
Motorhomes, The Illustrated History by Andrew Jenkinson
Motorsport in colour, 1950s by Martyn Wainwright
MR2 - Toyota's Mid-engined Sports Car by Brian Long
Nissan 300ZX & 350Z - The Z-Car Story by Brian Long
Pass the Theory and Practical Driving Tests by Clive Gibson & Gavin Hoole
Pontiac Firebird by Marc Cranswick
Porsche Boxster by Brian Long
Porsche 356 by Brian Long
Porsche 911 Carrera - The Last of the Evolution by Tony Corlett
Porsche 911R, RS & RSR, 4th Edition by John Starkey
Porsche 911 – The Definitive History 1963-1971 by Brian Long
Porsche 911 – The Definitive History 1971-1977 by Brian Long
Porsche 911 – The Definitive History 1977-1987 by Brian Long
Porsche 911 – The Definitive History 1987-1997 by Brian Long
Porsche 911 – The Definitive History 1997-2004 by Brian Long
Porsche 911SC Companion by Adrian Streather
Porsche 914 The Definitive History Of The Road & Competition Cars by Brian Long
Porsche 924 by Brian Long
Porsche 944 by Brian Long
Porsche 993 'King of Porsche' - The Essential Companion by Adrian Streather
RAC Rally Action by Tony Gardiner
Rolls-Royce Silver Shadow/Bentley T Series Corniche & Camargue Revised & Enlarged Edition by Malcolm Bobbitt
Rolls-Royce Silver Spirit, Silver Spur & Bentley Mulsanne 2nd Edition by Malcolm Bobbitt
Rolls-Royce Silver Wraith, Dawn & Cloud/Bentley MkVI, R & S Series by Martyn Nutland
RX-7 - Mazda's Rotary Engine Sportscar (updated & revised new edition) by Brian Long
Singer Story: Cars, Commercial Vehicles, Bicycles & Motorcycles by Kevin Atkinson
SM - Citroën's Maserati-engined Supercar by by Brian Long
Subaru Impreza 2nd edition by Brian Long
Taxi! The Story of the 'London' Taxicab by Malcolm Bobbitt
Triumph Motorcycles & the Meriden Factory by Hughie Hancox
Triumph Speed Twin & Thunderbird Bible by Harry Woolridge
Triumph Tiger Cub Bible by Mike Estall
Triumph Trophy Bible by Harry Woolridge
Triumph TR6 by William Kimberley
Turner's Triumphs, Edward Turner & his Triumph Motorcycles by Jeff Clew
Velocette Motorcycles - MSS to Thruxton Updated & Revised Edition by Rod Burris
Volkswagen Bus or Van to Camper, How to Convert by Lindsay Porter
Volkswagens of the World by Simon Glen
VW Beetle Cabriolet by Malcolm Bobbitt
VW Beetle - The Car of the 20th Century by Richard Copping
VW Bus - 40 years of Splitties, Bays & Wedges by Richard Copping
VW Bus, Camper, Van, Pickup by Malcolm Bobbitt
VW Golf by Richard Copping & Ken Cservenka
VW - The air-cooled era by Richard Copping
Works Rally Mechanic by Brian Moylan

First published in December 2005 by Veloce Publishing Limited, 33 Trinity Street, Dorchester DT1 1TT, England. Fax 01305 268864/e-mail info@veloce.co.uk/web www.veloce.co.uk orwww.velocebooks.com
ISBN 10: 1-904788-97-1. ISBN 13: 978-1-904788-97-3. UPC 36847-00397-5
© Robert Ackerson and Veloce Publishing 2005. All rights reserved. With the exception of quoting brief passages for the purpose of review, no part of this publication may be recorded, reproduced or transmitted by any means, including photocopying, without the written permission of Veloce Publishing Ltd. Throughout this book logos, model names and designations, etc, have been used for the purposes of identification, illustration and decoration. Such names are the property of the trademark holder as this is not an official publication.

Readers with ideas for automotive books, or books on other transport or related hobby subjects, are invited to write to the editorial director of Veloce Publishing at the above address.
British Library Cataloguing in Publication Data - A catalogue record for this book is available from the British Library. Typesetting, design and page make-up all by Veloce Publishing Ltd on Apple Mac.
Printed in India by Replika Press.

Jeep Wrangler

Robert Ackerson

VELOCE PUBLISHING
THE PUBLISHER OF FINE AUTOMOTIVE BOOKS

LONGMONT PUBLIC LIBRARY
LONGMONT, COLORADO

CONTENTS

A 1987 Wrangler Laredo in Olympic White with Silver striping. The front bumper extensions, tow hooks and chrome front bumper, grille panel, and headlamp bezels were included in the Laredo Package. (Author's collection)

to coast to ensure that at least one service technician from each dealership has received specialized training on the Wrangler prior to introduction."

Jocou explained that the instructors at each session "can train up to twelve service technicians at each two-day session, which means that every dealership can be covered in the space of a month". He also noted that Wranglers would not be shipped to dealerships until at least one of their technicians had participated in the training program.

Along with this program, AMC also added millions of dollars worth of parts inventory at its National Parts Distribution Center and regional parts warehouses in the US and Canada to ensure dealers access to Wrangler parts prior to its introduction.

"Our special training program would be of little help without having parts readily accessible," Jocou said, "so we are stocking the regional warehouses with the most critical Wrangler parts and are prepared to expedite other parts from the master warehouse.

"We have invested heavily in service training and in systems to improve parts distribution to make sure that Jeep Wrangler buyers get quality service and quality handling of parts."

For three consecutive years Jeep vehicles had received '4WD Vehicle of the Year' awards from major

A 1987 Wrangler with the Sport Decor Package. The striping and 'Wrangler' lettering were available in Silver or Tan. This example has the 15 x 7in aluminum wheels. (Author's collection)

The 1987 Base model Wrangler was equipped with four P215/75R Goodyear Wrangler BSW tires. The halogen fog lamps seen on this Wrangler were optional for both the Base and Laredo models. All had a padded roll bar and side bars as standard. (Author's collection)

"a virtually impassable assortment of huge rocks and boulders on an off-road course through the mountainous terrains of northern California."

Dedeurwaerder anticipated the Wrangler playing a major role in AMC's goal of setting back-to-sales records. "Our sales potential climbs with each new addition to the Jeep line-up", he said. "We have introduced new compact sports utility wagons and mid-size trucks the past two years. Now we have Wrangler as the newest addition to the Jeep family. We are confident it will help to increase Jeep's sales share in the four-wheel drive market."

Outwardly resembling the CJ-7, the Wrangler, which was formally announced on May 13, 1986, was based on a new set of design parameters. "The product philosophy behind the two vehicles," Castaing explained, "is completely different. Our market research told us that in recent years customers were using these types of vehicles more for personal transportation, as well as for recreational activities.

"For that reason we learned that in any future purchase consideration they would look for everyday comfort and those special amenities that vehicles such as the CJ-7 didn't provide."

As recently as 1978, only 17 per cent of vehicle buyers in the Wrangler's class used them for everyday transportation. By 1986 this figure had risen to 95 per cent. While 37 per cent of owners in 1978 said they frequently engaged in off-roading activities; only 7 per cent did so in 1986, however, this didn't mean that off-road performance wouldn't be important to Wrangler owners since 80 per cent reported some off-road usage.

As a result of these factors the Wrangler's designers and engineers were assigned four basic product objectives when design work began on what became the 1987 Wrangler.

First, they were asked to develop a completely new, small, sport utility vehicle. Second, it had to be a modern, open-design vehicle. Third, it was to have the traditional Jeep characteristic of rugged, durable, four-wheel drive capability. Finally, the Wrangler was envisioned as a sophisticated vehicle for its class with a modern exterior and interior appearance, smooth highway riding performance, easy rear access and convenient soft top fit, function and sealing, and the latest in corrosion protection.

The Wrangler's development lasted nearly five years, with its engineering production design program reaching the 'hands-on' testing stage in late 1983. At that time twelve 'mechanical mule' prototypes (incorporating the new chassis and power trains) had been constructed. They were used for design feasibility and durability testing.

In the spring of 1984, another nine 'skin' prototypes with the Wrangler's new sheet metal exterior were built. They were tested extensively for durability and reliability.

Concurrently, an assortment of packaging bucks (pre-production, hand-made interior assemblies) were assembled to finalize such items as design clearances, fit/function of the tops, interior instrumentation and creature comforts. In total, nearly 600,000 test miles were accumulated in the various stages of the Wrangler's engineering development.

To make certain that its dealers were prepared to meet the needs and expectations of Wrangler owners, AMC instituted a major training program for its service technicians prior to the Wrangler's May 1986 introduction. The training sessions began on April 1 at 14 company centers and 22 vocational school locations in the US and Canada. Supervising this operation was AMC's Managing Director of Parts and Service Operations, Pierre Jocou. "The Jeep Wrangler is new from the ground up," he said, "so we are providing intensive training courses from coast

1 THE NEW JEEP WRANGLER – THE POSSIBILITIES ARE ENDLESS

When Joseph Cappy, American Motors' Executive Vice President of Operations, announced on November 27, 1985 that production of the CJ Jeep would end early in 1986 (for calendar year 1986, a total of 18,414 CJ Jeeps were built), he remarked that "completion of CJ production will signal an end of a very important era in Jeep history." The CJ's popularity, along with its predecessor's achievements in World War II, had given the Jeep name virtually universal recognition. AMC reported that two polls taken in 1980, one in the US and the other in Japan, had concluded that "Jeep was the most popular and memorable vehicle in the world".

The Jeep's international appeal, based initially on its role in World War II, had been further stimulated by four decades of civilian production and extremely effective promotion of its virtues and versatility. It began in 1945 with the 'If you have tough jobs, get a Jeep' advertising theme. In the mid-sixties the message was 'The original Jeep – a work and hobby horse'. In 1973 came 'Jeep – Toughest 4-letter word on wheels'. Five years later Jeep was telling the world that 'We wrote the book on four-wheel drive'. Then, in 1984, came 'Only in a Jeep'.

Confident that the CJ's successor, the Wrangler, would get off to a solid start, Jose J Dedeurwaerder, President and Chief Executive Officer of American Motors, said on January 3, 1987 that "the debut of the Wrangler couldn't come at a better time because interest in Jeep is at an all-time high."

Building upon AMC's characterization of the Wrangler, as 'new-from-the ground', Francois A Castaing, AMC Vice President of Product Engineering, reported that the "Jeep Wrangler combines a classic, open air design with state-of-the-art, four-wheel drive engineering, including 'shift-on-the-fly' capability and a tuned, smooth-ride suspension. This new generation of small sport utility vehicles will offer very comfortable and enjoyable on-highway driving and superb off-road capability."

Underscoring the latter point was the Wrangler's successful traversing of the Rubicon Trail, described by AMC as

American Motors introduced the 1987 Wrangler on May 13, 1986. Joining a Wrangler Laredo (upper left) in this photo is a Base model with the Sport Decor option. The Laredo package included five 15 x 7in, 5-bolt, Sport, aluminum wheels. As seen here, they were optionally available for the Base Wrangler. Also shown are the hood and lower body striping and the P215/ 75R21015 All-Terrain OWL tires included in the Sport Decor Package. (Author's collection)

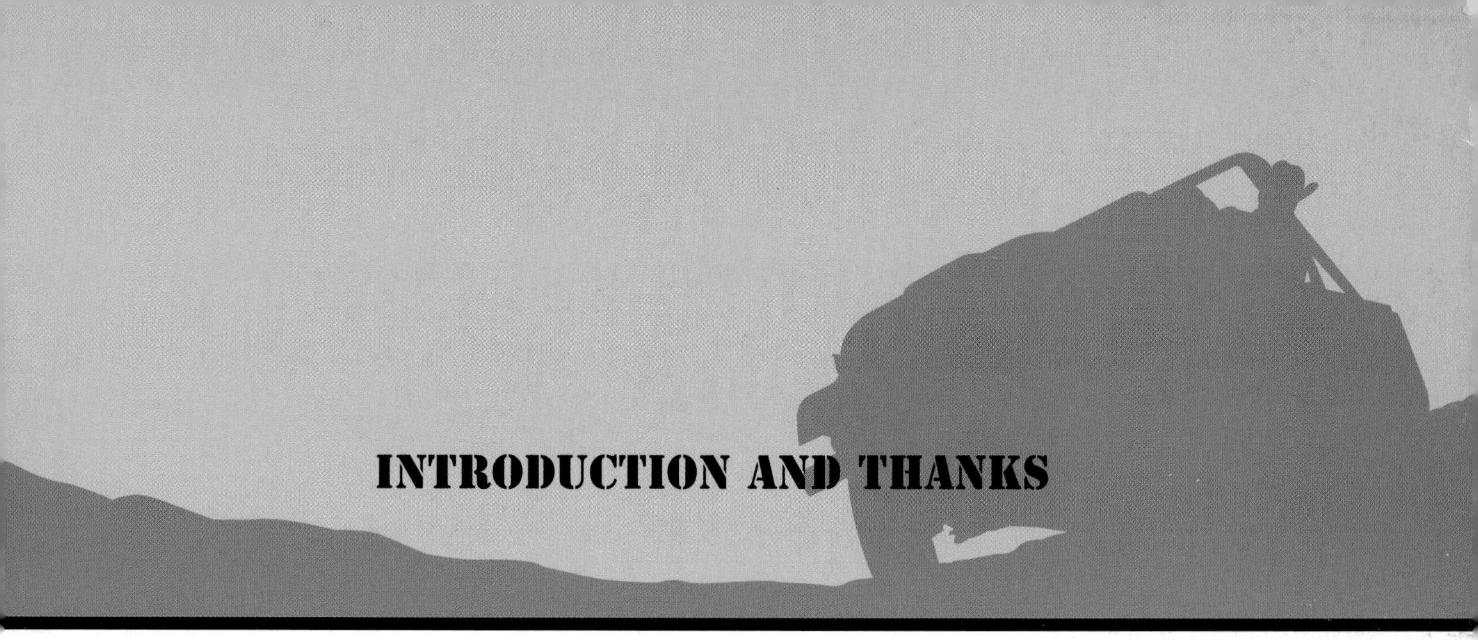

INTRODUCTION AND THANKS

When the Wrangler replaced the CJ-7 in 1987, there were some CJ enthusiasts who mourned its passing in a manner not unlike that of those Model T loyalists when they faced its replacement with the 1928 Model A. But in 1987, as in 1928, the world didn't come to an end when a transportation legend reached the end of its trail.

This was due in large part to the care American Motors took to maintain in the Wrangler all that was great in its predecessors and improve upon the best features of the design. The result was a Jeep that, with the exception of some minor missteps (such as its rectangular headlights), was quickly recognized as a Jeep worthy of its heritage.

Whereas the CJ's military origin predestined it, in the early years of its production life, to be valued primarily for its utility and adaptability to a wide range of work environments, the Wrangler arrived at a time when the CJ has evolved into a popular recreational vehicle. But that didn't mean the CJ had gone soft – the Wrangler was no less capable, and the latest Rubicon models may very well be the best-yet of the breed.

As with the first volume in this Jeep series, dealing with the history of the CJ models, my good friend Bruce Phillips was a major contributor. In the case of the present volume, his ownership experiences with an early 4-cylinder Wrangler and its successor, a 2004 Rubicon, provided the author with invaluable tales of off-road adventures proving that the latest Wrangler is as good a 4x4 as any and better than most. If racing improves the breed, then going off-road does the job even better.

Robert C Ackerson
Brainards Forge, New York

The Laredo's standard hard top, which was optional for the Base model, was a new design for 1987. The side and rear windows had flush-fitting tinted glass. Styled side vents improved interior airflow. The chrome bumperettes were also included in the Laredo Package. (Author's collection)

off-road publications in the United States and Europe. Vice President Francois A Castaing was confident the Wrangler would maintain this trend. "We believe," he remarked, "that the Wrangler will be a worthy and popular addition to the Jeep vehicle line-up."

One AMC press release was even more emphatic about the Wrangler's destiny, asserting that the Wrangler would be "taking its place beside the elite of the four-wheel drive community ... the debut of the Wrangler will be yet another milestone in a long list of historic Jeep vehicles."

This chronological list included these models:

1946 – CJ-2A
1946 – Model 463 Station Wagon
1947 – Panel Delivery and Pickup Trucks
1949 – Jeepster
1954 – CJ-5
1963 – Wagoneer
1967 – Jeepster models
1972 – Hard top CJ-5
1973 – Quadra-Trac
1974 – Cherokee
1976 – CJ-7
1984 – down-sized Wagoneer and Cherokee
1985 – 2WD Cherokee
1986 – Comanche pickup

Linking the Wrangler with these models, as well as the other members of the 1987 Jeep vehicle line-up, was a common grille design that was universally recognized as the Jeep's prime design cachet. Robert C Nixon, Director of Exterior Design for American Motors, noted that "the vertical grille is like a trademark for Jeep vehicles. It's a badge that stands for ruggedness and durability.

"We've made some subtle changes in the grille for the Wrangler. The vertical design peaks about three quarters from the top and then slopes slightly inward. But there's still no mistaking the Jeep look."

In terms of basic dimensions (if not in price) the Wrangler and CJ-7 were quite similar:

Model	Wrangler	CJ-7
Base price:	$9899	$7500
Wheelbase:	93.4in	93.4in
Overall length:	153.2in	152.0in
Overall width:	65.3in	66.0in
Front tread:	55.8in	58.0in
Rear tread	55.1in	58.0in
Front headroom:	40.0in	39.9in
Rear headroom:	40.5in	39.6in
Front legroom:	39.5in	39.1in
Rear legroom:	35.0in	35.0in

With the exception of doors and end gate, the Wrangler, from the firewall back, retained the CJ's body work. All front-end sheet metal ahead of the cowl was new, including hood, fenders, splash apron and the radiator grille guard. The use of rectangular headlights and the positioning of the parking lights at the outer edges of the grille gave the Wrangler what Nixon defined as a "brawny" appearance. Adding to this image were the standard flexible wheel flares and the hood's beveled edges

Incorporated into the Wrangler's exterior body sides were splash shields extending approximately 10 inches back from the front fenders. As an option, a full-length splash shield running from the front to the rear fender and including a built-in body side step was available.

The Wrangler's exterior body panels were constructed of galvanized steel. All body surfaces received a multi-part corrosion-resistant treatment that began with a phosphate cleaning bath and included priming and sealing prior to the paint application. Body components such as the hood, windshield frame, front fenders, doors and tailgate were fully immersed in a dip tank which electrostatically bound the primer coat directly to the metal. After the vehicle was assembled, a protective coating was applied to the underside. The final body coat was a baked-enamel finish.

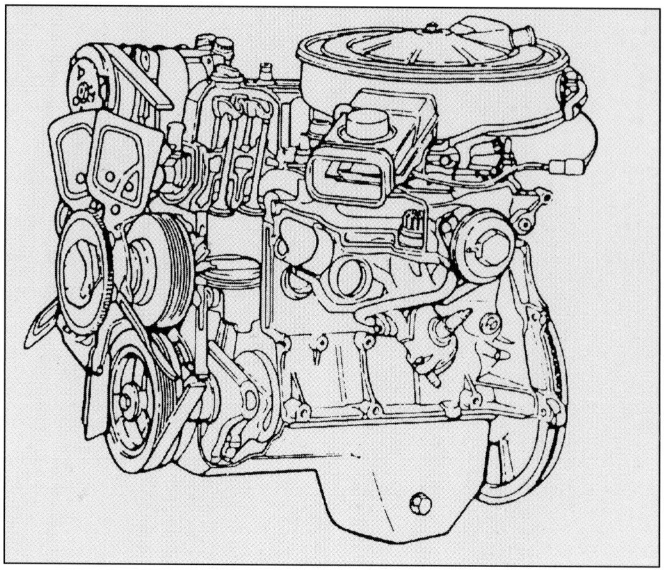

A perspective of the 1987 Wrangler's standard 2.5-liter, 4-cylinder engine, which was also used in the Jeep Comanche pickup as well as the Cherokee and Wagoneer wagons. (Author's collection)

All bolt-on assemblies such as the hood, fenders, grille guard and windshield were also cathodic electro-coated. In addition, plastic liners were used in the rear wheelhouse to resist water entry into body joints and an anti-corrosive paint was used on bumpers and exposed brackets.

The soft top Wrangler model was equipped with standard metal half-doors that, aside from enhancing the comfort level and quality of its interior, also played a role in the Wrangler's styling. As Robert Nixon explained: "The tops of the half-door are even with the rear quarter panels, while the forward parts slope upward to the door pillars to give the Wrangler more design continuity."

Both the Wrangler's soft top and its optional hard top had entirely new designs. The soft top incorporated adjustable snaps for a tight fit around the side rails and half-doors. Also helping to seal out the weather were Velcro fasteners. The soft top was factory installed to ensure a consistent quality fit, and included a retention system that minimized outside road noise and reduced air and water intrusions.

The soft top's bow structure design made folding the top a relatively simple operation. Contributing to the open-air nature of the Wrangler were the door's easily detached soft upper halves and the 'bikini top' effect created by the removal of the side and rear windows. Side curtains were still used on the soft top, but the hard top had roll-down, flush glass side windows and rear tailgate glass. Also part of the hard top's design were air extractors that improved performance of the heater and standard air vents. A new electric rear window defogger was optional for the hard top. Both versions had standard tinted glass for the windshield. The Wrangler, in either soft or hard top configuration, had a simple two-step tailgate operation. The spare tire was attached to a swingaway tailgate for convenient access to the Wrangler's rear compartment.

American Motors' claim that "the interior of the Wrangler was designed to capture the appearance and convenience usually found only in today's upscale passenger cars", was elaborated on by Vincent J Geraci, AMC's Director of Interior Design: "We've gotten away from the 'no frills' approach that is so commonplace in small utilities because our consumer research told us people wanted more creature comforts [but] we were careful not to abandon the rugged functional look."

The Wrangler's gauges and instrumentation were positioned for driver convenience. If an automatic transmission was installed, the gear selection panel was positioned directly in front of the steering column. To the column's left was a circular tachometer balanced by the speedometer (which included a trip odometer) on the right side of the column. Extending across the panel were smaller, circular gauges for the temperature, fuel level, clock, oil pressure and voltmeter. Controls for the windshield washer/wiper, high beam lights and, if installed, cruise control, were mounted on the steering column. The heating and ventilation systems were lever-activated. Integrated into the padded dash was the passenger assist panel, glove box and defroster ducts. Commenting on these aspects of the Wrangler's design, Geraci noted: "We've attempted to create a more comfortable interior environment for the Wrangler buyer. The interior trim is more eye appealing. It isn't just painted metal."

The Wrangler used a traditional separate body/chassis arrangement with a tubular, rectangular-shaped frame side-rail design which compared favorably with the three-sided 'C' channels found on many domestic small pickups. This arrangement eliminated the stresses usually associated with the welding of stamped steel channels. Additionally, the section modules were uniform throughout the side rails, providing the torsional strength and flexibility required for severe off-road use and long-term durability.

Many Wrangler chassis components, such as the steering system, brake assembly, transfer case, manual transmission, hydraulic clutch assembly, wheels and tires ,were derived from the Cherokee/Wagoneer models. The Wrangler used a modified Cherokee/Wagoneer front axle

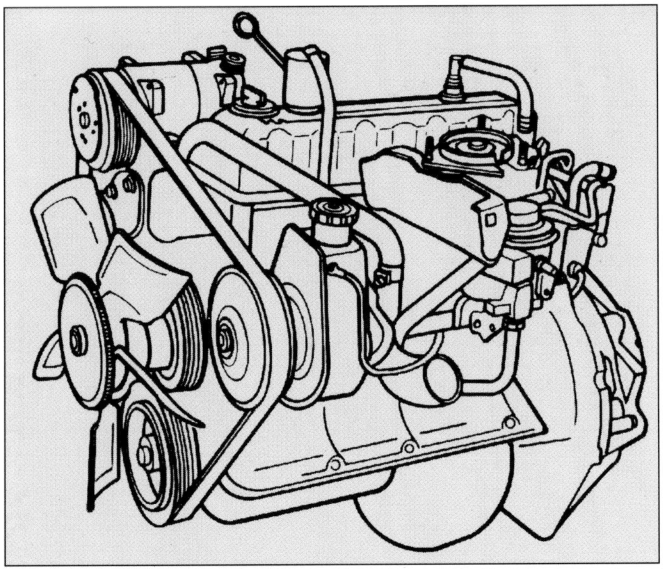

With 210lb-ft of torque at 2000rpm, the Wrangler's optional 4.2-liter, 6-cylinder engine was touted as having the highest torque rating in its class. (Author's collection)

with an inverted pinion design and a vacuum actuated disconnect. Its rear axle, a Dana 35C unit, was basically the same as the Cherokee's.

A tuned suspension system was used which included multi-leaf, longitudinal, semi-elliptical springs, 1.375in shock absorbers, a power steering system with a 14:1 ratio, front and rear track bars and a front stabilizer bar.

An optional Off-Road Package included high-pressure, gas-charged Fichtel and Sachs shock absorbers and P225/75 R15 Goodyear Wrangler tires. These replaced the standard P215/75R15 RBL Wrangler tires. Regardless of the type of suspension used, an 800lb payload was specified. Use of a New Process 207 transfer case gave the Wrangler the same 'shift-on-the-fly' capability as the Cherokee.

The Wrangler's standard engine was the electronically fuel injected 2.5-liter, 4-cylinder engine with 117hp at 5000rpm and 135lb-ft of torque at 3500rpm. As an option, the carbureted 4.2-liter, 6-cylinder was available. Its 112 horsepower rating trailed the 4-cylinder's but it produced 210lb-ft of torque at 2000rpm.

A 5-speed transmission (an Aisin unit with the 4-cylinder engine; a Peugeot model for the 6-cylinder) was standard with both engines. A 3-speed automatic was optional in combination with the 6-cylinder engine. Improved shifting performance relative to the CJ resulted from the use of a new shift linkage mounted on the engine.

Both engines gave the Wrangler good acceleration. When linked to the standard transmission, the 4-cylinder provided a 0-60mph time of 14 seconds. The larger engine, with the 5-speed manual, moved the Wrangler from 0-60mph in about 12 seconds.

Additional technical specifications of the Wrangler were as follows:

Exterior	
Front overhang:	23.9in (607mm)
Rear overhang:	
With P215 spare tire:	34.7in (882mm)
With P225 spare tire:	35.7in (908mm)
Overall height:	
Open body:	68.6in (1744mm)
Soft top:	72.0in (1828mm)
Hard top:	69.3in (1760mm)
Interior	
Headroom – front :	
Driver – soft top:	41.4in (1052mm)
Driver – hard top:	40.2in (1021mm)
Passenger-Soft top:	41.0in (1043mm)
Passenger – hard top:	40.0in (1016mm)
Headroom – rear:	
Soft top:	40.3in (1024mm)
Hard top:	40.5in (1029mm)
Leg room – front	
Driver:	39.5in (1003mm)
Passenger:	39.6in (1006mm)
Leg room – rear:	35.0in (889mm)
Shoulder room	
Front:	53.1in (1348mm)
Rear:	56.3in (1420mm)
Hip room	
Front:	53.1in (1348mm)
Rear:	36.0in (914mm)
Usable cargo volume	
Rear seat removed:	54.4ft³ (1.4m³)
Rear cargo area:	12.5ft³ (0.4m³)
Rear cargo area with seat folded:	43.2ft³ (1.2m³)
Ground clearance*	
Angle of approach:	37.77°
Angle of departure (to fuel tank):	36.37°

Angle of departure (to bumperette):	31.50°
Ramp break over angle:	24.64°
Rear axle to ground (running clearance):	8.14in (207mm)
Skid plate to ground (minimum running clearance):	9.65in (245mm)

*All ground heights at curb weight with P245/75R15 tires.

Power train

Engine:	Standard	Optional
Type:	I-4, ohv	I-6, ohv
Displacement	2.46-liter	4.2-liter
Bore x stroke	3.88 x 3.19in	3.75 x 3.895in
Compression ratio:	9.2:1	9.2:1

Transmission

Type	Aisin[1]	Peugeot[2]	Chrysler #999[3]
	M-5	M-5	A-3
Gear ratios			
1st:	3.93:1	4.03:1	2.74:1
2nd:	2.33:1	2.39:1	1.55:1
3rd:	1.45:1	1.53:1	1.00:1
4th:	1.00:1	1.00:1	–
5th:	0.84:1	0.72:1	–
Rev:	3.76:1	3.76:1	2.20:1

[1] 4-cylinder engine
[2] 6-cylinder engine
[3] 6-cylinder engine

Transfer Case:	New Process #207 part-time (early in the production run a switch was made to a New Process 231 unit)
4-Position Dual Range	
Ratios:	
High:	1.00:1
Low:	2.60:1
Drive line	
Front axle:	Dana Model 30, semi-floating
Ring gear diameter:	7.125in (180.98mm)
Rear axle:	Dana Model 35C, semi-floating
Ring gear diameter:	7.563in (192.09mm)
Final drive ratios:	
4-cylinder:	4.11:1
Optional:	None
6-cylinder:	3.08:1
Optional:	3.55:1
Prop shaft	
Universal joints:	Cardan

Chassis

Frame:	Tubular construction
Tires:	Goodyear 'Wrangler' All-Terrain steel-belted radial
Size:	P215/75R15 (P205/75R15 All-Weather vector tires and 15 x 6in Argent steel wheels required in the state of Maryland)
Wheel type:	5-stud, painted spoker with bright hub
Wheel size:	15 x 7.0JJ
Spare tire size:	P225/75D15 polyspare (full size optional)
Brakes:	Power, single diaphragm vacuum booster
Front:	Disc, vented cast-iron rotor
Caliber bore:	2.60in (66mm)
Rotor:	11.02in x 0.88in (279.9mm x 22.4mm)
Rear:	Drum
Dimensions:	9.84in x 1.77in (250mm x 45mm)
Parking brake:	Foot operated, hand release
Steering:	Saginaw recirculating ball
Turns lock-to-lock	
Power:	4.0
Manual:	5.25
Ratio:	
Power:	14:1
Manual:	24:1
Turning diameter (curb to curb):	33.67ft (10.26m)

Suspension

Front:	Hotchkiss leaf spring, mounted below axle
Spring rate:	113lb-in (at wheel)
Stabilizer bar:	Link type, 0.937in diameter (22.7mm)

This 1987 Wrangler has received its full-doors, indicating it will be equipped with the new hard top. A similar Wrangler can be seen in the background. (Author's collection)

A 1987 Wrangler body with the Sport Decor package being checked to ensure the fit of key components is within acceptable tolerances. (Author's collection)

Travel		
Jounce:		3.42in (86.9mm)
Rebound:		4.93in (125.2mm)
Roll center height:		16.1in (408.9mm)
Rear:		Hotchkiss leaf spring, mounted below axle
Spring rate:		170lb-in (at wheel)
Stabilizer bar:		None
Travel		
Jounce:		5.55in (140.9mm)
Rebound:		2.50in (63.5mm)
Roll center height:		21.8in (553.7mm)
Fuel capacity:		
Standard:		15-gallons (57-liters)
Optional:		20-gallons (76-liters)
Weights		
	4-cylinder	6-cylinder
Base curb:	2902lb (1316kg)	3028lb (1373kg)
Max GAWR:		
Front:	2200lb (998kg)	2200lb (998kg)
Rear:	2500lb (1134kg)	2500lb (1134kg)
Payload:	800lb (363kg)	800lb (363kg)
Estimated fuel economy ratings		
4-cylinder engine/manual 5-speed		
City:		18mpg
Highway:		20mpg
Combined:		19mpg

'Easy Does It!' A 1987 Wrangler receives its body on the Brampton, Ontario assembly line. (Author's collection)

6-cylinder engine/manual 5-speed	
City:	17mpg
Highway:	21mpg
Combined:	19mpg
6-cylinder engine/automatic 3-speed	
City:	16mpg
Highway:	18mpg
Combined:	17mpg

The Wrangler was marketed as the Jeep YJ in Canada. The Wrangler nameplates on the rear quarter panels were deleted on the Canadian models, and a YJ decal was added above the right-hand tail lamp. If the Sport Decor Group option was ordered for a YJ, the 'Wrangler' hood decals were also deleted. (Author's collection)

The Wrangler, identified as the Jeep YJ in Canada since General Motors already was marketing a full-sized Suburban as a Wrangler, was offered in Base, Sports Decor and Laredo hard top form. The Base model had this array of standard equipment:

Interior

- -Front ashtray
- -Cigarette lighter
- -Gauges for tachometer, speedometer (with trip odometer), engine coolant temperature, fuel, clock, oil pressure, voltmeter
- -Indicator lights for high beam, seat belts, 4WD, turn signals, brake warning
- -Heater and defroster
- -Front mini carpet mat
- -8.5in day/night rearview mirror
- -Padded sun visors
- -Padded instrument panel
- -Passenger safety rail
- -Padded sport bar
- -High-back front bucket seat with seat belts
- -Fold-and-tumble rear seat with lap belts
- -3-spoke, soft-feel, sport steering wheel
- -Trim: Jeep denim vinyl seats, injection molded half-door trim panels (optional full-door with hard top had vinyl trim panel)

Exterior

- -Black painted front bumper
- -Front frame overlay
- -Lights: halogen headlamps, parking, tail and stop, backup, directional signals, side safety markers and 4-way hazard flashers
- -Outside left mirror (windshield hinge mounted)
- -Black painted rear bumperettes
- -Soft top with half-hard lower and removable soft upper doors; storage sleeves for side windows
- -Swing-away tailgate with integrated spare tire mounting
- -Tinted windshield
- -Wheel-lip extensions (front extensions integrated with ⅓ length mud guards)
- -Wrangler name plate on rear quarter panels (deleted for Canadian market, replaced by 'YJ' decal above right-hand tail lamp)

Functional

- -12-volt, 56amp alternator
- -12-volt battery (55.421 cold crank)
- -Permanent type engine coolant (50/50 mix) with Hi-Temp thermostat
- -Single exhaust system
- -Tank and in-line fuel filters
- -Fuel tank skid plate

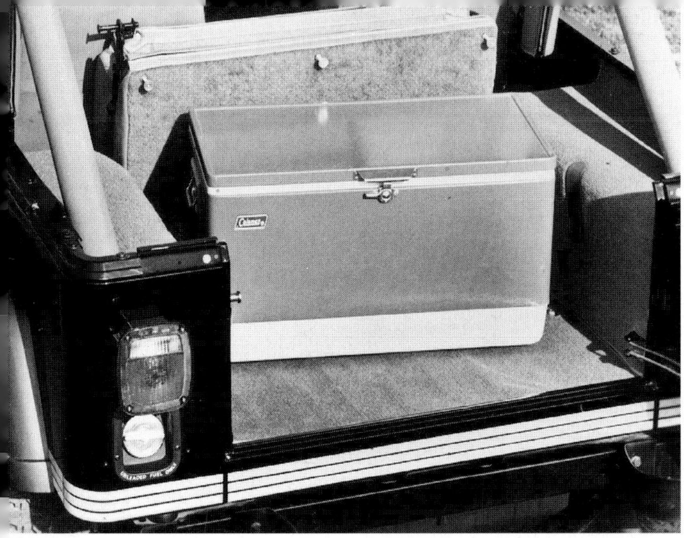

Clockwise from top left: The 1987 Wrangler's new vertically-hinged door opened to provide easy access to 43.2ft3 of cargo space with the standard fold-and-tumble rear seat in place. If the seat was fully removed, cargo space increased to 53.4ft^3. (Author's collection). The soft upper/hard lower door of a 1987 Wrangler with the Sport Decor Package. It also has the optional integrated body side steps. (Author's collection). This integrated side step and full-length mud guard were standard for the 1987 Wrangler Laredo. (Author's collection)

- -Single horn
- -P225/70D15 Polyspare with Black 15 x 6in wheel
- -Vinyl spare tire cover with Jeep logo; Black with Black or White top, Honey with Honey top
- -Tools: Bottle-type jack, separate wheel wrench and jack handle (stored under hood)
- -2-speed electric windshield wipers with washers
- -Rear wheelhouse liners, splash deflector in front wheelhouse
- -Full underbody protective spray coating

The Sport Decor Group option offered many items adding to or replacing equipment found on the Base model, including an AM/FM monaural radio, Black side cowl carpet (full color-keyed carpeting was optional), Special 'Wrangler' hood decals (deleted in Canada), and striping on the lower body side in either silver or tan, Goodyear All-Terrain P215/75R15 Outline White Letter steel-belted radial tires (replaced by the previously noted P205/75R15 tires and Argent steel wheels in Maryland), conventional-size spare tire with wheel lock and Convenience Group. The latter contained courtesy lights with door switches, engine compartment light, intermittent wipers and glove box locks.

The Laredo model's equipment in addition to, or in place of, that of the Base model's, was as follows:

Interior

- -AM/FM mono radio
- -Buffalo grain vinyl seat trim*
- -Front and rear carpet
- -Center console
- -Extra Quiet Insulation Package (included carpeting for floor front and rear, cargo, tailgate panel, trimmed inner side panels, belt line moldings and hood insulation)
- -Leather-wrapped steering wheel
- -Jeep nameplate on glove box door
- -Special door trim panels with carpeted lower third and map pocket

Reading from left to right: the 1987 Wrangler's standard gauges for engine coolant temperature, fuel level, clock, oil pressure, and voltmeter. The Wrangler also had a standard tachometer. This model is also equipped with an AM/FM radio. (Author's collection)

-Front and rear floor protective mats
*Vincent J Geraci summing up the Laredo's interior said, "It has that Western feel and suggests an extension of the name, Wrangler."

Exterior
-Chrome front bumper, rear bumperettes, grille panel, headlamp bezels and tow hooks
-Color-keyed wheel flares
-Deep tint glass (Gray tone with Black or White top, Bronze tone with Honey top)
-Left and right side door mounted R-5 type mirror
-Bumper Accessory Package
-Hard top with full hard doors
-Special hood and body side stripes in silver or brown with 'Laredo' lettering in the lower body side stripes
-Color-keyed body side step integrated with full-length mudguard
-Textured overlay panel in door offset

Functional
-Convenience Group
-15 x 7in, five-spoke, sport, cast-aluminum wheels with 'Jeep' lettering
-P215/75R215 Goodyear Wrangler OWL All-Terrain radial tires (except as previously noted for the state of Maryland)
-Conventional spare tire mounted on a matching aluminum wheel with wheel lock

The Wrangler was available with numerous factory installed, regular production options, many of which were found in the Laredo and Sport Decor Group options:

A – available
NA – not available

Item	Standard	Laredo
Automatic transmission:	A	A
Rear Trac-Lok differential:	A	A
Air conditioning:	A	A
Heavy-duty alternator:	A	A
Heavy-duty battery:	A	A
Bumper Accessory Package (Black finish on Base):	A	S
Front and rear carpeting:	A	S
Center console:	S	A
Cold Climate Group (heavy duty battery and alternator, engine block heater):	A	A
Convenience Group:	A	S
Heavy-Duty Cooling System (6-cylinder engine only, includes extra capacity radiator):	A	A
Cruise control (6-cylinder with auto trans only):	A	A
Deep tinted hard top glass:	A	A
Draw bar:	A	A
Extra capacity (20-gallon) fuel tank:	A	A
Extra Quiet Insulation Package (hard top only):	A	S
Protective floor mats:	A	S
Halogen fog lamps:	A	A
Exterior passenger side mirror:	A	S
Power steering:	A	A
AM/FM mono radio:	A	S
AM/FM ETR stereo radio:	A	A
AM/FM cassette ETR stereo radio with Dolby:	A	A
Rear window defogger for hard top:	A	A
Leather-wrapped steering wheel:	A	S
Body side step:	A	S
Heavy Duty Suspension (heavy duty front and rear springs and shock absorbers):	A	A
Off-Road Package (heavy duty front and rear gas filled Fitchell and Sachs shock absorbers, and Goodyear P255/75R15 Wrangler tires):	A	A
Tilt steering wheel (includes intermittent windshield wipers, required with auto trans):	A	A

Hard top with tinted glass and full-doors:	A	S
Four White 15 x 7in styled-steel wheels:	S	NA
Five Sport 15 x 7 aluminum wheels:	A	S
P215/75R15O OBL Goodyear Wrangler All-Terrain radial tires:	S	NA
P215/75R OWL Goodyear Wrangler or Michelin All-Terrain radial tires (5):	A	S
P225/75R15 OWL Goodyear Wrangler Off-Road radial tires (5):	A	A
Conventional spare tire (P215/75R15 OBL):	A	A
Jeep-print denim grain vinyl interior trim:	S	NA
Buffalo grain vinyl interior trim:	NA	S
Metallic paint:	A	A
Special (non-recommended) color combinations of regular production exterior colors/interior trim/stripe:	A	A

The Wrangler's seat, trim and color availability was as follows:

A – available *NA – not available*	**Base**		**Sport Decor**		**Laredo**	
Trim Color	Black	Honey	Black	Honey	Black	Honey
Standard Exterior Colors						
Olympic White	A	A	A	A	A	A
Classic Black	A	A	A	A	A	A
Beige	A	A	A	A	NA	NA
Colorado Red	A	A	A	A	NA	NA
Sun Yellow	A	A	A	NA	A	NA
Metallic Exterior Colors						
Mist Silver	A	NA	A	NA	A	NA
Medium Blue	A	NA	A	NA	NA	NA
Autumn Brown	A	A	A	A	NA	NA
Mocha Brown	A	A	A	A	A	A
Garnet	A	A	A	A	A	NA

The Laredo's standard Buffalo grain vinyl, high-back bucket seats were available in Black, as seen here, or Honey. (Author's collection)

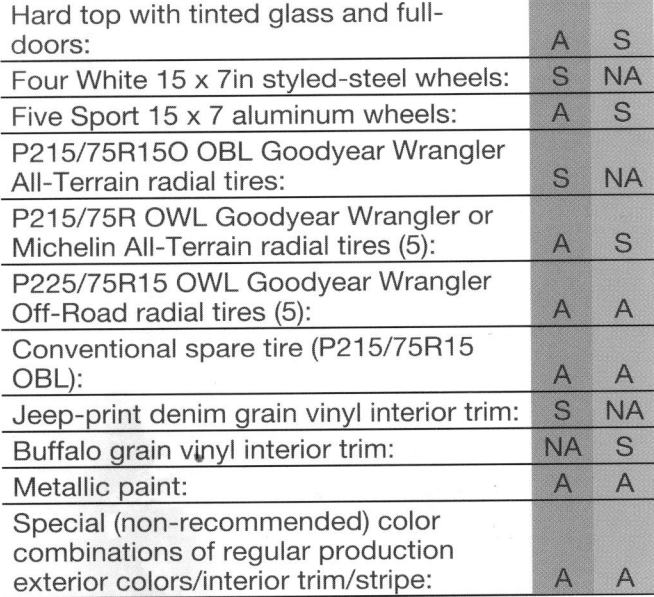

This fold-and-tumble rear seat was a standard 1987 Wrangler feature. (Author's collection)

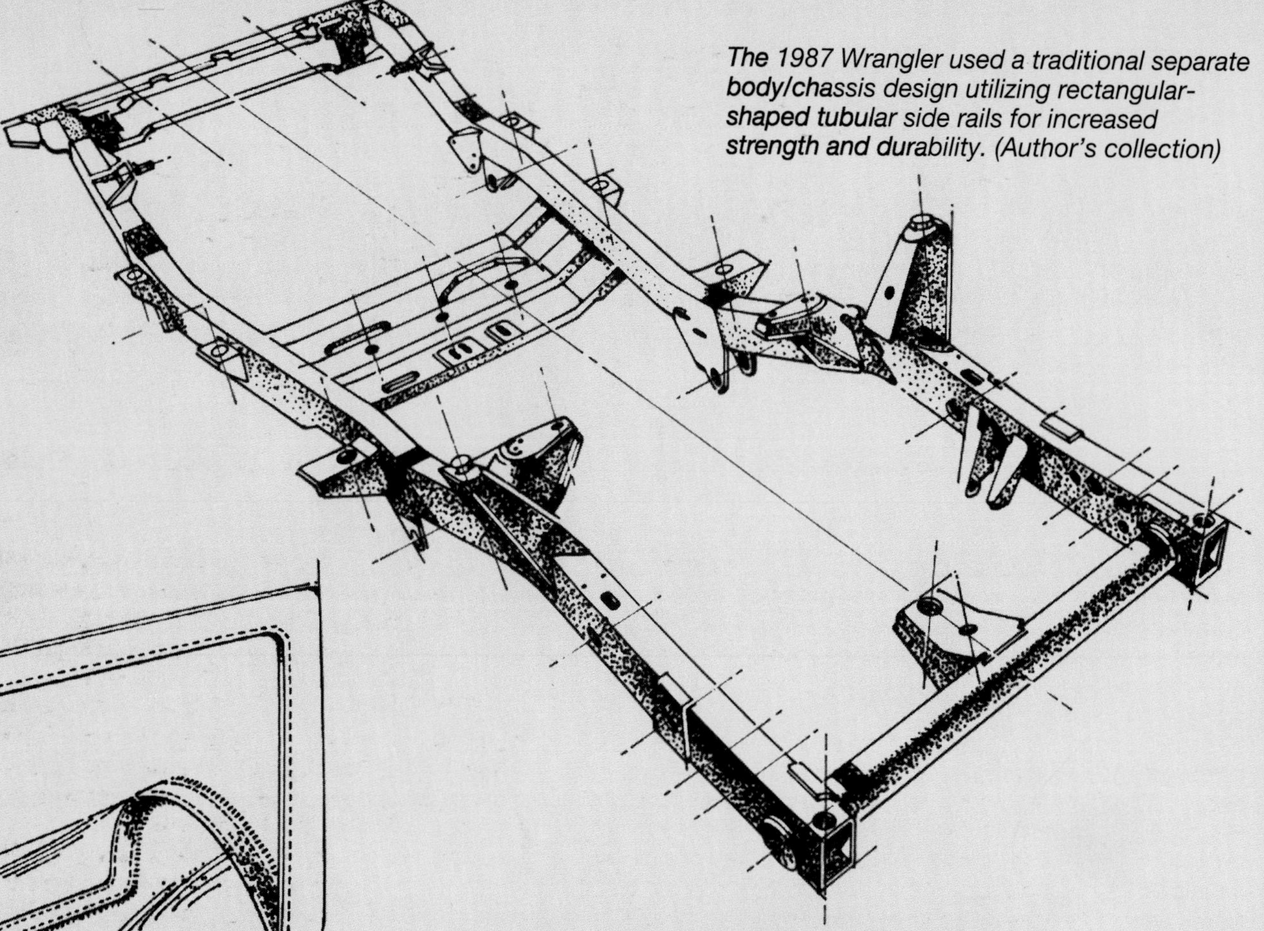

The 1987 Wrangler used a traditional separate body/chassis design utilizing rectangular-shaped tubular side rails for increased strength and durability. (Author's collection)

Depictions of the new Wranglers' standard half-doors and soft top. The view of the half-door shows the means by which the soft upper top is installed and the zip-down design of the side windows. The second sketch shows a Wrangler with its soft top and windows ready for a season of inclement weather. (Author's collection)

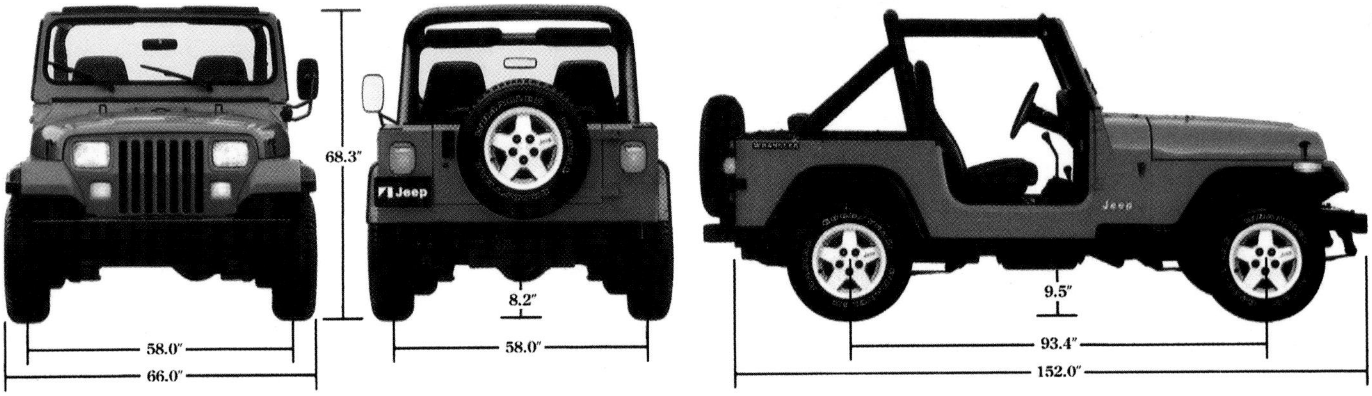

Three views of a Colorado Red 1987 Wrangler with optional 15 x 7in, 5-bolt, Sport, aluminum wheels. (Author's collection)

American Motors prepared a comprehensive marketing plan for the Wrangler that was intended to communicate the unique benefits of owning the latest Jeep model to a broad cross section of motorists. Wrangler advertisements were aired on all major cable and network television systems.

The commercial began with a view of a cowboy asleep in his red Wrangler as dawn breaks on an Arizona desert. The camera slowly made a 350° pass around the Wrangler as its radio picked up disc jockeys around the country commenting on ideal weather for a day of outdoor activities. The promotion ended with the announcement: "New Jeep Wrangler ... the possibilities are endless", as the phrase "Only in Jeep" appeared on the screen.

Coinciding with the Wrangler's mid-May introduction was a direct-mail campaign to a half-million prospective customers. AMC also made arrangements for numerous promotional tie-ins with many associations and corporations such as:

-The Stetson Cologne sweepstakes and mall shows backed by a $2 million advertising campaign by Stetson.
-Mailings to 18 million American Express card holders.
-A major promotion with Pennzoil featuring the Wrangler in over $4 million of radio and television advertising.
-A program in association with S&H saving stamps including point-of-sale displays at 350 major truck stops, 1100 supermarkets and 150 newspaper ads.
-Wrangler vehicle displays at all American Quarter Horse Association events, IPRA rodeos, Arabian horse shows and 4-H Club state and county fairs.
-A Hardee's sweepstakes contest at 2500 stores, along with vehicle displays and ten million, four-color, four-page Sunday newspaper inserts.
-A $500,000 television campaign featuring battery-operated Wrangler 'go-karts' manufactured and sold by Kransco.

Graphically illustrating the Wrangler's combination of on-road riding comfort with off-road ruggedness was its 16-page catalog which was actually two catalogs in one. It had two separate sections and covers, back-to-back. One focused on the Wrangler's 'on-road' attributes with the other detailing its 'off-road' capabilities.

The Wrangler was covered by a 12-month/12,000-mile limited warranty as well as extended power train protection for an additional 12 months or 12,000 miles. In addition, the Wrangler's warranty also included coverage against corrosion for three years.

According to Pierre Jocou, Managing Director of Parts and Service Operations for American Motors, the Wrangler's extended power train protection included a number of specified engine, transmission, transfer case and front- or rear-drive components. Owners were required to pay the first $100 per repair visit for repair or replacement of covered items during the period of the extended power train protection.

American Motors' Service Security Plan, in either standard or deluxe form, was also available to Wrangler purchasers as an option. It provided protection against major repair bills for up to five years or 50,000 miles. Car rental assistance and towing expenses were also included in both forms.

Tentative prices for the Wrangler were announced by AMC on March 20, 1987:

Model	**Price***
Base soft top:	$9899
Sport Decor:	$10,620
Laredo:	$12,205

*The Wrangler's destination charge was $391.

On May 8, 1987 AMC expanded the Wrangler model line by introducing the Wrangler S which was depicted as "an entry level sport utility vehicle aimed at new four-wheel

The entry level Wrangler S, priced at $8795, was introduced on May 8, 1987. It was available in two exterior colors – Olympic White and Classic Black. (Author's collection)

Three perspectives of the 1988 Wrangler Sahara. The brush/ grille guard and front winch were dealer-installed accessories. When Chrysler acquired American Motors for approximately $2 billion, including debt assumption in 1987, Chrysler management made no secret that Jeep was the prize of the acquisition. (Author's collection)

This 1988 Wrangler Laredo combines a Tan hard top with an Olympic White body. Standard Laredo features seen here include the chrome grille panel, front bumper and headlamp bezels, full-length mud guards and special Laredo striping. (Author's collection)

drive buyers". With a base price of $8795, the Wrangler S was positioned to compete in-between the high-line Suzuki Samurai and light four-wheel drive compact trucks such as the Ford Ranger, Dodge Ram 50 and Toyota pickup models.

"Price is the top motivating factor for the buyers in this market," said William E Enockson, Group Vice President, North American Sales and Marketing, "but they are also looking for versatility, fuel economy and the fun associated with four-wheel drive vehicles. We expect that approximately 25 per cent of the buyers will be women who are becoming increasingly important in this segment and, like men, are attracted by the price, utility and smaller size of the vehicle."

The Wrangler S was equipped with the 2.5-liter engine, 5-speed transmission, soft top, P205/75R15 Wrangler tires and Argent steel wheels. It was available in only two exterior colors, Olympic White or Classic Black. Options were limited to a rear seat, full carpeting, power steering and a choice of radios.

Earlier, at the Geneva, Switzerland Auto Show (March 5-15, 1987), the first public showing of a new Wrangler model for 1988 – the Sahara – took place. The Sahara went on sale in the US later in the year. European sales began in 1988.

AMC depicted the Sahara as "combining today's 'in' products – Jeep vehicles – with today's 'in' fashion – safari clothing".

In the view of William E Enockson, "The Sahara will project a unique and sophisticated image that fits right in with the current trend toward exotic travel and safari-type clothing and merchandise".

The Sahara was available in two exterior colors, Khaki Metallic or Coffee. It was also identified by unique tape stripes, 'Sahara' logos on the body side and spare tire cover, khaki-colored spoker wheels, khaki soft top (a tan hard top was optional), and khaki-colored interior trim appointments. Other exterior standard equipment features included special fender-mounted fog lights, color-keyed wheel flares and integrated body sidesteps.

The Sahara interior had a Trailcloth seat fabric in khaki with tan accents, khaki-colored 20-ounce carpeting, map

Jeep described the new 1988 Sahara model as "designed to accommodate changing consumer usage patterns". When the Sahara was first announced in early 1987, Jeep was part of American Motors. Shortly thereafter, AMC was purchased by Chrysler. Eager to assure Jeep loyalists that all was well, Chrysler released this statement: "It has been called an America Legend. Jeep. The most rugged, most versatile, most recognizable four-wheel drive vehicle ever built. And it is now part of the Chrysler stable of quality cars and trucks." (Author's collection)

pocket pouches on both door sides, a leather-wrapped steering wheel, center console with padded cover plus an AM/FM electronically-tuned stereo radio. Dealer-installed options for the Sahara included a brush-grille guard, bug screen kit, and a bikini soft top with boot.

The 1988 Wrangler was available in many new interior and exterior colors. There were seven new exterior colors (Pearl White, Coffee, Sand Dune Yellow, Metallic Silver, Metallic Spinnaker Blue, Khaki and Vivid Red), two new soft and hard top colors (Charcoal and Tan) and two new interior trim colors (also Charcoal and Tan). The Laredo had the same Trailcloth water resistant seat fabric as used on the Sahara as well as red and blue exterior colors for 1988.

The Sport Decor Group was revised for 1988 to increase what AMC depicted as "its visual impact". Changes included the addition of net door map pockets and the availability of Trailcloth fabric seats as an option.

All 1988 Wranglers were covered by the Jeep New Vehicle limited warranty, providing 12-month/12,000-mile coverage on vehicle components and three years' corrosion protection. Major engine and power train components were covered for 36 months/36,000 miles.

2 LEGENDARY AND RUGGED – THE 1989-1995 WRANGLERS

The 'theme concept' philosophy of marketing the Wrangler was given new expression in 1989 with the introduction of the Islander model. Chrysler regarded the latest Wrangler as a "sporty, fun-to-drive 'niche' vehicle".

Moses Ludel, (*Off-Road* magazine, April 1989), praised this strategy: "The marketing genius behind the special edition Wranglers deserves recognition. Someone's paying close attention to the American consumer. Personalized, self-enhancing products abound in the current marketplace, with individual taste and style more important than ever. The Jeep Islander finds its perfect outlet among the youthful, free-spirited, financially solvent, recently revived 'Now Generation'."

In the Wrangler hierarchy the Islander was positioned behind the Sahara and Laredo models. Major exterior graphics of the Islander consisted of a hood stripe, lower-body side stripes, body side steps integrated with full-length mud guards, an 'Islander' sunburst decal/logo and a Wrangler decal. The stripes were offered in Midnight Blue with Yellow-Orange and Bright Orange Red accent colors. A spare tire cover with a special Islander logo was standard. The optional hard top was offered in Black, Charcoal and Sand. The Islander was equipped with standard Charcoal vinyl seats. Trailcloth fabric seats were optional. Also included in the Islander's standard interior appointments were removable front and rear carpeting (including tailgate) and vinyl door trim panels with map pockets.

The 1989 Wrangler S was described by Chrysler Corporation as an entry-level sport utility vehicle. (Author's collection)

Once again functioning as a low-priced entry vehicle, the Wrangler S was equipped with the following standard equipment items: 56amp alternator; Dana Model 30 semi-floating front axle; Dana Model 35C semi-floating rear axle; 12-volt battery with 55-421 cold crank amps; front 11.02in diameter disc brakes; 10.00 x 1.75in rear drum brakes; foot-lever-actuated parking brake operating on rear wheels; 2.5-liter, 4-cylinder engine; 15-galllon fuel tank; skid plates for fuel tank and transfer case; recirculating ball manual steering with 24:1 ratio; P205/75R15 Goodyear Wrangler, steel-belted, radial, Outline White Letter tires with Polyspare P225/75D15 spare tire mounted on a 015 x 6in wheel; 15 x 6in eight-spoke argent styled steel wheels; electric windshield washer/wiper with 2-speed column-mounted controls; front black bumper; rear black bumperettes; black fender flares with one-third length mud guards; tinted windshield glass; passenger-side grab handle; heater/defroster; instrument cluster gauge group consisting of tachometer, voltmeter, oil pressure and engine coolant temperature gauges; fuel gauge, clock and trip odometer; instrument-panel-mounted ashtray and

The 1989 Wrangler Sahara's exterior graphics included narrow striping running from the leading edge of the front fenders and around the rear deck. (Author's collection)

The new Wrangler Islander was described by Chrysler Corporation as being "aimed at the image-conscious, younger, single, well-educated buyer who is an adventurous outdoor person." (Author's collection)

cigarette lighter; padded instrument panel and sun visors; 8.5in day/night rearview mirror; padded, color-keyed sport bar with side bars; front, high-back, Jeep Denim vinyl bucket seats; and a soft-feel, 3-spoke, sport steering wheel.

The optional equipment offered for the Wrangler S was again limited to the hard top, rear fold-and-tumble seats, carpeting and a choice of radios consisting of an AM monoaural with two speakers, an AM/FM electronically tuned stereo with two speakers, or an AM/FM electronically tuned stereo Dolby unit with cassette tape player and two speakers.

A step up from the Wrangler S, the Wrangler Base, featured the following items in place of, or in addition to, the content of the Wrangler S: P215/75R15 Goodyear Wrangler, black, steel-belted radial tires; 15 x 7in, six-spoke, silver-painted wheel with bright hub covers; left and right side door-mounted exterior mirrors; spare tire cover; AM monoaural radio; and a rear fold-and-tumble seat with lap belts. Following the Wrangler Islander, the Wrangler Sahara added these items to the Islander's standard equipment: gas-filled shock absorbers; P215/75R15 Goodyear Wrangler, black, steel-belted tires; 15 x 7in, six-spoke, khaki-painted, steel wheels; halogen fog lamps; special exterior Yellow/Red tape stripes and Sahara decals; AM/FM electronically tuned radio with two speakers; Convenience Group consisting of courtesy lights with door switches; engine compartment light; intermittent windshield wipers; glove box light and center console; front, high-back bucket seats finished in Trailcloth Sand-colored fabric with khaki accents; and a leather-wrapped steering wheel.

The top-of-the line Wrangler, the Laredo, featured a high level of standard equipment including the 4.2-liter, 6-cylinder engine and a hard top with full-doors. Additional standard features replacing, or in addition to, those found on the Sahara consisted of P215/75R15 Goodyear Wrangler, Outline White Letter, steel-belted radial tires (four of these tires were provided for the Islander; the Sahara was also equipped with a spare tire of these specifications); five 15 x 7in, sport, aluminum wheels; front chrome bumper with bumper extensions and tow hooks; rear chrome bumperettes; deep-tinted gray tone or bronze tone rear quarter windows; special hood and body side stripes with 'Laredo' cutouts on lower body side; chrome grille and headlamp bezels; special door panels with carpeted one-third lower portion and map pocket; extra-quiet insulation including hood insulation and trimmed inner side panels; protective floor mats; and front high-bucket seats in Trailcloth fabric. The Laredo's stripes were offered in either Light Medium Silver/Dark Silver or Light Sand/Dark Sand.

Nine exterior colors were available for the 1989 Wrangler: Pearl White, Classic Black, Bright Red, Sand, Silver Metallic, Spinnaker Blue Metallic, Malibu Yellow, Pacific Blue Metallic and Khaki Metallic. The metallic colors were extra cost items.

The 1989 Wrangler Islander's spare tire cover had a distinctive logo complementing its special body graphics. (Author's collection)

The 1989 Wrangler Islander had P215/75R15 OWL tires and 15 x 7in, six-spoke, silver-painted steel wheels as standard equipment. (Author's collection)

The Wrangler S was offered in four exterior colors: Pearl White, Classic Black, Sand and Bright Red. The Sahara was available in either Sand or Khaki Metallic. Color choices for the Islander consisted of Malibu Yellow, Bright Red, Pearl White or Pacific Blue Metallic.

Optional equipment and prices for the 1989 were:

Model	MSRP
Wrangler S:	$8995
Wrangler Base:	$11,022
Wrangler Islander:	$11,721
Wrangler Sahara:	$12,853
Wrangler Laredo:	$14,867
Destination charge:	$435
Item price	
4.2-liter engine (not available for Wrangler S):	$417
3-speed automatic transmission:	$497
Saginaw power steering (14:1 ratio):	$294
Air conditioning[1]:	$861
Rear Trac-Loc differential:	$273
Trailcloth fabric seats (Islander):	$105
Hard top (S and Base models):	$596
Hard top with deep-tinted glass (Islander and Sahara):	$748
California emissions package:	$125
Metallic paint (Base, Islander, Laredo):	$170
Carpet (Base and S):	$134
Convenience Group[2] (Base and Islander):	$182
Convenience Group (with tilt steering column):	$121
Cruise control[3] (Sahara and Laredo):	$218
Rear defogger for hard top[4]:	$161
20-gallon fuel tank[4]:	$61
Heavy duty Alternator and Battery Group[4]:	$132
Floor mats (Base, Islander and Sahara)[5]:	$32
Off-Road Package[6]:	$190-$316
AM radio (Wrangler S):	$98
AM/FM stereo ET radio (Wrangler S):	$265
AM/FM stereo ET radio (Base and Islander):	$167
AM/FM stereo ET radio with cassette (Wrangler S):	$524
AM/FM stereo ET radio with cassette (Base and Islander):	$426
AM/FM stereo ET radio with cassette (Sahara and Laredo):	$259
Folding rear seat (Wrangler S):	$446
Tilt steering column (Base and Islander):	$184
Tilt steering column (Sahara and Laredo):	$122

A Malibu Yellow 1990 Wrangler Islander. The Islander's striping combined Midnight Blue with Yellow-Orange and Bright Orange-Red accents. This example is equipped with the optional 15 x 7in, five-spoke, Sport, aluminum wheels. (Author's collection)

Tires:	
Five 215/75R15 OWL (Base and Sahara):	$224
Five 225/75R15 OWL (Base and Sahara):	$411
Five 225/75R15 OWL (Islander):	$313
Five 225/75R15 OWL (Laredo):	$187
Alloy wheels:	
Islander with 215 OWL spare:	$411
Base and Sahara with 215 black tires:	$424
Islander with 205 OWL spare:	$424
215 OWL conventional spare tire (Islander):	$126
215 black conventional spare tire (Base and Sahara):	$109
205 OWL spare (Base, Islander and Sahara):	$109

[1]Required 4.2-liter engine and power steering.
[2]Included courtesy lights, intermittent windshield wipers, glove box lock, engine compartment light, and center console.
[3]Required 4.2-liter engine.
[4]Not available for Wrangler S.
[5]Required carpet.
[6]The Off-Road Package consisted of heavy-duty, gas-filled shock absorbers, draw bar, tow hooks and conventional spare tire. The Off-Road Package was available only for the Base and Islander. The price varied according to the tire installed on those models.

The Jeep Wrangler entered the 1990 model year with 21 consecutive record sales months (dating back to September 1987) to its credit. Nine exterior colors were available for the Wrangler. Carried over from 1989 were Sand, Malibu Yellow, and Khaki Metallic. New colors were Bright White, Black, Graphic Red, Pacific Blue, Charcoal Gray Metallic, and Navy Blue Metallic. The lateral support for the front seats was improved and an AM/FM Stereo radio was standard on the Base, Islander, Sahara, and Laredo models. All soft top models with half-doors had a new lock system while a rear window wiper/washer was included with the hard top.

As this comparison of the 1989 and 1990 models indicates, although the entry level S model's option list

The 1990 Wrangler S was the only model not equipped with standard dual exterior mirrors. A passenger side mirror was supplied with the optional hard top. (Author's collection)

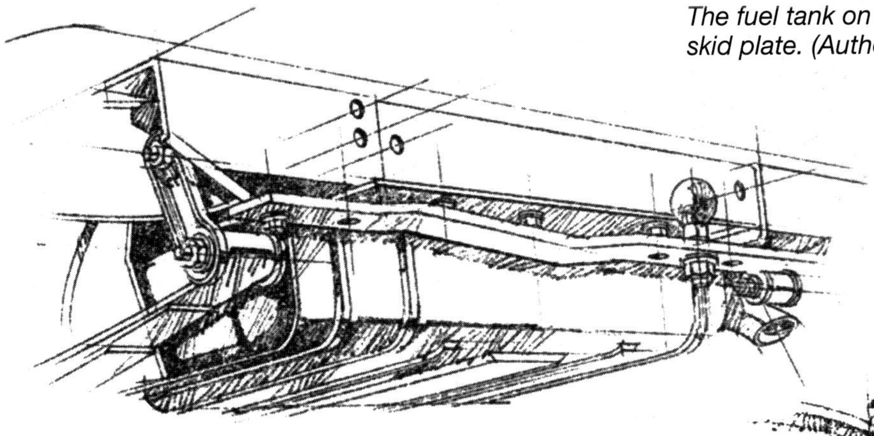

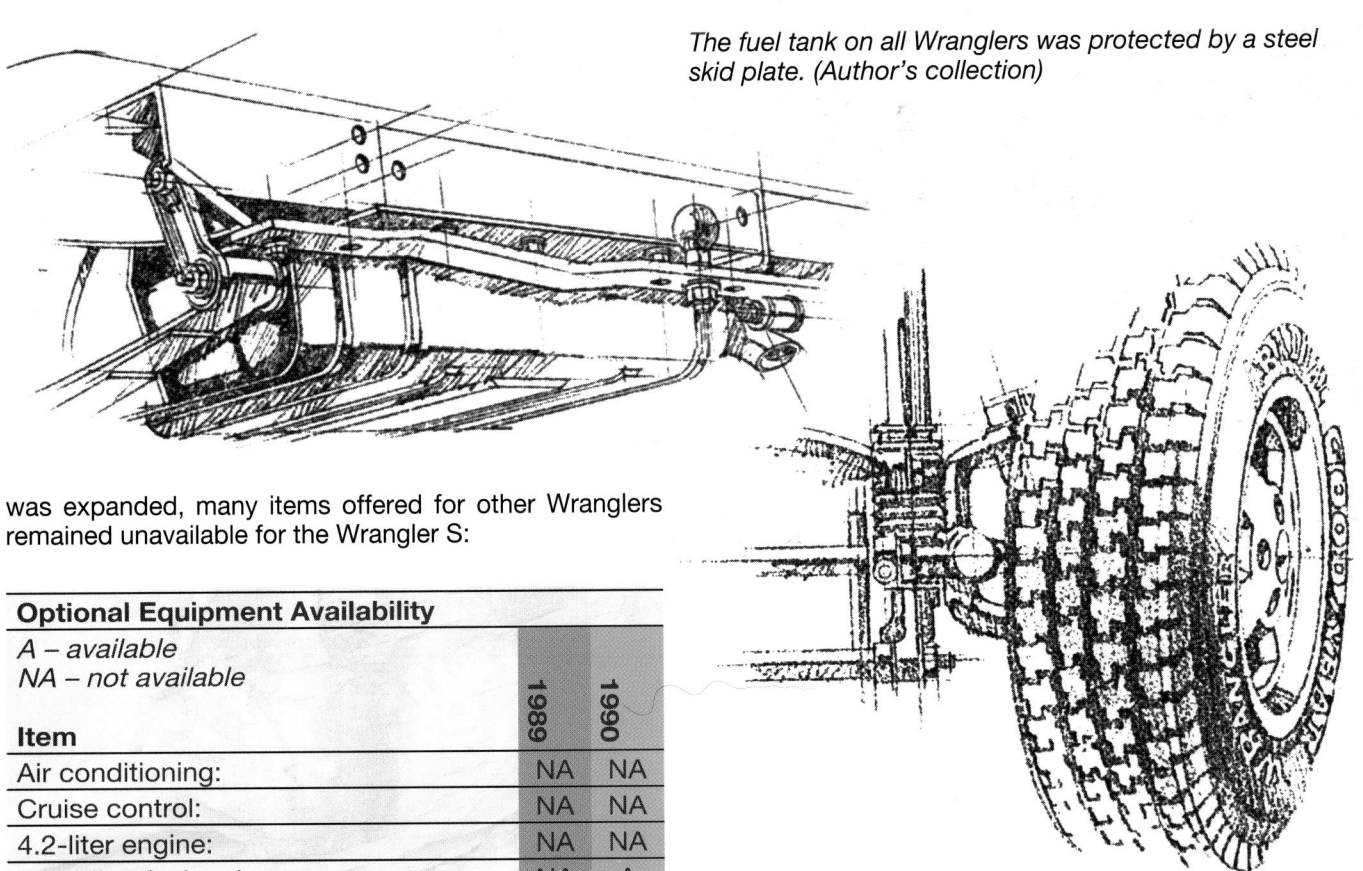

The fuel tank on all Wranglers was protected by a steel skid plate. (Author's collection)

was expanded, many items offered for other Wranglers remained unavailable for the Wrangler S:

Optional Equipment Availability *A – available* *NA – not available* **Item**	**1989**	**1990**
Air conditioning:	NA	NA
Cruise control:	NA	NA
4.2-liter engine:	NA	NA
20-gallon fuel tank:	NA	A
Heavy-Duty Alternator and Battery Group:	NA	A
Gas-charged shock absorbers:	NA	NA
Power steering:	A	A
Off-Road Package:	NA	NA
P215/75R15 Goodyear Wrangler OWL tires:	NA	A
P225/75R15 Goodyear Wrangler OWL tires:	NA	NA
Conventional full-size spare with 15 x 6in wheel:	NA	A
Trac-Lok rear differential:	NA	NA
Automatic transmission:	NA	NA
15 x 7in, six-spoke, silver-painted wheels:	NA	A
15 x 7in, five-spoke, Sport, aluminum wheels:	NA	NA
Body side steps with full-length mud guards:	NA	NA
Front chrome bumpers:	NA	NA
Rear chrome bumperettes:	NA	NA
Fender flares:	NA	NA
Halogen fog lamps:	NA	NA
Hard top:	A	A
Chrome grille/headlamp bezels:	NA	NA
Door-mounted left-side exterior mirror:	NA	S
Door-mounted right-side exterior mirror:	NA	A
Metallic paint:	NA	NA
Spare tire cover:	NA	NA
Convenience Group:	NA	A
Interior door trim:	NA	NA
Extra-quiet insulation:	NA	NA
Protective floor mats:	NA	NA
Hard top rear window defroster:	NA	A
High-back, Trailcloth bucket seats:	NA	NA
Leather-wrapped steering wheel:	NA	NA
Tilt steering column:	NA	A

A depiction of the key elements of the 1990 Wrangler's optional Off-Road Package's high-pressure gas-charged shock absorbers and P225/75R15 tires. (Author's collection)

An overhead view of a 1990 Wrangler Sahara. (Author's collection)

Added to the Wrangler hard top in 1990 was this rear window wiper/washer system. (Author's collection)

The 1990 Wrangler Sahara's interior combined Trailcloth fabric seats and full floor carpeting with a leather-wrapped steering wheel. (Author's collection)

A 1990 Wrangler demonstrating Jeep's assertion that it "has the guts and the gumption to turn an uphill battle into the time of your life". (Author's collection)

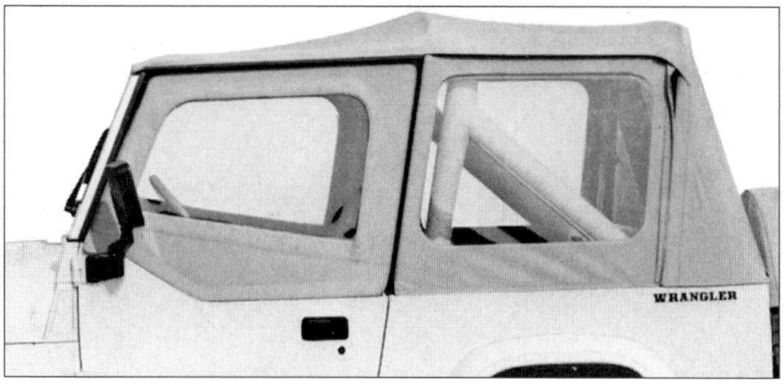

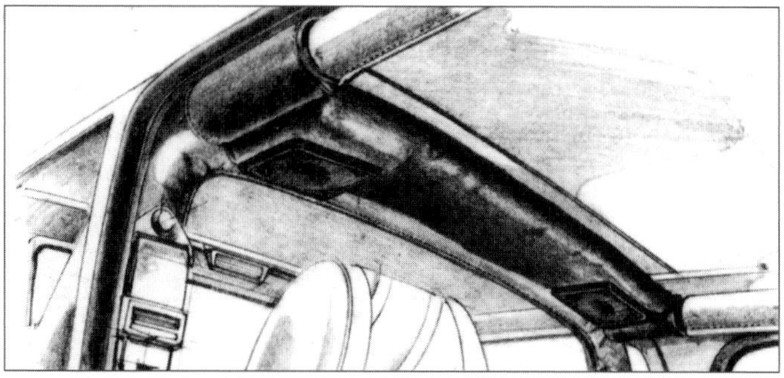

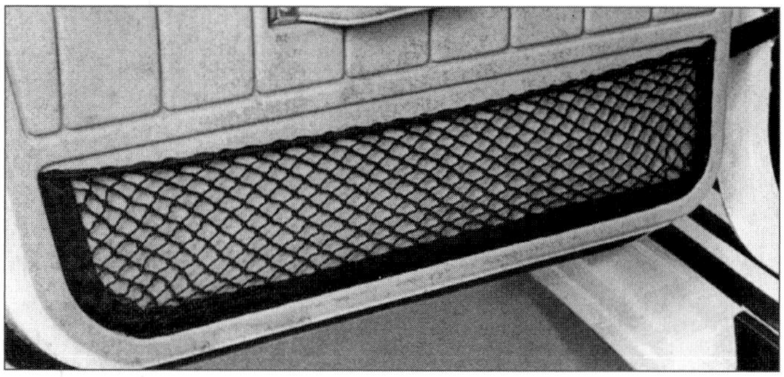

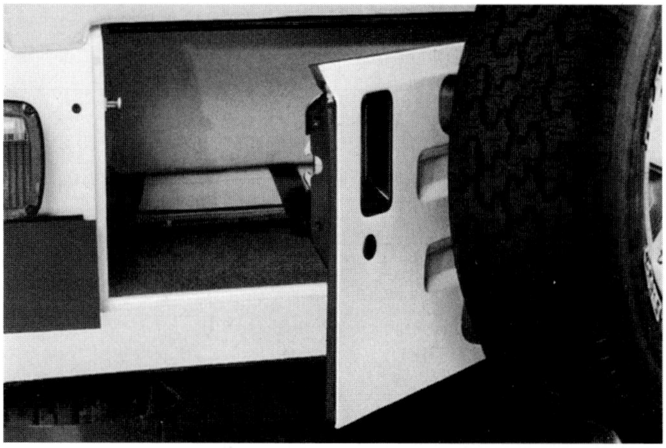

Anti-clockwise from left: All 1991 Wranglers had this soft top with lockable half-hard doors as standard; New for 1991 was this optional (not available on the S model) rear sound system with two speakers; Exclusive to the Wrangler Islander soft top models were net stowage pockets on the driver and passenger door trim panels; This spare tire carrier mounted on the vertically-hinged, swing-away tailgate was standard Wrangler equipment for 1991. The Renegade had a tailgate 'hold-open' feature which would hold it open even when the Wrangler was parked on an incline. (Author's collection)

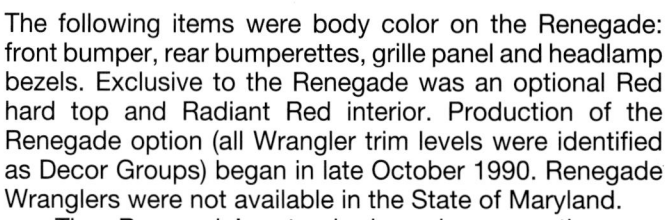

Sahara and Laredo models had a 20-gallon fuel tank as standard equipment. The other Wrangler models continued to use the 15-gallon fuel tank with the larger unit available as an option. Content of the Off-Road option was modified to include five P225 OWL tires. All 1990 model Wranglers had side-marker, turn-signal flashers.

Replacing the Laredo as the top level Wrangler for 1991 was the Renegade, which Jeep depicted as "unquestionably the ultimate fun and freedom machine". The new Renegade featured: Trailcloth fabric, high-back front bucket seats; floor carpeting; front floor mats; leather-wrapped steering wheel; color-keyed fender flares; full mud guards with integrated body side steps; vinyl soft top with half-doors; left and right door-mounted mirrors; special stripes with 'Renegade' decal; Convenience Group; 20-gallon fuel tank; fog lamps (positioned in the fenders with mesh protectors); power steering; 29 x 9.5R15Lt OWL, Wrangler All-Terrain radial tires; 5-hole, 15in x 8in aluminum wheels; and off-road gas shock absorbers.

The following items were body color on the Renegade: front bumper, rear bumperettes, grille panel and headlamp bezels. Exclusive to the Renegade was an optional Red hard top and Radiant Red interior. Production of the Renegade option (all Wrangler trim levels were identified as Decor Groups) began in late October 1990. Renegade Wranglers were not available in the State of Maryland.

The Renegade's standard engine was the new 4.0-liter 'Power Tech Six', which replaced the 4.2-liter engine available in 1990. The specifications, optional for the Base, Islander and Sahara, are detailed below.

Displacement:	4.0-liters ($242in^3$)	
Bore and stroke:	3.88in x 3.41in	
Compression ratio:	8.8:1	
Fuel system:	Sequential multipoint fuel injection	
Comparative power rating of the 1990 and 1991 6-cylinder engines:		
	1991 4.0-liter	1990 4.2-liter
Horsepower:	180 @ 4750rpm	112 @ 3000rpm
Torque:	220lb-ft @ 4000rpm	210lb-ft @2000rpm

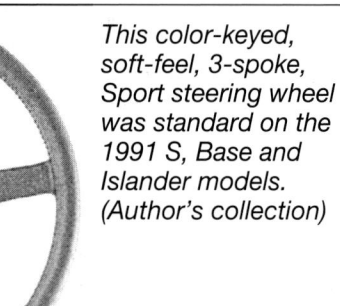

This color-keyed, soft-feel, 3-spoke, Sport steering wheel was standard on the 1991 S, Base and Islander models. (Author's collection)

The 1991 Sahara and Renegades had this color-keyed, leather-wrapped, 3-spoke, Sport steering wheel as standard equipment. (Author's collection)

The standard engine for the other Wrangler decor groups was the 2.5-liter, 4-cylinder with a sequential multipoint fuel-injection system in place of the previous throttle body unit. Peak power for the 2.5-liter was now 126 horsepower @ 5250rpm and 148lb-ft of torque @ 3000rpm.

Jeep attributed the sequential multipoint fuel-injection system, which was similar to that used on the Power Tech Six, as the primary source of the increased horsepower. A new intake manifold with longer and larger runners helped improve torque. Other upgrades adding power and enhancing durability and fuel efficiency included better flowing intake and exhaust ports, plus a new serpentine drive belt system.

The 4.0-liter engine shared many components and systems with the 2.5-liter including the complete cylinder chamber from the cylinder head to the piston cavity and bore diameter. Other shared parts were as follows:

- Connecting rods
- Oil pumps
- Rod bearings
- Piston pins and ring set
- Main bearings
- Head bolts
- Rod cap bolts
- Main bearing cap bolts, retainers and several other fasteners
- Intake valves
- Exhaust valves
- Stem seals
- Valve springs, retainers and keepers
- Rocker arms, pivots and fasteners
- Hydraulic valve lifters

A new single-board engine control computer (SBECII) monitored engine functions on all models. Improved electrical system protection was provided by the addition of plug-in maxi fuses that opened at lower levels of overload current. Accompanying these developments was the addition of 'Check Engine' and 'Maintenance Required' lights to the instrument cluster.

The EPA provided these mileage estimates (city/highway) for the two Wrangler engines:

Engine	5-speed man trans	3-speed auto trans
2.5-liter:	18/20mpg	–
4.0-liter:	17/22mpg	15/17mpg

The introduction of the new 4.0-liter engine provided the Wrangler buyer with this choice of power train combinations, all of which were combined with a New Process 231 Command Trac Part-Time 4-Wheel Drive System

A – available
NA – not available
S – standard

Eng/Trans	Axle	S	Base	Islander	Sahara	Renegade
2.5-liter/5-speed man	4.11	S	S	S	S	NA
4.0-liter/5-speed man	3.08[a]	NA	A	A	A	A
4.0-liter/3-speed auto	3.55	NA	A	A	A	A

[a] A 3.55 ratio was standard with the optional Trac-Lok rear differential and standard with High Altitude Emission Control System. Engines require the High Altitude Emission Control System on vehicles sold for principal use in countries wholly located at elevations above 4000 feet.

All 1991 models had new front seats with wider cushion and backrest pads. Optional for the S, and standard on all other Wranglers, were front seats incorporating driver and passenger backseat recliners. New for all Wranglers except the S was an optional Sound Bar with two Jensen speakers mounted on the sport bar. Common to all Wranglers was a new standard battery (58-390 cranking

A set of four of these 15 x 6in Argent steel wheels with a Black hub cover was standard for the 1991 Wrangler S. (Author's collection)

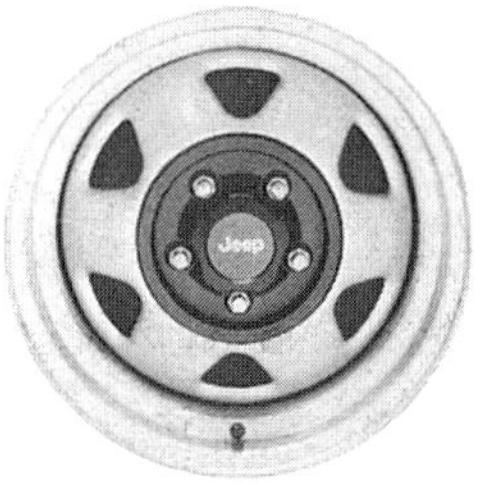

Standard for the 1991 Base and Islander models was this 15 x 7in, six-spoke, Silver, styled wheel. A set of five was supplied. (Author's collection)

The 1991 Sahara was delivered with four of these 15 x 7in, six-spoke, Khaki, styled steel wheels. (Author's collection)

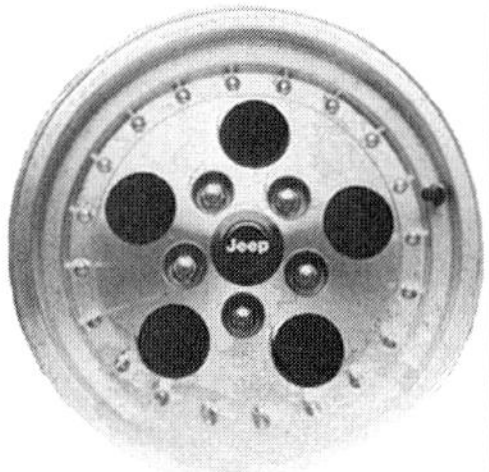

Exclusive to the 1991 Renegade was this 15 x 8in cast-aluminum wheel. Five wheels were supplied. (Author's collection)

This 15 x 7in, five-spoke, steel wheel was optional for all 1991 models except the Renegade. It required P215 or P225 tires and a full-size spare. Five wheels were provided. (Author's collection)

capacity), a 75amp alternator and double-bitted keys. Standard on all hard top-equipped Wranglers was a redesigned rear window wiper/washer system. Use of a glass-mounted, single speed wiper motor and washer nozzle prevented interference with rear window operation. The wiper/washer was operated by an instrument-panel-mounted rocker switch. Pressing the top of the switch turned the wiper on. Depressing the switch's bottom activated the washer.

White replaced Charcoal as a color choice for the Wrangler's soft and hard tops. The complete Wrangler top availability was as follows:

Vinyl soft tops with half-doors

A – available
NA – not available

Color	**S**	**Base**	**Islander**	**Sahara**	**Renegade**
Black	A	A	A	NA	A
White	A	A	A	NA	A
Dark Sand	A	A	NA	NA	NA
Khaki	NA	NA	NA	A	NA
Hard tops with full-doors and deep tinted glass					
Black	A	A	A	NA	A
White	A	A	A	NA	A
Deep Sand	A	A	NA	A	NA
Red	NA	NA	NA	NA	A

This listing of selected standard equipment for the five versions of the Wrangler illustrates their similarities and differences.

S – standard

Item	**S**	**Base**	**Islander**	**Sahara**	**Renegade**
Alternator (75amp):	S	S	S	–	–
Alternator (90amp):	–	–	–	S	S
Front ashtray:	S	S	S	S	S
Front Black bumper:	S	S	S	S	–
Front body color bumper:	–	–	–	–	S
Black rear bumperettes:	–	S	S	S	–
Body color rear bumperettes:	–	–	–	–	S
Front bumper extensions:	–	–	–	S	–
Front mini mat carpet:	S	S	–	–	–
Front and rear floor carpet:	–	–	S	S	S
Cigar lighter:	S	S	S	S	S
Front console with cupholders:	–	–	–	S	S
Hood decals:	–	–	S	–	–
Hood stripe:	–	–	–	–	S
Door map pockets:	–	–	S	S	S
2.5-liter engine:	S	S	S	S	–
4.0-liter engine:	–	–	–	–	S
Fender flares:	S	S	–	–	–

Fender flares with integrated mud guard and color-keyed body side steps:	–	–	S	S	S
Floor mats (2):	–	–	–	S	S
Fog lamps:	–	–	–	S	S
Front frame overlay:	S	S	S	S	S
Fuel tank (15gal):	S	S	S	–	–
Fuel tank (20gal):	–	–	–	S	S
Fuel tank skid plate:	S	S	S	S	S
Tinted windshield:	S	S	S	S	S
Glove box lock:	–	–	–	S	S
Heater and defroster:	S	S	S	S	S
Engine compartment light:	–	–	–	S	S
Glove box light:	–	–	–	S	S
Interior courtesy light:	–	–	–	S	S
Left side exterior mirror:	S	S	S	S	S
Right side exterior mirror:	–	S	S	S	S
Padded sun visors:	S	S	S	S	S
Padded instrument panel:	S	S	S	S	S
Power steering:	–	–	–	S	S
AM/FM ET radio:	–	S	S	S	S
Front bucket seats, Denim vinyl, non-reclining:	S	–	–	–	–
Front bucket seats, Denim vinyl, reclining:	–	S	S	–	–
Front bucket seats, Trailcloth fabric, reclining:	–	–	–	S	S
Fold-and-tumble rear seat:	–	S	S	S	S
Gas off-road shock absorbers:	–	–	–	S	S
Compact P225/75RD15 spare tire with 15 x 6in wheel:	S	S	S	S	–
Full size 29 x 9.5R15LT OWL spare tire with 15 x 6in wheel:	–	–	–	–	S
Vinyl spare tire cover:	–	–	S	S	–
Spare tire mount with swing away tailgate:	S	S	S	S	S

Three-spoke, soft-feel steering wheel:	S	S	S	–	–
Three-spoke, leather-wrapped steering wheel:	–	–	–	S	S
Tape stripes:	S	–	–	–	–
Tires:					
P205/75R15 BSW Wrangler (4):	S	–	–	–	–
P215/75R15 BSW All-Terrain (4):	–	S	–	S	–
P215/7R15 OWL All-Terrain (4):	–	–	S	–	–
29 x 9.5R15LT OWL All-Terrain (5):	–	–	–	–	S
Soft top with half metal doors:	S	S	S	S	S
Tow hooks:	–	–	–	S	–
Wheels:					
Styled-steel Argent 15 x 6in with Black hubs (4):	S	–	–	–	–
Styled steel Silver six spoke 15 x 7in with Black hubs (4):	–	S	S	–	–

Standard for all 1991 Wranglers, except the Renegade, the 2.5-liter, 4-cylinder engine was retuned for greater output. It was only available with a 5-speed manual transmission. (Author's collection)

Styled steel Khaki six spoke 15 x 7in with Black hubs (4):	–	–	–	S	–
Aluminum five hole 15 x 7in (5):	–	–	–	–	S
2-speed windshield wiper washer:	S	S	S	–	–
Intermittent windshield wiper washer:	–	–	–	S	S

Five new exterior colors were introduced for 1991: Navajo Turquoise Metallic, Steel Blue Low Gloss Metallic (late availability), Navy Blue Metallic, Canyon Blue Metallic and Radiant Fire Red. Canceled for 1991 were Sand, Graphic Red, Pacific Blue and Charcoal Gray.

Color availability for the five 1991 Wranglers was:

A – available *NA – not available* **Standard exterior colors**	S	Base	Islander
Bright White:	A	A	A
Black:	A	A	NA
Radiant Fire Red:	A	A	A
Malibu Yellow:	A	A	A
Extra cost metallic colors			
Gray Mist:	NA	A	NA
Navajo Turquoise:	NA	NA	A
Canyon Blue:	NA	A	A
Navy Blue:	NA	A	NA
Steel Blue Low Gloss:	A	A	NA

Standard exterior colors	Renegade	Sahara
Bright White:	A	NA
Black:	A	NA
Radiant Fire Red:	A	NA
Khaki Metallic:	NA	A

The following stripe colors were offered:

Islander	Midnight Blue with Yellow Orange and Bright Orange-Red accent colors
Sahara	Yellow/Red
Renegade	Medium Silver/Black

Items dropped for 1991 were cruise control, P205/75R OWL tires, bronze tone deep tinted glass and the Charcoal soft and hard tops.

The 1991 Wrangler's tire availability consisted of these combinations:

A – available *NA – not available* **Tire size and type***	S	Base	Islander	Sahara	Renegade
P205/75R15 BSW Goodyear Wrangler:	S	NA	NA	NA	NA
P215/75R15 BSW Goodyear Wrangler:	NA	S	NA	S	NA
P215/75R15 OWL Goodyear Wrangler:	A	A	S	A	NA
P225/75R OWL Goodyear Wrangler:	A	A	A	A	NA
LT29 x 9.5 OWL Goodyear Wrangler:	NA	NA	NA	NA	S
Polyspare P225/75D15 with black15 x 6in wheel:	S	S	S	S	NA
Conventional full-size spare with matching fifth wheel and wheel lock:	A	A	A	A	S

*All tires were steel-belted radials

Prices for the 1991 Wranglers and options were as follows:

A – available at extra cost
NA – not available
NC – *no cost*
S – standard

Model	**Price***
Wrangler S (with soft top):	$9910
Wrangler Base (with soft top):	$12,356

*US destination charge was an additional $485

Prices listed were issued April 25, 1991

Model Availability

Option	S	Base	Islnder	Sahara	Renegade	**Price**
Metallic paint:	NA	A	A	S	NA	$173
Bucket vinyl seats with Jeep Denim trim (Non-reclining):	S	NA	NA	NA	NA	NC

(Reclining)[1]:	A	S	S	NA	NA	$75
Fabric bucket seats with Trailcloth trim						
(Non-reclining):	NA	NA	NA	S	NA	NC
(Reclining):	NA	NA	A	NA	S	$107
Black vinyl soft top with half-door:	S	S	S	NA	S	NC
White vinyl soft top with half-door:	S	S	S	NA	S	NC
Dark Sand vinyl soft top with half-door:	S	S	NA	NA	NA	NC
Khaki vinyl soft top with half-door:	NA	NA	NA	S	NA	NC
White, Black or Dark Sand hard top with full-doors, wiper/washer, with tinted glass:	A	A	NA	NA	NA	$755
with Gray tone deep tinted glass:	NA	NA	A	NA	A	$923
Dark Sand hard top with full-doors, wiper/washer with Gray tone deep tinted glass:	NA	NA	NA	A	NA	$755
Red hard top with full-doors, wiper/washer with Gray tone deep tinted glass:	NA	NA	NA	NA	A	$923
4.0-liter engine included heavy-duty engine cooling:	NA	A	A	A	S	$612
3-speed automatic transmission/ part-time 4WD[2]:	NA	A	A	A	A	$673

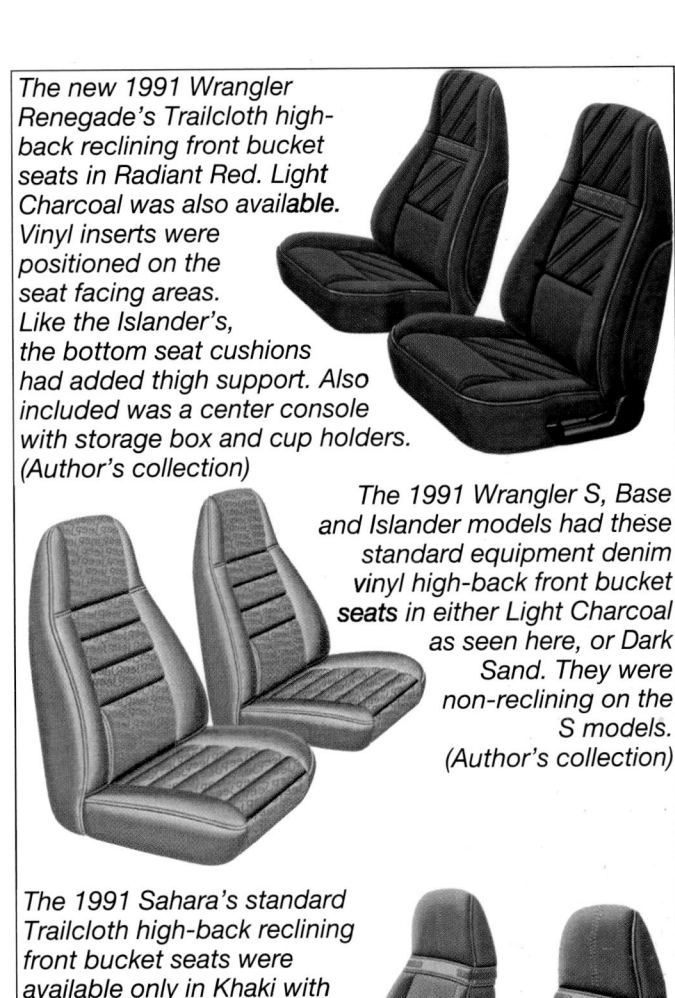

The new 1991 Wrangler Renegade's Trailcloth high-back reclining front bucket seats in Radiant Red. Light Charcoal was also available. Vinyl inserts were positioned on the seat facing areas. Like the Islander's, the bottom seat cushions had added thigh support. Also included was a center console with storage box and cup holders. (Author's collection)

*The 1991 Wrangler S, Base and Islander models had these standard equipment denim vinyl high-back front bucket **seats** in either Light Charcoal as seen here, or Dark Sand. They were non-reclining on the S models. (Author's collection)*

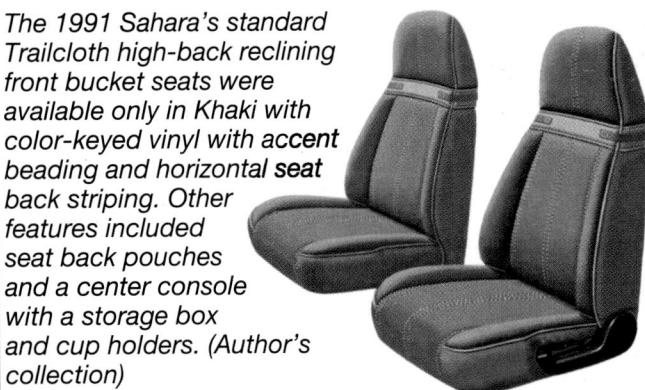

The 1991 Sahara's standard Trailcloth high-back reclining front bucket seats were available only in Khaki with color-keyed vinyl with accent beading and horizontal seat back striping. Other features included seat back pouches and a center console with a storage box and cup holders. (Author's collection)

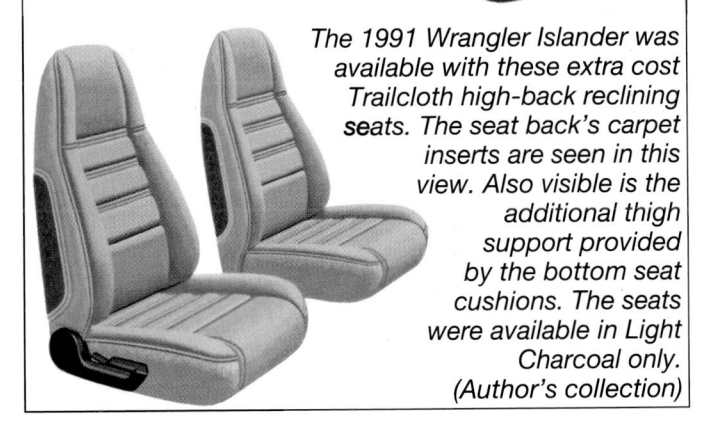

*The 1991 Wrangler Islander was available with these extra cost Trailcloth high-back reclining **seats**. The seat back's carpet inserts are seen in this view. Also visible is the additional thigh support provided by the bottom seat cushions. The seats were available in Light Charcoal only. (Author's collection)*

Rear Trac-Lok differential[3]:	NA	A	A	A	A	$278
California Emission System:	A	A	A	A	A	$128
High Altitude System:	A	A	A	A	A	NC
Islander Decor Group[4]:	NA	NA	A	NA	NA	$738
Sahara Decor Group[5]:	NA	NA	NA	NA	A	$4226
Renegade Decor Group[6]	NA	NA	NA	A	NA	$1886
Air Conditioning[7]:	NA	A	A	A	A	$878
Body side steps:	NA	A	A	A	A	$73
Floor carpet[8]:	A	A	S	S	S	$137
Convenience Group[9]:	A	A	A	S	S	$233
Rear window defroster[10]:	A	A	A	A	A	$164
Extra capacity 20-gallon fuel tank:	A	A	A	S	S	$62
Heavy Duty Alternator and Battery Group[11]:	A	A	A	S	S	$135
Right side exterior mirror[12]:	A	S	S	S	S	$27
Off-Road Package[13]:	NA	A	NA	NA	NA	549
Power steering:	A	A	A	S	S	$300
AM/FM stereo radio with two speakers:	A	S	S	S	S	$270
AM/FM cassette stereo radio with two speakers:	A	NA	NA	NA	NA	$534
As above	NA	A	A	A	A	$264
Sound Bar:	NA	A	A	A	A	$173
Rear seat[14]:	A	S	S	S	S	$455
Tilt steering column[15]:	A	A	A	NA	NA	$193

As above	NA	NA	NA	A	A	$130
Tires: P205/75R14 Black 'Wrangler' All-Terrain steel radials (4):	S	NA	NA	NA	N	NC
P215/75R14 OWL 'Wrangler' All-Terrain steel radials (4):	NA	NA	S	NA	NA	NC
P215/75R14 OWL 'Wrangler' All-Terrain steel radials (5)[16]:	A	NA	NA	NA	NA	$272
As above	NA	A	NA	A	NA	$228
P225/75R15 OWL 'Wrangler' All-Terrain steel-belted	A	NA	NA	NA	NA	$463
As above	NA	A	NA	A	NA	$419
As above	NA	NA	A	NA	NA	$319
29 x 9.5R15LT OWL 'Wrangler' All-Terrain steel radial:	NA	NA	NA	NA	S	NC
Conventional spare tire[17]:						
With P215/75R15 OWL:	NA	NA	A	NA	NA	$129
With P215/75R15 Black:	NA	A	NA	A	NA	$111
With P205/75R15 OWL	A	A	A	A	NA	$110
15 x 7in, six-spoke, silver wheels[18]:	A	S	S	S	NA	Pkg
15 x 7in, five-spoke, aluminum wheels[19]:	A	A	A	A	NA	$339
15 x 8in, five-hole, aluminum wheels:	NA	NA	NA	NA	S	NC

[1]Required carpeting and rear seat on Wrangler S.
[2]Required 4-liter engine and tilt steering column.
[3]Included a 4.11:1 ratio with I-4 and 3.55 with I-6

All 1991 Wranglers had a full-length instrument panel with tachometer, oil pressure, engine coolant temperature, and fuel level gauges, clock and trip odometer. New for 1991 were warning lights for maintenance and service reminders. (Author's collection)

engine. Required conventional spare tire.
[4]Included: floor carpeting; net door map pocket; denim vinyl, high-back front bucket seats; color-keyed fender flares and full mud guard with integrated body side step; spare tire cover with 'Jeep' logo; exterior graphics; hood stripe; lower body stripes; 'Jeep' decal/logo; 'Wrangler' decal; P215/75R15 OWL 'Wrangler' All-Terrain radial tires; and silver, six-spoke, styled wheels with black hubs.
[5]Included Khaki floor carpeting, Sand with Khaki accent door map pouches, Trailcloth fabric high back front bucket seats, leather-wrapped steering wheel, Khaki vinyl soft top, spare tire cover with special logo, special tape stripes/decal, color-keyed fender flares and full mud guard with integrated body side steps, front Black bumper extensions and tow hooks, Convenience Group, fog lamps, power steering, extra capacity fuel tank, front floor mats, off-road shocks, P215/75R15 BSW Wrangler AT tires (4), and Khaki, six-spoke, styled steel wheels with black hub covers (4).
[6]Included: Trailcloth fabric, high-back front bucket seats; floor carpeting; front floor mats; leather-wrapped steering wheel; color-keyed fender flares and full mud guard with integrated body side steps; body color front bumper; rear bumperettes; grille panel; headlamp bezels; vinyl soft top with half-doors; left and right door-mounted mirrors; special stripes with 'Renegade' decal; Convenience Group; extra capacity (20 gallon) fuel tank; fog lamps; power steering; 29 x 9.5R15LYT OWL 'Wrangler' All-Terrain radial tires; 15 x 8in, five-hole, aluminum wheels; off-road shock absorbers, 4.0-liter engine.
[7]Required power steering, carpeting and 4.0-liter engine.
[8]Front and rear, removable, included passenger area and wheel housing. Required trim and rear seat option on 'S'.
[9]Included courtesy light with door switches, engine compartment light, intermittent wipers, glove box lock, center console with cup holders. Tilt steering wheel could be included for an additional $170.00.
[10]Required hard top.
[11]Included heavy duty battery (58-500 amp) and heavy duty 90amp alternator.
[12]Standard with hard top.
[13]Included heavy duty, gas-filled shock absorbers (front and rear), draw bar and tow hooks. Black 225/75R15 OWL tires were available for off-road equipped Islander models for an additional $449.00.
[14]Fold-and-tumble design; required with reclining seats, required carpet option.
[15]Included intermittent wipers; required with automatic transmission; available with either manual or automatic transmission.
[16]Required either six-spoke or five-hole wheels.
[17]Replaced Polyspare, included spare tire lock.
[18]Wrangler S required P215 OWL tires; Khaki wheels on Sahara.
[19]Wrangler S required P215 OWL tires; required conventional spare tire.

For 1992 the Sahara Decor Group was 'freshened' via new Low-Gloss paints (Sand, Sage Green and Hunter), a new Dark Green interior color, unique 15 x 7in, full-face, steel wheels painted Low-Gloss Sand with Sand or Argent colored hub covers, and new graphics.

The radio now included a clock function. Purchasers of the Wrangler S had to order a factory radio in order to get a clock. Three-point rear seat belts were adopted. Integrated into the Gauge Pack was a 4WD indicator graphic. All Wrangler models were offered with Customer Preferred Option Packages.

The availability of certain options was expanded for 1992. These included rear bumperettes for the S model, a Bright Package and cloth seats for the Base Wrangler, and a leather-wrapped steering wheel for both the Base and Islander Models.

Commencing with the 1993 model year, Wrangler

Clockwise from left: a 1992 Wrangler Islander in Radiant Fire Red. Its striping color was Midnight Blue with Yellow-Orange and Bright Orange-Red accent colors; the appearance of the Wrangler Renegade differed radically from that of the other Wranglers. It is seen here in proximity to two other important Jeep vehicles for 1992, the Jeep Comanche Eliminator pickup and the Cherokee Limited; another view of the Sand Beige Low Gloss Metallic 1992 Wrangler Sahara showing its Sahara logo; a 1992 Wrangler S model. For the first time it was available with optional rear bumperettes. The 'S' identification was not used in the 1992 edition of The Jeep Book sales brochure; this 1992 Wrangler S in Radiant Fire Red was equipped with the optional fold-and-tumble sear seat. (Author's collection)

This 1992 Wrangler Sahara had a Limited Edition Sand Beige Low Gloss Metallic finish. The Sahara was also available in Hunter Green (late availability), and two additional Limited Edition Low Gloss colors: Sage Green and Steel Blue. (Author's collection)

A 1992 Wrangler S model. For the first time it was available with optional rear bumperettes. The 'S' identification was not used in the 1992 edition of The Jeep Book *sales brochure. (Author's collection)*

production was transferred from Brampton, Canada to Chrysler's Toledo, Ohio assembly plant.

The Islander model was not offered for 1993. The 4.0-liter engine was now standard for the Sahara as well as the Renegade. Four-wheel anti-lock brakes was a new option for the Renegade, Sahara and Base Wrangler models equipped with the 4.0-liter engine. This system, which was active in both two-wheel and four-wheel drive modes, was essentially the same as used on the Cherokee. Minor changes from that system included the use of a different master cylinder and the repositioning of components (the deceleration switch used with four-wheel drive was located under the driver's seat).

Also new for 1993 was a tamper resistant odometer. This feature had been first introduced on the 1992 Cherokee and involved the positioning of a clear acrylic lens over the odometer wheel which prevented tampering with the reading.

As with all 1993 Chrysler vehicles, the Wrangler was fitted with seven-tumbler locks. Use of the additional tumbler increased the number of possible key combinations by three times, reducing the probability of unlocking the wrong car and the possibility of theft through use of substitute keys.

Also found on the 1993 Wrangler was a stainless steel exhaust system. All exhaust system connectors had industry-standard slip joints in place of the flanged connections used in 1992.

Blue/gray tinted quarter and rear windows were new additions to the soft top. Aside from their impact upon the Wrangler's appearance, these windows reduced radiant heating of the interior and reduced glare for rear seat passengers.

A new Sport Package for the Base model, with a MSRP of $1640, debuted in 1993. Chrysler described it as "a new graphic package intended to have a sportier image than the Islander package it replaces".

An early 1993 *Jeep Wrangler Code Guide*, issued in May 1992, noted that its content consisted of these items: body side steps (body-color); P215/75R15 OWL All-Terrain tires (5); full-face, 15 x 7in, Argent steel wheels with hub covers (5); fender flares (body color); Sport tape stripes; Convenience Group; passenger and cargo area floor carpeting; 20-gallon fuel tank; power steering; Sound Bar; and tilt steering column. The major Jeep sales brochure for 1993, *The Jeep Book*, also included the Convenience Group in the Sport Package, but it described the fender flares as black and noted the 20-gallon fuel tank was an option. However, the *1993 Jeep Wrangler Code Guide* issued on January 26, 1993 did not include the 20-gallon fuel tank, tilt steering column and the Convenience Group in the content of the Sport option.

A pair of 1992 Wranglers. The Radiant Fire Red soft top model has the standard 15 x 6in, Argent styled wheels. The Bright White Wrangler has a Spice-colored, extra-cost hard top with locking full-doors. The hard top was also available in Black or White for the Wrangler, Base and Islander models. This example also has the optional 15 x 7in, five-spoke, aluminum wheels, P225/75R15 Goodyear Wrangler OWL tires and, as indicated by its tow hooks, the Off-Road Package. (Author's collection)

A 1993 Wrangler Base with the optional Sport Package. in Canyon Blue Metallic. The Sport Package was also available in Flame Red, Black, Bright White and Navajo Turquoise. (Author's collection)

New web-locking front Unibelt retractors were standard for all 1993 Wranglers. In a crash, these retractors gripped the belt webbing where it exited the retractor to minimize webbing deflection. These retractors were webbing and vehicle sensitive, thus they locked in response to a sharp pull on the webbing and to sudden deceleration of the vehicle.

Replacing Cinder/Spice as a choice for the Tweed Vinyl seats on the S and Base models was a Spice color. New exterior colors for 1993 were Flame Red, Gray Mist, Light Champagne and Deep Blue. Along with the elimination of the low gloss colors (all 1993 colors had a clearcoat finish), the result was this color selection and availability for 1993:

A – available
NA – not available

Color	S	Base*	Sahara	Renegade
Flame Red	A	A	NA	A
Deep Blue Metallic	NA	A	NA	NA
Canyon Blue Metallic	NA	A	NA	A
Hunter Green Metallic	NA	A	A	NA
Bright White	A	A	NA	A
Black	A	A	NA	A
Navajo Turquoise Metallic	NA	A	NA	NA
Gray Mist Metallic	NA	A	NA	NA
Light Champagne Metallic	NA	A	A	NA

*Base models with the Sport Package were only available in Flame Red, Canyon Blue Metallic, Black or Gray Mist Metallic.

With the elimination of the Islander, the tire selection for the remaining Wrangler models was as follows:

A – available
NA – not available
S – standard

Tire size and type	S	Base	Sahara	Renegade
P205/75R15 Goodyear Black Wrangler (4):	S	NA	NA	NA
P215/75R15 Goodyear Black Wrangler (4):	NA	S	S	NA
P215/75R Goodyear OWL Wrangler (4):	A[1]	A	A	NA

P225/75R OWL (5):	A[1]	A	A	NA
LT29 x 9.5 OWL (5):	NA	NA	NA	S
Polyspare P225/75D15 with Argent 15 x 6in wheel:	S	S	S	NA
Conventional full-size spare with matching fifth wheel and wheel lock:	A	A	A	S

[1]Required 15 x 7in wheels and a full-size spare tire.

Prices of the 1993 Wrangler models and their options were as follows:

Model	MSRP*
Wrangler S:	$10,925
Wrangler Base:	$13,343
Wrangler Sahara:	$15,842

*The Destination Charge for 1993 was an additional $495.

Both the Sahara and Renegade Wranglers were considered as packages, priced respectively at $2499 and $4266 above the MSRP of the Base model.

A – available
NA – not available
S – standard

Item	S	Base	Sahara	Renegade	Price
4.0-liter engine:	NA	A	S	S	$612
3-speed auto trans:	NA	A	A	A	$598
Air conditioning:	NA	A	A	A	$878
Anti-lock brakes:	NA	A	A	A	$599
Black rear bumperettes:	A	S	S	NA	$36
Bright Exterior Group:	NA	A	NA	NA	$197
Floor carpet:	A	A	S	S	$137
Convenience Group:	A	A	S	S	$233
Hard top:	A	A	A	A	$755[1]

A 1993 Wrangler Base model, also in Flame Red, with optional 15 x 7in, five-spoke, cast-aluminum wheels. Flame Red Wranglers were prominently displayed in Jeep sales brochures for good reason; based on 1992 sales rates, it was regarded as the 'preferred' color for 1993. (Author's collection)

A Flame Red 1993 Wrangler Renegade. Jeep Wrangler buyers, at an average age of 29, were younger than most sport utility buyers. (Author's collection)

A 1993 Wrangler S in – what else? – Flame Red. For 1993, production of the Wrangler was shifted to the Toledo, Ohio plant. (Author's collection)

Rear window defroster for hard top:	A	A	A	A	$164
Engine block heater (Alaska only):	A	A	A	A	$31
Extra capacity 20-gallon fuel tank:	A	A	S	S	$62
Heavy Duty Alternator and Battery Group:	A	A	S	S	$135
Right side black exterior mirror[2]:	A	S	S	S	$27
Off-Road Group:	NA	A	NA	NA	$129
AM/FM ET Stereo Radio:	A	S	S	S	$270
AM/FM ET Stereo Radio with cassette:	A	A	A	A	$534[3]
Rear seat:	A	S	S	S	$455
Sound Bar:	NA	A	A	A	$204
Power steering:	A	A	S	S	$300
Leather-wrapped steering wheel:	NA	A	S	S	$48
Body side steps:	NA	A	S	S	$73
Tilt steering column:	A	A	A	A	$193[4]
P215/75R15 OWL All-Terrain tires (5):	A	A	A	NA	$272[5]
P225/75R15 OWL All-Terrain tires (5):	A	A	A	NA	$463[6]
Conventional spare tire:	A	A	A	S	$111
Trac-Loc rear differential:	NA	A	A	A	$278
15 x 7in styled steel wheels:	NA	A	S	NA	$102
15 x 7in sport aluminum wheels:	A	A	A	NA	$339[7]
California Emission System[7]:	A	A	A	A	$128

[1]Price listed is for Wrangler S and Base with non-metallic paint. For other colors and models the price ranged from $923 to $1096.
[2]Standard with hard top.
[3]Price listed is for the Wrangler S. The price for the remaining Wranglers was $264.
[4]If the Convenience Group was ordered in conjunction with the tilt steering column, its price was reduced to $170.
[5]Price listed was for the Wrangler S. The price for the Base and Sahara Wrangler ranged from $117 to $228 depending on additional options ordered.
[6]Price listed is for Wrangler S. The price for the Base and Sahara Wrangler ranged from $191 to $419 depending on additional options ordered.
[7]Price listed is for Wrangler S. If ordered for Base,

Use of this 15 x 6in, Argent steel wheel with black hub cover was restricted to the Wrangler S in 1993. A set of four was provided. (Author's collection)

This wheel, in a set of five, was standard for the 1993 Base Wrangler. It was also included in the P215 and P225 All-Terrain OWL tire options for the Wrangler S. (Author's collection)

The 1993 Wrangler S, Base and Sahara models were available with this 15 x 7in, five-spoke, aluminum wheel. (Author's collection)

As in previous years, use of this 15 x 8in, cast-aluminum wheel was limited in 1993 to the Wrangler Renegade. (Author's collection)

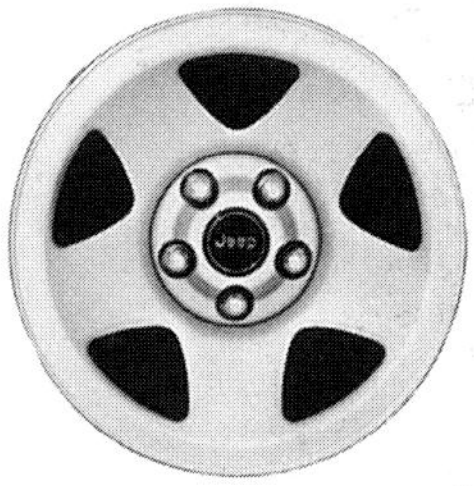

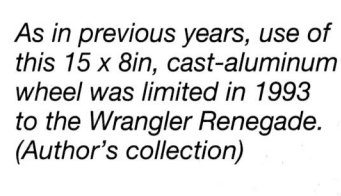

A set of five of these 15 x 7in, Argent, full-face, steel wheels with bright hub covers was standard for the 1993 Sahara. They were available on the Base model for $102. (Author's collection)

This color-keyed, soft-feel, 3-spoke, Sport steering wheel was standard for the 1993 Wrangler S and Base models. (Author's collection)

The 1993 Base Wrangler could be equipped, for an additional $48, with this color-keyed, perforated-leather-wrapped steering wheel. It was standard equipment for both the Sahara and Renegade. (Author's collection)

the price was $211. The price for the Sahara was $237.

[8]Mandatory and available only in the state of California.

The Renegade model was dropped for 1994. With the introduction of the SE model and the elimination of the Wrangler Base, the line-up for 1994 consisted of the Wrangler S, SE, Sport and Sahara models.

All 1994 Wranglers were equipped with a center high-mounted stoplight (CHMSL). These had been required on passenger cars for several years and were mandated for trucks and multi-purpose vehicles for 1994. The Wrangler's CHMSL was mounted on the tailgate. A goose-necked bracket attached to the tire carrier positioned the light at the proper height. Contact 'buttons' in the hinge area provided power to the light when the tail gate was closed.

For the first time since its introduction in 1987, availability of the 3-speed automatic transmission was extended to the 2.5-liter engine.

This Model 30RH transmission was phased in as a running change during the model year. Its features included a computer-controlled lockup torque converter that reduced engine noise at highway speeds and

Both the 1993 Wrangler S and Base model had these standard tweed vinyl high-back bucket seats. Reclining versions were used on the Base. As an alternative to the Spice color seen here, they were also offered in Cinder/Light Charcoal. (Author's collection)

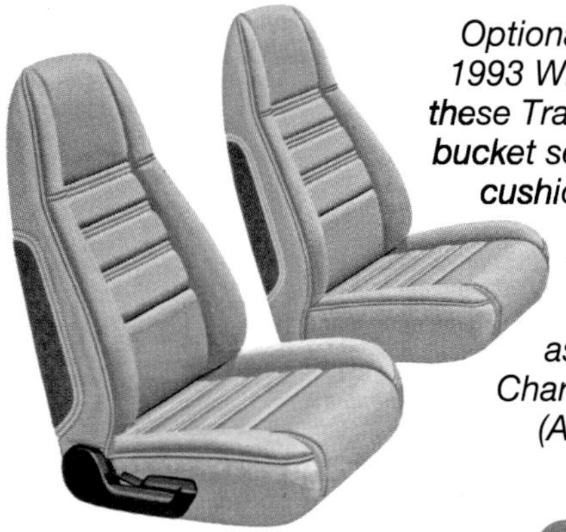

Optional, at $107, for the 1993 Wrangler Base were these Trailcloth, high-back, bucket seats. Their bottom cushions had additional thigh support. They were offered in Spice as well as this Cinder/Light Charcoal combination. (Author's collection)

The 1993 Sahara's standard Trailcloth, high-back, reclining bucket seats featured color-keyed vinyl accent beading, horizontal seat back striping and seat back pouches. Not shown is the center console with storage box and cup holders. The only color offered was this Cinder/Dark Green combination. (Author's collection)

The 1993 Renegade's Trailcloth fabric, high-back, reclining bucket seats in Cinder/Radiant Red. A Cinder/Light Charcoal combination was also available. The seats had vinyl inserts on seat facing areas as well as additional thigh support. The Renegade was equipped with a center console with storage box and cupholders. (Author's collection)

This 1994 Wrangler Sahara has a Hunter Green Metallic finish and a dealer-installed vinyl Sun Bonnet. Its Tonneau Cover was also a dealer-installed extra. (Author's collection)

contributed to fuel economy. Its ratios were 2.74, 1.54 and 1.00:1. The transmission's internal components were sized to the relatively low weight and low power of the 4-cylinder engine.

A new torque converter with a 7.5 per cent higher stall torque ratio was used in the automatic transmission available for Wranglers with the 4-liter engine. Along with the higher stall torque, it had a slightly rising speed-torque characteristic that Chrysler said provided a "good performance 'feel'". It also had an electronically controlled converter clutch that contributed to highway fuel economy and low engine noise.

The Power Train Control Module (PCM) used on both Wrangler engines met all previous California requirements. In addition, the PCM now turned on the instrument panel's 'Check Engine' warning lamp if a monitoring sensor failed. Previously such a failure only set a fault code in memory for access during diagnostic analysis.

The Add-A-Trunk option offered late in 1993 was continued into 1994. This was a steel container mounting behind the Wrangler's rear seat and was bolted to the rear wheel houses. It was open at the rear and had a hinged top with prop rod for easy loading when the tail gate was open. The security of the trunk's contents was enhanced by the inclusion in the lid of dual latches that were inoperative when the locking tailgate was closed. The lid was flush with the tops of the rear wheel houses and had a carpeted cover.

Beginning in January 1994, a non-CFC R-134A refrigerant replaced the more commonly used freon gas in the Wrangler's air conditioning system. This ozone-preserving substance had been introduced on the Jeep Grand Cherokee in 1993. Changes made in the air conditioning system, making it compatible with the new refrigerant, included means of preventing it from venting into the atmosphere, a new compressor lubricant, new moisture-removing material in the filter-dryer assembly and new seal and gasket materials throughout the system.

As was the case with all Chrysler-built engines for 1994, the Wranglers' had new engine oil filter caps with a new engine oil graphic logo created to identify engine oils meeting the most critical requirements specified by the vehicle manufacturer. The higher quality requirements were developed by the American Automobile Manufacturers Association.

Also coming on line during the model year was an optional 'easy-operating' soft top using the hard top's full-doors rather than the standard soft top's half-doors and side curtains. Except for the doors, the erected appearance of the new top was comparable to that of the standard soft top. Included in the top's linkage were over-center tension bars making folding and raising of the top a straightforward, one person operation. Molded rubber header latches at the top of the windshield aided in releasing the top for folding. The top and frame folded together and were secured when folded by elastic straps. Providing a nice finishing touch was a boot to cover the folded top. Both the top's rear side curtains and rear window attached in the same manner as the standard soft top's.

Wranglers with optional full-doors had dual door, hinge-mounted outside mirrors that were the same as the standard soft top mirrors. For 1994 they were larger than their predecessors for improved rearward visibility. The availability of the Sound Bar option was extended to the S model. With the addition of two new exterior Pearlcoat colors (Brilliant Blue and Dark Blue), the Wranglers were available in the following colors for 1994:

A – available *NA – not available* **Color**	S	SE	Sport	Sahara
Flame Red:	A	A	A	NA
Black:	A	A	A	NA
Bright White:	A	A	A	NA
Hunter Green Metallic:	NA	A	NA	A
Light Champagne Metallic:	NA	A	NA	A
Navajo Turquoise Metallic:	NA	A	A	NA
Dark Blue Metallic	NA	A	NA	NA
Brilliant Blue Metallic:	A	A	A	NA
Gray Mist Metallic:	NA	A	NA	NA

The revised Wrangler model line-up resulted in this availability of options and standard equipment content for 1994:

A – available *M – Mopar dealer* *NA – not available* *S – standard* **Item**	S	SE	Sport	Sahara
Alternator, 75amp:	S	S	S	NA
Alternator, 90amp:	A	A	A	S
Axle ratio, 3.73:1[a]:	S	S	S	S
Axle ratio, 3:44:1[b]:	A	A	A	A
Battery, 430 cold amps:	S	S	S	NA
Battery, 500 cold amps:	A	A	A	S
Anti-lock 4-wheel brakes:	NA	A	A	A
2.5-liter engine:	S	NA	NA	NA
4.0-liter engine:	NA	S	S	S
15-gallon fuel tank:	S	S	S	NA
20-gallon fuel tank:	A	A	A	S
Heavy-Duty Alternator and Battery Group:	A	A	A	S
Off-Road Package:	NA	A	A	NA
Gas-charged shock absorbers:	NA	A	A	S
Manual steering:	S	S	NA	NA
Power steering:	A	A	S	S
P205/75R15 Goodyear Wrangler BSW (4):	S	NA	NA	NA
P215/75R15 Goodyear Wrangler BSW(4):	NA	S	NA	S
P215/75R15 Goodyear Wrangler OWL (5):	A	A	S	A
P225/75R15 Goodyear Wrangler OWL (5):	A	A	A	A
Polyspare P225/75D15 with Argent 15 x 6in wheel:	S	S	NA	NA
Conventional full-size spare with matching wheel and wheel lock:	A	A	S	S
Front tow hooks (black):	NA	A	A	S
Trac-Lok rear differential[c]:	NA	A	A	A
2-speed NP 231 Command Trac transfer case, 2.72:1 low-range and shift-on-the-fly capability:	S	S	S	S
5-speed manual transmission:	S	S	S	S
3-speed automatic transmission:	A	A	A	A
15 x 6in, Argent, styled steel wheels with black hub covers (4):	S	NA	NA	NA
15 x 7in, six-spoke, steel, silver-painted with black hub covers (4)[d]:	A	S	NA	NA
15 x 7in, full-face, Argent-painted with bright hub covers (4)[e]:	NA	A	S	S
15 x 7in, five-spoke, Sport, aluminum wheels:	A	A	A	A
2-speed electric windshield wipers with washer:	S	S	NA	NA
Intermittent electric windshield wipers with washer:	A	A	S	S
Rear window wiper/washer (included with optional hard top only):	A	A	A	A
Bike Carrier[f]:	M	M	M	M
Body side steps integrated with mud guards:	NA	A	S	S
Bright Package[g]:	NA	A	A	NA
Black front bumper[h]:	S	S	S	S
Black rear bumperettes:	A	S	S	S
Color-keyed fender flares with full-length mud guards and integrated side steps:	NA	NA	S	S

Black fender flares with ⅓ length mud guards:	S	S	NA	NA
Tinted windshield glass:	S	S	S	S
Tinted rear quarter hard top windows[i]:	A	A	A	A
Sport body side graphics:	NA	NA	S	NA
Special tape strips and 'Sahara' decals:	NA	NA	NA	S
Grille brush guard[j]:	M	M	M	M
Halogen fog lamps:	NA	NA	NA	S
Light bar:	M	M	M	M
Left-side swingaway exterior mirror:	S	S	S	S
Right-side swingaway exterior mirror[k]:	A	S	S	S
Ski carrier:	M	M	M	M
Spare tire cover with Sahara logo:	NA	NA	NA	S
Sun bonnet (vinyl):	M	M	M	M
Tonneau cover (vinyl):	M	M	M	M
Hard top:	A	A	A	A
Air conditioning:	NA	A	A	A
AM/FM ET radio with clock:	A	S	S	S
AM/FM ET radio with cassette:	A	A	A	S
AM/FM pullout radio with CD:	M	M	M	M
Sound Bar:	NA	A	A	S
Sound Package[l]:	A	NA	NA	NA
Convenience Group[m]:	A	A	S	S
Front mini carpet mat:	S	S	NA	NA
Front floor mats:	M	M	M	M
Front and rear removable carpeting[n]:	A	A	S	S
Rear window defroster (for hard top):	A	A	A	A
Tweed, vinyl, high-back bucket seats:	S	NA	NA	NA
Tweed, vinyl, high-back reclining bucket seats[o]:	A	S	S	NA
Trailcloth fabric, reclining, high-back bucket seats:	NA	A	A	NA
Trailcloth fabric, reclining, high-back bucket seats with seatback map pouches[p]:	NA	NA	NA	S
Rear fold-and-tumble seat[q]:	A	S	S	S
Soft-feel, three-spoke steering wheel:	S	S	S	NA
Leather-wrapped steering wheel:	NA	A	A	S
Tilt steering wheel[r]:	A	A	S	S
Add-A-Trunk[s]:	A	A	A	A

[a]Optional for 2.5-liter engine; in place of standard 4:11:1 ratio
[b]Optional for 4.0-liter engine; in place of standard 3.07:1 ratio.
[c]Required conventional full-size spare tire.
[d]Five wheels on Wrangler SE.
[e]Champagne painted on Sahara with Light Champagne exterior. Sport model had Argent hub covers and 5 wheels.
[f]Mounts to spare tire, holds two bicycles.
[g]Included bright front bumper, bright rear bumperettes, bright grille overlay and headlight bezels.
[h]Included bumper extensions and tow hooks on Sahara.
[i]Deep tint on Sahara.
[j]Available in silver, gold, gun metal blue, black, aluminum or black steel.
[k]Standard with hard top.
[l]Included Sound Bar, top sport bar padding and AM/FM ET radio with clock.
[m]Included courtesy lights with door switches, engine compartment light, intermittent wipers, glove box lock, and center console with cup holders.
[n]Included carpeted wheelhouses and, on Sahara, cowl-side carpet.
[o]Required carpeting and rear seat.
[p]Seats were Dark Green with Spice accents.
[q]Required carpeting.
[r]Included intermittent wipers; required with automatic transmission.
[s]Included color-keyed carpeted top; required rear carpeting on S and SE models.

One of the major attractions of the Chrysler Jeep stand at the October 1994 British International Motor Show was the Jeep ECCO, publicized as Chrysler's vision of how the Jeep of the future could look. Chrysler said the key aspect of the ECCO's design was to have it be in harmony with the 21st century. As a result, explained Chrysler, "ECCO is lightweight, yet strong, versatile and durable. It is fully recyclable and is powered by the engine of the future– an advanced, lean-burn two-stroke which is mounted amidships."

As had been the case so many times in the past

Jeep used this 1994 Navajo Turquoise Metallic SE equipped with the 4.0-liter engine to illustrate both the Wrangler's exterior dimensions and major off-road clearances. (Author's collection)

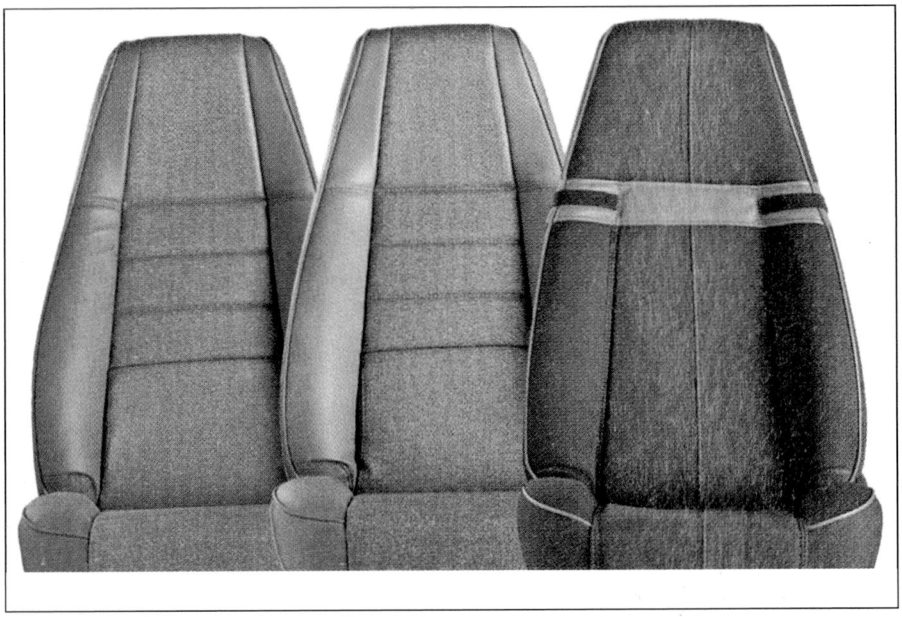

From left to right, the Tweed Vinyl seat in Spice and Light Charcoal that was standard for the 1994 S, SE and Sport models; and the Sahara's Dark Green Trailcloth fabric seat. (Author's collection)

whenever design changes were suggested, there were simultaneous assurances that the Jeep's core values would remain untarnished, Thus Chrysler added, "But ECCO hasn't lost sight of Jeep's original 'go anywhere, do anything' principles. With a permanent four-wheel drive system, high ground clearance and a wide track for optimum stability, the two-door four-seater ECCO continues Jeep's established excellence on and off the beaten track."

Indicative of the environmentally-friendly nature of its design, the ECCO made extensive use of recyclable aluminum and plastic body components.

The ECCO's engine was developed by Chrysler's Alternative Engine Task Force, a group of 15 engineers involved in developing a two-stroke engine meeting 1994 emissions regulations while also producing acceptable levels of power and fuel economy. In the case of the ECCO, this resulted in it having an all-aluminum, 1.5-liter, 3-cylinder, two-stroke engine with direct fuel injection.

With 85 hp and 120lb-ft of torque, this engine, along with the ECCO's relatively aerodynamic shape, provided what Chrysler considered "lively performance coupled with impressive fuel economy".

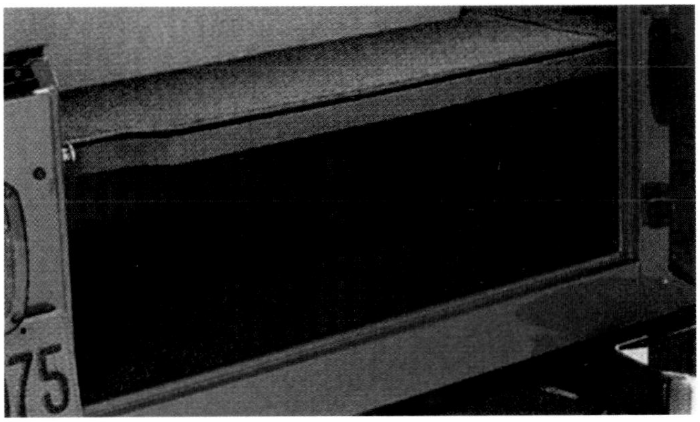

A comparison of the ECCO with the contemporary Wrangler indicates the similarities and differences:

Model:	**ECCO**	**Wrangler Sport**
Engine Material:	Alloy	Cast-iron
Engine type:	Two-stroke	Four-stroke
Number of cylinders:	3	4
Displacement:	1500cc	2464cc
Horsepower:	85 @ 4200rpm	122 @ 5300rpm
Torque:	120lb-ft @ 2700rpm	147lb-ft @ 3200rpm
Dimensions		
Wheelbase:	100.3in	93.4in
Length:	143.0in	152.7in
Width:	70.6in	66.0in
Height:	64.7in	72.0in
Front and rear track:	61.0in	58.0in

The 1995 Wrangler was carried through an 18 month product cycle. The major development of 1995 was a

A peek at the Wrangler's new-for-1994 Add-A-Trunk option showing its access via the swing-out tailgate. (Author's collection)

This 1995 Wrangler Rio Grande has a Light Pearlstone Pearlcoat finish. (Author's collection)

new Rio Grande Edition Group option for the S model. Described as "featuring an American Southwest look", it included a Spice interior with specially trimmed Pueblo cloth seats, exterior Rio Grande graphics, an AM/FM stereo radio with cassette player, Sound Bar, full-face wheels, P215 All-Terrain tires, front and rear carpeting, reclining front seats and bumperettes.

The latest Sahara was fitted with Moss Green seats with Spice accents. A Late Availability Option was the addition of a dome light to the Sound Bar.

The combination of five new and five carry-over colors provided the Wrangler with the color selection detailed in the table opposite.

When the 1996 Jeep line was introduced, Chrysler announced "the current generation Jeep Wrangler is preparing to take its place in the legendary 55 year history of Jeep. The 1995 Wrangler, the icon of the Jeep brand, will be succeeded early in the 1996 calendar year by an all-new 1997 model. Wrangler will not be available as a 1996 model."

The one-year gap in Wrangler model-year succession was not matched by any significant pause in production. Construction of the 1995 model year Wranglers at the Toledo plant was extended from July 1995 to December 1995 when the plant was readied for assembly of the Wrangler's successor.

Although the Wrangler was not available as a 1996 model, those '1995' models built in the 1996 model year for other Jeeps had a number of unique features, the most significant being refined 4- and 6-cylinder engines improved in NVH (Noise-Vibration-Harshness) subjective sound ratings and overall sound quality.The 2.5 engine that the Wrangler S shared with the Cherokee SE had new

A – available
NA – not available

Color	S	Rio Grande	SE	Sport	Sahara
Flame Red:	A	NA	A	A	NA
Black:	A	NA	A	A	NA
Bright White:	A	A	A	A	NA
Moss Green Pearlcoat*:	NA	A	A	NA	A
Emerald Green Pearlcoat*:	A	NA	A	A	NA
Aqua Pearlcoat*	NA	A	A	A	NA
Light Pearlstone Pearlcoat*:	NA	A	A	NA	A
Bright Mango*:	NA	A	A	NA	NA
Brilliant Blue Pearlcoat*:	A	NA	A	A	NA
Dark Blue Pearlcoat:	NA	NA	A	NA	NA

*New colors for 1995. Brilliant Blue was listed as a Metallic color in 1994.

Jeep reported that "with a look inspired by the rugged landscape of the Southwest, the new Wrangler Rio Grande Edition blends off-highway capability with colorful cloth seating, an AM/FM cassette stereo, and a two-speaker overhead Sound Bar." The Spice-colored Pueblo Cloth seat trim seen here was exclusive to the Rio Grande. (Author's collection)

strutless and tapered lightweight pistons that were more flexible than previously. The pistons also had elliptical skirts and thinner rings with less tension to reduce noise.

Also new was an accessory drive with a revised routing and a direct mount power steering pump that reduced NVH levels and improved accessory belt life by reducing the belt span and providing a more accurate alignment of the pump pulley. The belt spans were reduced to minimize vibration and belt squeal.

The 4-liter engine standard for the Wrangler SE and Sahara was also used for the 1996 Cherokee Sport and Country as well as all Grand Cherokee models. Its new pistons had the same design features as those used for the latest 2.5-liter engine. It also had the same accessory drive and belt span revisions as the 2.5 engine.

Additional changes for 1996 included the use of additional ribs in the engine block to stiffen the walls, thus reducing deflection and vibration. The main bearing brace now had a ladder design that tied the main bearing caps together, significantly reducing the number of possible bending modes. The valve cover used a new rubber and steel gasket. By further isolating the valve cover from the rest of the engine, it reduced airborne valve train noise. Also contributing to lower noise levels were revised camshaft lobe profiles that diminished valve train seating velocities. Not used on the Wrangler were the 6-cylinder's new Jeep-Truck Engine Controller (JTEC) microprocessor and ORBII (On-Board Diagnostics Second Phase) system.

The replacement of Bright White with a new Stone White shade and the deletion of Brilliant Blue, Emerald Green and Aqua resulted in this exterior color selection detailed below.

The conclusion of Wrangler production in December 1995 ended a nine-year model run that was capped off by a calendar year sales record of nearly 75,000 units in 1994, its last full sales year.

Paying tribute to the first generation Wrangler, Michael Kane, Jeep Marketing Manager, noted that "Wrangler is the original legendary Jeep ... Buyers tell us authenticity and ownership of an original are their primary reasons for purchase ... There is a mystique about this brand that no one else has quite been able to copy. There may be a lot of imitators but there still is only one Jeep."

A – available *NA – not available* **Color**	**S**	**Rio Grande**	**SE**	**Sport**	**Sahara**
Flame Red:	A	NA	A	A	NA
Black:	A	NA	A	A	NA
Stone White:	A	A	A	A	NA
Moss Green Pearlcoat:	NA	A	A	NA	A
Light Pearlstone Pearlcoat:	NA	A	A	NA	A
Dark Blue Pearlcoat:	NA	NA	A	NA	NA

Jeep
WRANGLER
SAHARA
EDITION
NOH 740

Facing page: A 1995 Wrangler Sahara in Moss Green Pearlcoat, a new color for 1995. It is fitted with the standard 15 x 7in, full-face, steel argent wheels with Argent hub covers. (Author's collection)

A 1995 Wrangler Sport with its 'color splash' graphics and optional 15 x 7in, five-spoke, aluminum wheels. (Author's collection)

Except for their reclining feature, the SE's standard front seats were virtually indistinguishable from those of the S model. Like that model's seats they were offered in tweed vinyl in either Light Charcoal or Spice. (Author's collection)

The standard tweed vinyl, high-back, non-reclining front seats for the 1995 Wrangler S. They were also available in Light Charcoal. (Author's collection)

The only front seats available for the 1995 Wrangler Sahara were these Trailcloth Fabric, high-back, reclining buckets in Moss Green with Spice vinyl accent beading, horizontal seat back stripe and seat back pouches. A center console with storage box and cup holders was standard. These seats, in Light Charcoal or Spice, were optional for the Wrangler SE. They were also available in Light Charcoal for the Sport. (Author's collection)

These Pueblo cloth high-back reclining bucket seats were included in the Rio Grande Edition Decor Pack for the 1995 Wrangler S. Their bottom seats cushions provided added thigh support. They were only available in the Spice design shown here. (Author's collection)

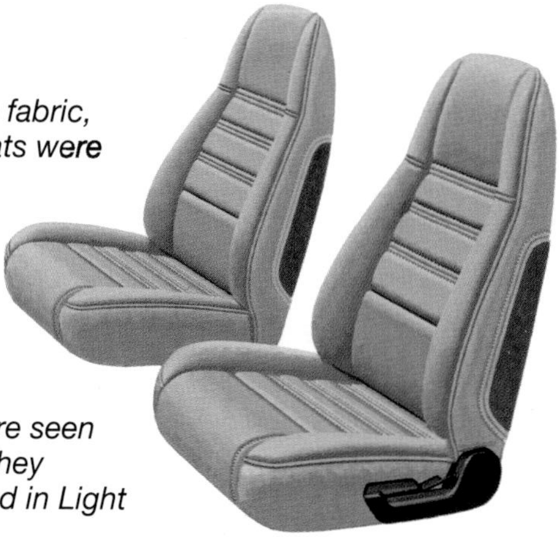

These Trailcloth fabric, front bucket seats were optional for the 1995 Wrangler S. Bottom seat cushions provided added thigh support. They are seen here in Spice. They were also offered in Light Charcoal. (Author's collection)

3 MERGING HISTORY WITH THE FUTURE – THE 1997 WRANGLER

Throughout the decades following the end of World War II, each successor to the 1941 Willys MB, from the 1945 CJ-2A to the 1987 Wrangler, had improved upon its predecessor's capability and refined its attributes without compromising what had become universally recognized as the Jeep's unique character.

Perhaps Chrysler could be accused of being a bit too exuberant, but few open-mined automotive enthusiasts would challenge its assertion that "with the all-new 1997 Wrangler, the world sees the rebirth of an automotive legend."

But unlike that of its predecessors, the 1997 Wrangler's creation took place in a new era of unified design and engineering. For its designers the new Wrangler represented a holistic approach to vehicle development since its interior and exterior were developed in the same studio.

Recalling this watershed experience, John Sgalia, Manager of the Jeep Exterior Design Studio, explained, "It was a natural marriage, since the Wrangler is an open vehicle where the inside and outside become one."

Development of the all-new 1997 Wrangler, code-named the TJ model – which debuted in the spring of 1996 – began in 1993. Serving as the performance and functional capability benchmarks for the new model were the previous Wrangler and CJ models. Competing sport-utility vehicles were targeted for comfort and convenience attributes.

While every body panel, with the exception of the doors and tailgate were new, the 1997 Wrangler retained the essential shape and styling cues of its predecessors. Along with outstanding off-road performance, those elements were identified by Chrysler as the "Jeep heritage of function-driven design".

Although the program budget for the 1997 Wrangler was a relatively low $260million, the major reason for the new model's close allegiance to preceeding design was not economic. Rather, it was intended to meet one of the nine major global customer requirements consumer research had indicated existed for the new Wrangler – that it look like a Jeep. The entire list was as follows:

1. Reliability
2. Off-road capability
3. Comfort/convenience
4. Fun-to-drive
5. Versatile and adaptable
6. 'Looks like a Jeep'
7. Safety and security
8. Affordability
9. Easy field repair and recovery

Alongside these nine prerequisites were five major global functional objectives based on priorities established in the consumer research. In each case the target was to better the previous Wrangler's level, in all cases achieving best in class. The objectives were:

-Greater off-highway capability with increased operating comfort
-Improved ride quality on normal paved roads
-More ergonomic interior – 'friendlier' and easier to use
-Better soft top sealing
-Enhanced HVAC (heating, ventilation, and air conditioning) system performance and capabilities.

These factors were embraced by the Wrangler's designers who, said Chrysler, "developed an 'almost religious' ethic that prioritized function and customer satisfaction over all other considerations".

Reflecting on the deceptively straightforward nature of these requirements, Tony Richards, General Manager, Jeep and Truck Business Operations, remembers that

A 1997 Wrangler Sport in Lapis Blue. It is equipped with standard five-spoke, 15 x 7in, full-face, steel wheels. (DaimlerChrysler Media Services)

As seen here on the Wrangler Sport, for 1997 the Jeep decal on the cowl side was placed on a continuous stamping plateau rather than on individual letter plateaus as on the previous Wrangler. (DaimlerChrysler Media Services)

"on the surface, managing a development program for a vehicle such as the Wrangler may appear fairly simple and straightforward. That couldn't be further from the truth. The reality is that planning and executing the Wrangler development program was a truly unique challenge."

Richards had no difficulty in justifying his 'relatively modest' depiction of the Wrangler's $260million program budget. "We wanted to improve Wrangler's capability, function and quality. We planned to add an interior with dual air bags. In the end, 77 per cent of all the parts going into the Toledo Assembly plant were new. Furthermore, we set out to satisfy the wide-ranging needs of customers in more than 100 countries worldwide, some of which view Wrangler as an entry-level lifestyle vehicle, while others consider it to be a utilitarian vehicle well-suited for primitive roads. All of that notwithstanding, we didn't dare compromise the authentic character that has enabled this vehicle line to thrive for more than a half a century."

Inherent in maintaining the Wrangler's appeal to a diverse global customer base was an ability to stand up to use under extreme conditions. Ensuring that the Wrangler was up to exceeding expectations was the reasoning behind 'duty-cycle' durability testing that included: high-humidity, low-speed traffic jams in Bangkok; high-speed driving over sand dunes in Saudi Arabia; jarring washboard roads and frigid temperatures in Alaska; and even Jeep Jamborees.

Tony Richards had words of praise for the lessons learned from these operations: "Due in no small part to the diversity of duty-cycle testing, all Wrangler customers benefit from a far more robust vehicle."

Consumer expectations that the new Wrangler had to 'look like a Jeep' were rooted in Jeep history since every successor to the original 1941 Willys MB had refined the Jeep image without compromising its essential character. In this process, the CJ/Wrangler Jeeps had become among the most recognizable vehicles in the world. Reflecting upon the final form of the 1997 Wrangler, Jeep/Truck Design Director Trevor Creed noted: "The new Wrangler contrasts with all modern styling cliches. It is a timeless yet contemporary design which keeps the legendary character of the vehicle."

Changes to the Wrangler's exterior appearance were predicated on this common sense position that as one of the most recognizable industrial products in the world, any design changes should be approached with extreme caution.

The result was a subtle, but nearly complete, redesign of the classic Wrangler form. The designers claimed it represented the most significant changes in the Jeep's half-century history while still bearing numerous examples of the firm grip of its heritage.

This was evident from virtually every perspective from which the new Wrangler was viewed, but nowhere was it more apparent than at its front. Chrysler explained that "sporting the signature Jeep grille and round headlights from earlier Jeep models, the '97 Wrangler's exterior design represents a refined and improved interpretation of its rugged character and function."

The use of the signature Jeep grille on the new Wrangler was a foregone conclusion. Yet, with the use of a coil front spring suspension similar to the Grand Cherokee's

The 1997 Wrangler's round headlights and the uninterrupted straight up-and-down form of its grille were clear indications that its designers deliberately intended to establish a historical link between 1997 and 1941. (DaimlerChrysler Media Services)

mandating front end changes, the Wrangler's designers had an opportunity at the start of a new model cycle to rectify a controversial feature of the 1987 Wrangler – its rectangular headlights.

Dealing diplomatically with this issue, Chrysler remarked that "the round headlamps, reminiscent of earlier Jeep models, give the new Wrangler an expressive personality while conforming to most international lighting regulations as well."

John Sgalia, forthrightly commented on this issue: "The change to round headlamps not only recaptured the familiarity of older Jeep models, but gave us an opportunity to offer a better headlamp at a reduced cost. On top of that, Wrangler owners – in true outspoken fashion – started wearing T-shirts that read, 'Real jeeps don't have square headlamps'."

This negative reaction to the geometries of the original Wrangler's headlamps illustrates what a Chrysler representative meant by saying "When you have one of the most recognizable industrial products on the face of the earth, common sense suggests that the Wrangler receive minimal exterior design changes, if any. Wrangler buyers belong to a 'functionalist' school of thought that accepts function-driven changes but not cosmetic ones. As a result, the 1997 Wrangler exterior is a subtle but nearly complete redesign of the classic Wrangler form."

A Black 1997 Wrangler Sahara with standard 15 x 7in, Grizzly, cast-aluminum wheels. Its optional full top was equipped with full-doors, roll-up windows, rear cargo lamp, rear wiper/washer and tinted glass. (DaimlerChrysler Media Services)

A cutaway view of the 1997 Wrangler illustrating many of its features. The engine is the 181hp, 4-liter, 6-cylinder. The Pueblo cloth seats were optional for the SE and Sport models. This example also has the 30 x 9.5in All-terrain tires, the largest ever offered on Wrangler, and the 15 x 8in, 8-hole, cast-aluminum wheels that were packaged with the 30in tires. (DaimlerChrysler Media Services)

Aside from returning the faithful to the fold, the 1997 Wrangler's round, seven-inch halogen lamp's light output and beam pattern was superior to those used in 1995. Similarly, the light output of its new halogen fog lamps was greater than the previous model's. The headlamps were more widely spaced than in 1995 and the amber park and turn signal lamps, located below the headlamps in 1995, were now recessed in the forward top corners of the fender flares. The grille's appearance was basically unchanged. All models had a body color grille and chrome headlight bezels. New halogen fog lamps provided increased light output compared to the previous lamps. Their appearance was changed by eliminating the grid over the lenses, which also contributed to increased output.

Far less emotional than the headlamp issue was the modest redesign of the front fenders which, along with the front and rear wheel openings and rear wheelhouses, was higher to accommodate the increased wheel travel allowed by the new suspension. These changes were also needed to accommodate the Wrangler's new optional 30 x 9.5in tires, which were one inch (25mm) larger than the largest previously available for the Wrangler. Even with the use of these tires, the new wheelhouse design allowed the rear seat to be six inches wider. New body side panels also contributed to the clearance for the new tires. The tailgate's forged aluminum hinges were stiffer and stronger than in 1995. They were also less likely to corrode than steel and easily supported the new 30in tire on the spare tire bracket.

The park and turn lamps were now located on the front fenders. The hood hinges and fasteners remained exposed to, said Chrysler, "communicate function and aggressiveness, but are now flush, with the surrounding sheet metal for both a cleaner appearance and in order to conform with European homologation requirements". The fixed half of the hinge was concealed by a removable cowl plenum cover. The Wrangler's tow hooks, door and swing gate hatches were also similarly arranged to enhance the Wrangler's look and to meet world standards.

In order to accommodate the increased wheel travel

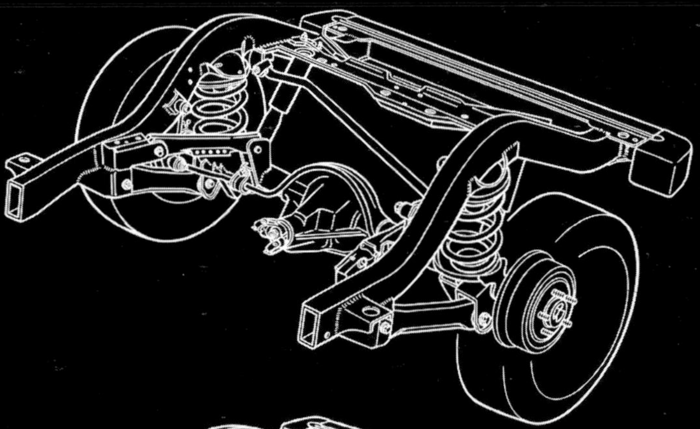

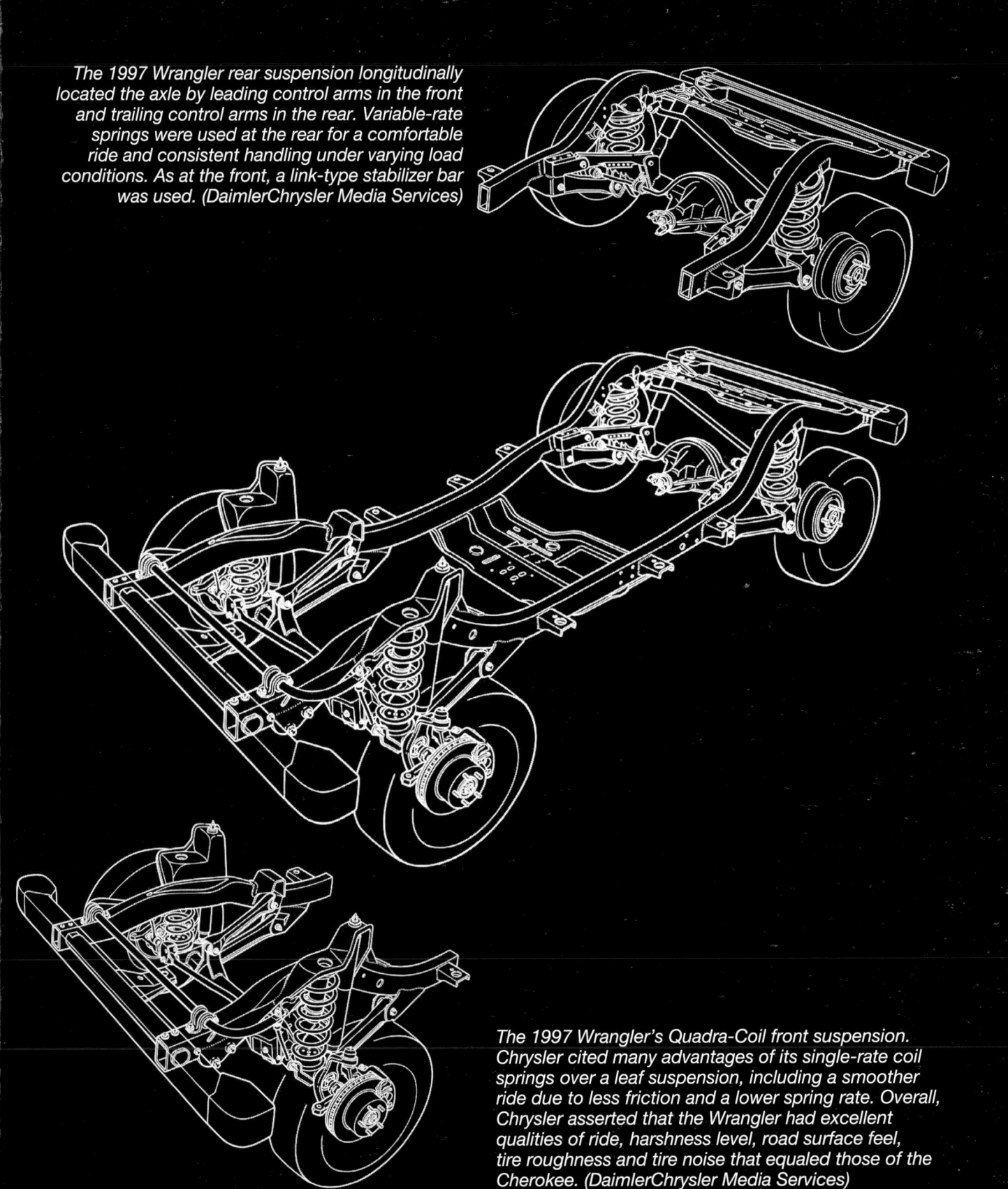

The 1997 Wrangler rear suspension longitudinally located the axle by leading control arms in the front and trailing control arms in the rear. Variable-rate springs were used at the rear for a comfortable ride and consistent handling under varying load conditions. As at the front, a link-type stabilizer bar was used. (DaimlerChrysler Media Services)

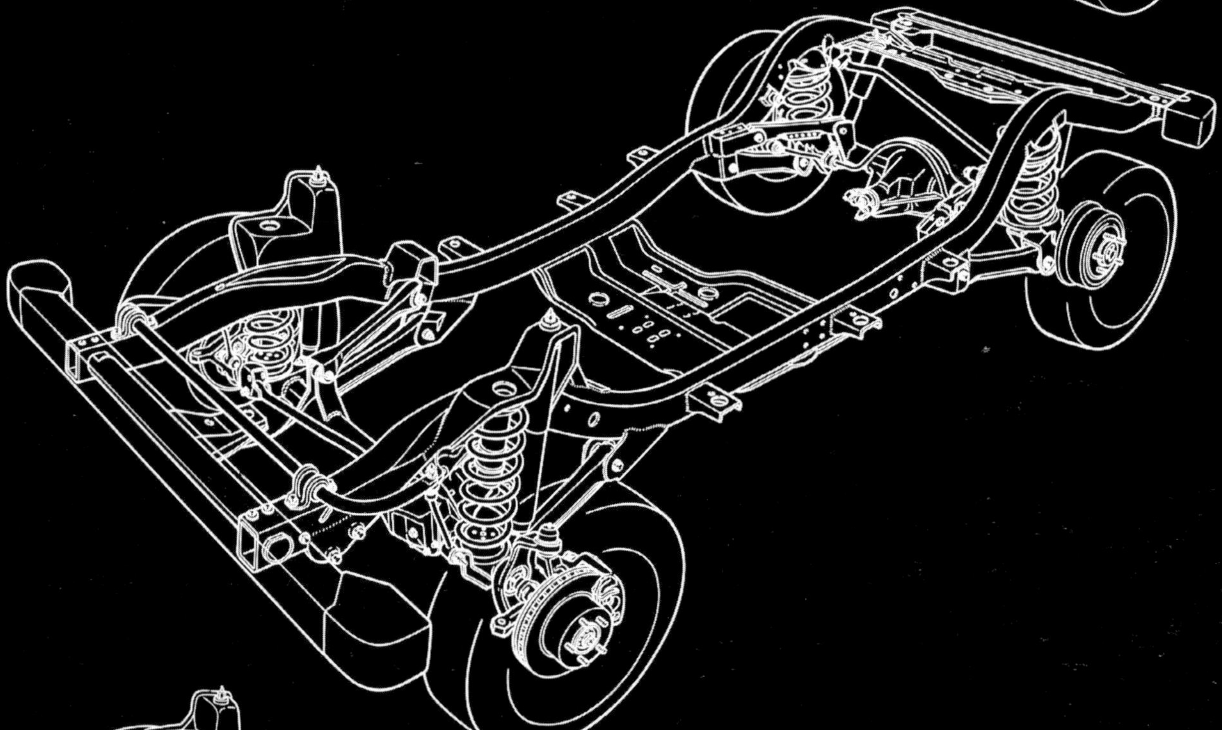

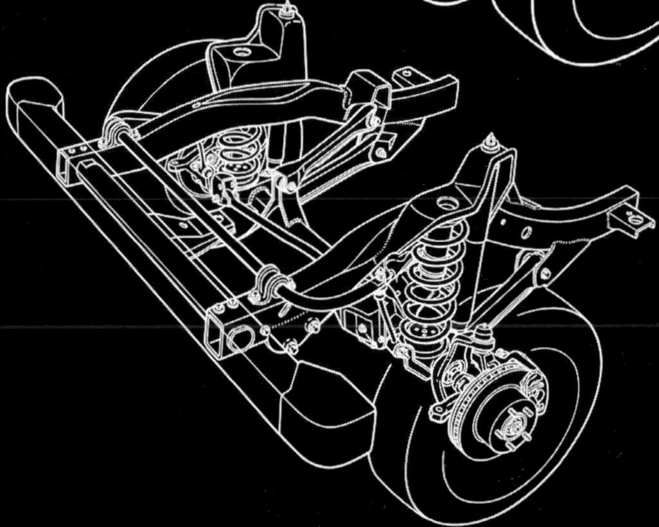

The 1997 Wrangler's Quadra-Coil front suspension. Chrysler cited many advantages of its single-rate coil springs over a leaf suspension, including a smoother ride due to less friction and a lower spring rate. Overall, Chrysler asserted that the Wrangler had excellent qualities of ride, harshness level, road surface feel, tire roughness and tire noise that equaled those of the Cherokee. (DaimlerChrysler Media Services)

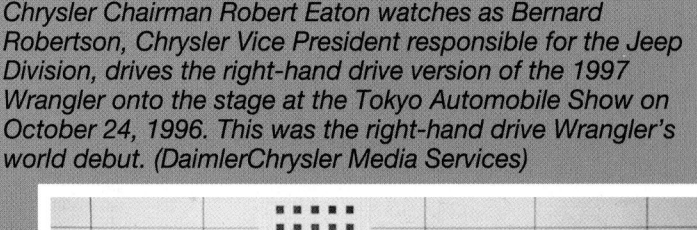

Chrysler Chairman Robert Eaton watches as Bernard Robertson, Chrysler Vice President responsible for the Jeep Division, drives the right-hand drive version of the 1997 Wrangler onto the stage at the Tokyo Automobile Show on October 24, 1996. This was the right-hand drive Wrangler's world debut. (DaimlerChrysler Media Services)

Robert Eaton and Bernard Robertson enjoying a moment or two of relaxation after Robertson's mishap-free arrival in the new right-hand drive Wrangler. (DaimlerChrysler Media Services)

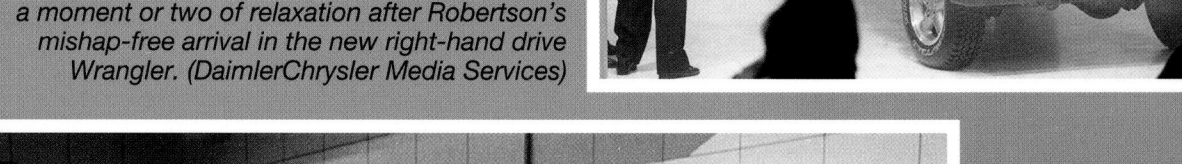

Robert Eaton admiring the right-hand drive 1997 Wrangler after its introduction at the Tokyo Auto show. (DaimlerChrysler Media Services)

Comparison views of the interiors of the left- and right-hand drive 1997 Wranglers. The placement of many elements and controls in a center 'stack' common to both versions greatly simplified their assembly. (DaimlerChrysler Media Services)

of the new suspension, the Wrangler's front fenders were redesigned to provide more tire clearance. "We knew that many of our customers liked to put larger tires on their Wranglers," said John Sgalia, "so the redesigned front fenders gave us the opportunity to offer larger tires initially, thereby benefiting our customers."

Another functional change that was motivated by customer feedback was the location of the new Wrangler's fuel-filler cap. On previous models the fuel-filler was located behind the license plate. The fuel-filler on the 1997 models was recessed in the left quarter panel aft of the rear wheel, increasing the ease of fueling and eliminating fuel spit-back. A black, molded plastic bezel trimmed the opening between the cap and the quarter panel. The license plate was now protected by a molded bracket. The fuel tanks were molded of a new monolayer plastic. The standard tank's capacity remained at 15-gallons (57-liters). The optional tank held 19-gallons (72-liters). A fuel tank skid plate was standard.

Although it was highly unlikely that anyone would confuse the 1997 Wrangler for any other vehicle but a Jeep, virtually every body panel was new and their assembly was far more refined than in the past. Relocated spot welds and improved welding techniques contributed to the Wrangler's smoother body sides. Exterior spot welds were unobtrusively located whenever possible such as under fender flares, in wheelhouses and under sills. When it was not practical or possible to locate welds in this manner, evidence of welding was held to a minimum by using welding guns with large flat back-up electrodes on the exposed side of the panel.

Stampings were consolidated to simplify assembly, and assembly procedures were revised to improve body fit conditions in these ways:

-One-piece underbody stiffeners gave a consistent floor pan mounting surface to confirm dimensional accuracy
-The dash-to-floor-pan joint was a slip plane – a joint letting the panels slide over one another rather than butting together – making assembly easy and accurate
-The radiator guard and grille opening panel assembly had fewer parts than its predecessor for easier assembly
-Simplified longitudinal grille opening panel support struts eliminated four brackets and their attachments
-One-piece front fenders simplified processing in the body shop
-The windshield frame used only a partial inner structure while maintaining structural requirements
-A new battery support eliminated several bolt-on pieces
-One-piece inner splash aprons provided mounting locations for major under hood systems
-The sports bar was designed to allow consistent windshield frame angular adjustment for an even gap to minimize noise and prevent water leaks
-Automated welding and automated fixturing were used to eliminate manual operations wherever possible
-Advanced dimensional control strategies were used throughout the body design process

This restored 1942 Willys MB from the Chrysler Jeep Imports collection was used to publicize the availability of the 1997 Wrangler in the UK in factory-built RHD form. (Chrysler Media UK Services)

Contributing to a one-third improvement in the vehicle's overall structural stiffness was the 100 per cent increase in the torsional stiffness of the Wrangler body. By contrast, the previous body contributed twenty per cent of the overall stiffness. Combined torsional stiffness of the body-frame combination was up 20 per cent and bending stiffness was increased by 37 per cent. Integrating the sports bar into the body structure provided between 60 and 70 per cent of the total gain in body stiffness. The sports bar was attached to the windshield pillars, door lock pillars, floor pan and rear wheel houses. Its main hoop was further forward than its predecessor, increasing rear passenger visibility. It aligned with the windshield pillar in the side view for a consistent flow of lines when the top was down. The bar's rear legs were parallel with the Jeep's center line and aligned with the forward extensions, helping to provide both an integrated appearance and improved rear passenger head clearance.

Both the Wrangler's soft and hard tops were revamped for improved weather sealing, reduced wind noise and ease of operation. The all-new soft top was easier and quicker to raise and lower than its predecessor. Either operation could be done by one person from outside the vehicle. Folding and set up times were reduced to less than a third of those required previously. Maximum force required to fold or raise the top was less than 25 pounds. The top was supported by three hinged bows which folded rearward in a manner similar to that of conventional convertible tops.

The Mopar bike carrier is seen here in the hitch-mount configuration on a 1997 Wrangler. The carrier was designed to carry two bikes. The carrier had a black E-Coat/Powder Coat finish. The carriers include a feature allowing the lift gate to be opened without removing bikes or skis. (Author's collection)

When carefully folded, the top extended approximately 3 inches (76mm) above the body opening.

The new soft top worked in conjunction with a new door sealing system to minimize wind noise and water leaks. Common door sealing surfaces, used with both the hard top and soft top, allowed the use of full-doors with the soft top for the first time. The door opening upper frames, against which the doors sealed, were independent of the top to facilitate top operation. They could be left in place when the top is folded. The soft top side curtains used with half-doors had heavier gauge frames for improved stability and resistance to aerodynamic forces.

The Wrangler's hard top was completely redesigned for easier installation and removal, and better sealing. It weighed 20 per cent (approximately 15lb) less than the older version, was fitted with quick-release header latches similar to those used with the soft top and had its rear body attachments reduced from eight to six. The lift gate window was wider and three inches (76mm) taller for improved rear visibility. The top's design allowed the lower edge of the glass to extend down to a bonded weatherstrip carrier that sealed against the tailgate. Other features of the Wrangler's modern hard top included new high-flow air exhausts in the rear corners for improved front-to-rear ventilation and longitudinal gullies molded into the roof to channel water away from the door openings. Full-doors had new one-piece windows for improved visibility and sealing. Vent windows were eliminated.

On the older top, power to the rear window defroster had been delivered through circuits internal to the gas props; it was now carried by telephone-style coiled wires.

In order to package the HVAC unit and a passenger air bag, the cowl was raised approximately one inch giving the hood a sloping profile line. The design team also relocated the windshield wiper motor from the inside cabin to the plenum. This made it possible to use taller glass for the Wrangler's windshield.

The windshield header remained in its former location while the base of the glass was moved forward, increasing its angle by four degrees to accommodate the air bag. The edge of the glass was now closer to the cowl, allowing the wipers to park at the base of the glass. The wipers were one inch longer than in 1995 and swept a larger area of the windshield. The wipers also had new over-center arm hinges allowing them to stand off the glass for easier cleaning of both the windshield and the wiper blades.

A more robust windshield pillar appearance resulted from leaving the rear line of the pillar in its prior location and making the pillar thicker. This also allowed the use of the previous models' outer door panels.

The Wrangler's folding windshield returned, said Chrysler, "by popular demand". Common fasteners for the sports bar forward extensions and the windshield lock made folding the windshield easier than before. A special tool was required for this operation, but it was the same tool for all fasteners. Returning the windshield to its upright position was now easier since the hinge lock and sports bar extension were preset, requiring no adjustment. When the windshield was folded for off-highway operation, the sports bar's forward extensions were removed and stored under the rear seat.

Chrysler Corporation readily admitted that "an aerodynamic Wrangler may be an oxymoron", but the new Wrangler had between ten and twelve per cent less drag than the older model. Moving the windshield forward at the base improved aerodynamics while retaining its familiar fold-down capability.

The hard top model's drag coefficient was 0.55 while that of the soft top was 0.58. Corresponding figures for 1995 were 0.63 and 0.65.

Because of the need to maintain its basic profile, alterations made in the Wrangler's form were subtle. Changes included:

-A refined shape for the leading edge of the hood
-The addition of a lip at the top of the windshield header
-The addition of rounded soft top and hard top windshield headers
-Rounded windshield pillars
-Removal of the upstanding flanges on the windshield pillars and windshield header with the soft top

A 1997 Wrangler equipped with a spare-tire-mounted ski carrier showing its maximum capacity of four pairs of skis. Cables and tabs were included with both the hitch and spare mounts to lock bikes and skis in the carrier and the carrier to the Wrangler for 'double-lock' security. (Author's collection)

In addition to contributing to the Wrangler's reduced wind resistance, these changes also benefited the Wrangler's occupants. By reshaping the leading edge of the hood and adding a rounded windshield header to the soft top, top flapping was minimized as air flow was kept attached to the vehicle's envelope, thus reducing the turbulence that causes flapping.

These refinements also stabilized air flow at the cowl plenum, reducing pressure pulsations inside the Wrangler, making the HVAC system's performance more stable. Rounded windshield pillars also reduced buffeting and wind noise around the soft top's side curtains. Along with the windshield header lip, the reshaped pillars also smoothed the air flow around the windshield, minimizing buffeting of occupants when the top was down.

"The instrument panel posed one of our more interesting challenges," Jeep Platform General Manager, Craig Winn, said. "We were not only designing an instrument panel from scratch but also adding two air bags, integrating the HVAC system and allowing for the easy assembly of left- and right-hand drive versions. Furthermore, we had to maintain a rugged look and a water resistant capability."

Going back to the project's basic goal, he added that "once again, we were meshing the past with the future." Though all-new, it retained a rugged functional characteristic consistent with Jeep history. The instrument panel's analog gauges were set in a modern cluster with black-on-white gauges inspired by the simplicity of World War II vehicles and early Willys' designs. A central stack arrangement provided access to the Wrangler's radio, HVAC controls, accessory switches and ashtray. Vent outlets were integrated into the instrument panel and a glove compartment replaced what had been an open box.

The creation of the new Wrangler's instrument panel exemplified the difficulties designers faced when their vehicle was sold in countries worldwide calling for specific configurations meeting numerous regulatory standards.

"We arranged all of the HVAC, radio and other controls on a center stack on the instrument panel," explained Jeep Product Manager Patrick Dilworth. "Then we replaced the foot-operated parking brake for a hand-operated brake lever located on the transmission housing. This configuration is common to both left-and right-hand drive models, vastly reducing component and assembly complexity. A simple but clever solution." Aside from this consideration, market research indicated that this new location was preferred by customers. The lever had a molded handle. A noteworthy feature found just above the center stack was a recessed storage tray with a removable rubber mat that reduced small object movement noise.

Alongside the panel's 'modular matrix' design were new consoles with floor-mounted shifters (previously, the automatic transmission had a column-mounted shifter). On Sport/SE models with standard mini-consoles, an accordion-pleated rubber boot surrounded the parking brake mechanism. The full console (standard on the Sahara) concealed the mechanism, making the boot redundant.

Seen here is Mopar's AM/FM Stereo radio with CD and graphic equalizer for the 1997 Wrangler. Either a single CD player or a six-disc changer could be installed. The former unit mounted in the rear cargo area and included a viscous silicon damping system for resistance to skips on rough roads. (Author's collection)

New one-piece molded polypropylene door trim panels included map pockets with slotted lower edges for a 'wash-out' capability. Also contributing to this traditional Jeep feature was the use of a water resistant air bag electronic control unit with a sealed wiring connector and its mounting on the floor forward of the console. As in earlier years, the carpeting was removable, the seat fabrics were water resistant, and floor pan plugs were positioned in several locations.

The full- and half-door versions were alike in design, but differed in detail since the half-doors were cut lower than the full-doors and inside hardware was in different locations. Both designs included a pull handle. The inside door handles on both the half-doors and full-doors now faced rearward – a reversal of the operation in 1995 – to meet European homologation requirements.

Major efforts to upgrade the stiffness and dimensional accuracy of the Wrangler's doors for 1997 included new structural reinforcements in the cowl side, lock pillars, door hinge pillars, and door inner panels to give the doors a more solid feel and reduce closing effort. The upper frames of the full-doors were welded into the lower sections at the belt line, improving their firmness for a better seal.

All-new reclining high-back front bucket seats offered increased comfort and better lateral support than the previous Wrangler seats. The day/night inside rearview mirror was relocated for compatability with the new seating position and previously mentioned revised windshield angle.

A patented tip-and-slide mechanism on the passenger seat facilitated entry and exit for rear seat passengers.

Six analog gauges were provided: 100mph (160kph) speedometer with secondary metric scale, electronic combination odometer and trip odometer, tachometer, fuel level, oil pressure, engine coolant temperature and electrical system voltmeter. The main odometer read up to 999,999 miles; the trip odometer read to 999.9 miles on all models. Warning lamps were provided for low fuel, high beam, seat belt, 4WD, turn signals, brakes, shift indicator (with manual transmission), 'check gauges', 'check engine', air bag, and anti-lock brakes (if equipped).

All-new seats (based on Grand-Cherokee-derived frames) provided an additional 1.6in (42mm) of travel at the front and, due to redesigned wheel well housings, 9in (229mm) more hip room at the rear than the older units. The seat was 6in (152mm) wider and 3in (76mm) taller than before. The rear floor pan riser was over 3in (76mm) further rearwards than in the previous Wrangler, increasing rear passenger foot room. Also adding to rear passenger foot room was the repositioning of the sports bar's floor pan mounting points forward and outboard of their original locations. The floor pan's smaller tunnel and the use of front-seat-mounted inboard seat belt buckles also enhanced front and rear foot room.

Summing up the total interior package, Trevor Creed said, "The interior of the new Wrangler is a much more modern design. It has been more carefully executed and is significantly more ergonomic. It was a major accomplishment for our designers to package so many components in a relatively small amount of space."

One of the major engineering challenges was to improve on-road ride and off-road capability while

The new Mopar hard top, seen here on a 1997 Wrangler Sahara, included tinted side quarter and lift gate windows. It also had high-flow air exhausts in the rear corners to enhance front-to-rear ventilation. (Author's collection)

maintaining the handling characteristics of the previous Wrangler.

Craig Winn explained: "Our goal for the new Wrangler was pretty straightforward: to make an acceptable road vehicle an exceptional off-road vehicle." This philosophy followed the pattern of previous redesign and revisions that had been targeted to improve upon the predecessor's capability and refine its comfort without compromising its authentic Jeep character. Market research indicated that serious off-road enthusiasts preferred solid axles. As a result the new Wrangler maintained the traditional Jeep body-on-frame construction, but the ladder frame was strengthened to increase overall chassis stiffness. Illustrating this, the 1997 Wrangler's frame had 15 per cent higher torsional stiffness than the previous model's. Contributing to this improvement was a 15 per cent thicker, flanged transfer case skid plate. The skid plate also included provision to support the transmission mount. Also contributing to frame stiffness was a new two-piece, box section, fuel tank cross member with corner gussets. The new frame also had thirty per cent higher bending stiffness which helped reduce vibration and harshness. The stiffer frame also reduced the transmission of low frequency vibrations from the suspension to the body. The frame's side rails retained the basic rectangular tube construction and cross-section of the 1995 Wrangler's frame but the walls were 25 per cent thicker. Frame corrosion protection was significantly improved through the use of a new cleaning process and new solvents in the paint.

This frame enabled use of a new all-coil spring Quadra-Coil suspension with an additional seven inches of articulation over the previous leaf spring set-up, as well as improved ground clearance and approach and departure angles. Market research disclosed that serious off-highway enthusiasts preferred solid axles and the use of this coil spring suspension with front and rear solid axles was a logical design choice.

Chrysler asserted that "coil springs are inherently better for both ride and off-highway operation than leaf

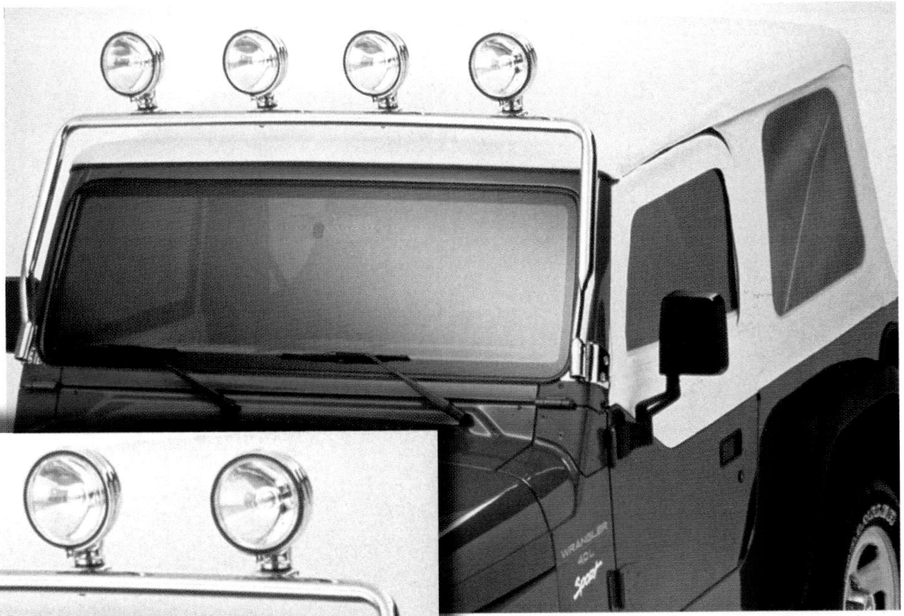

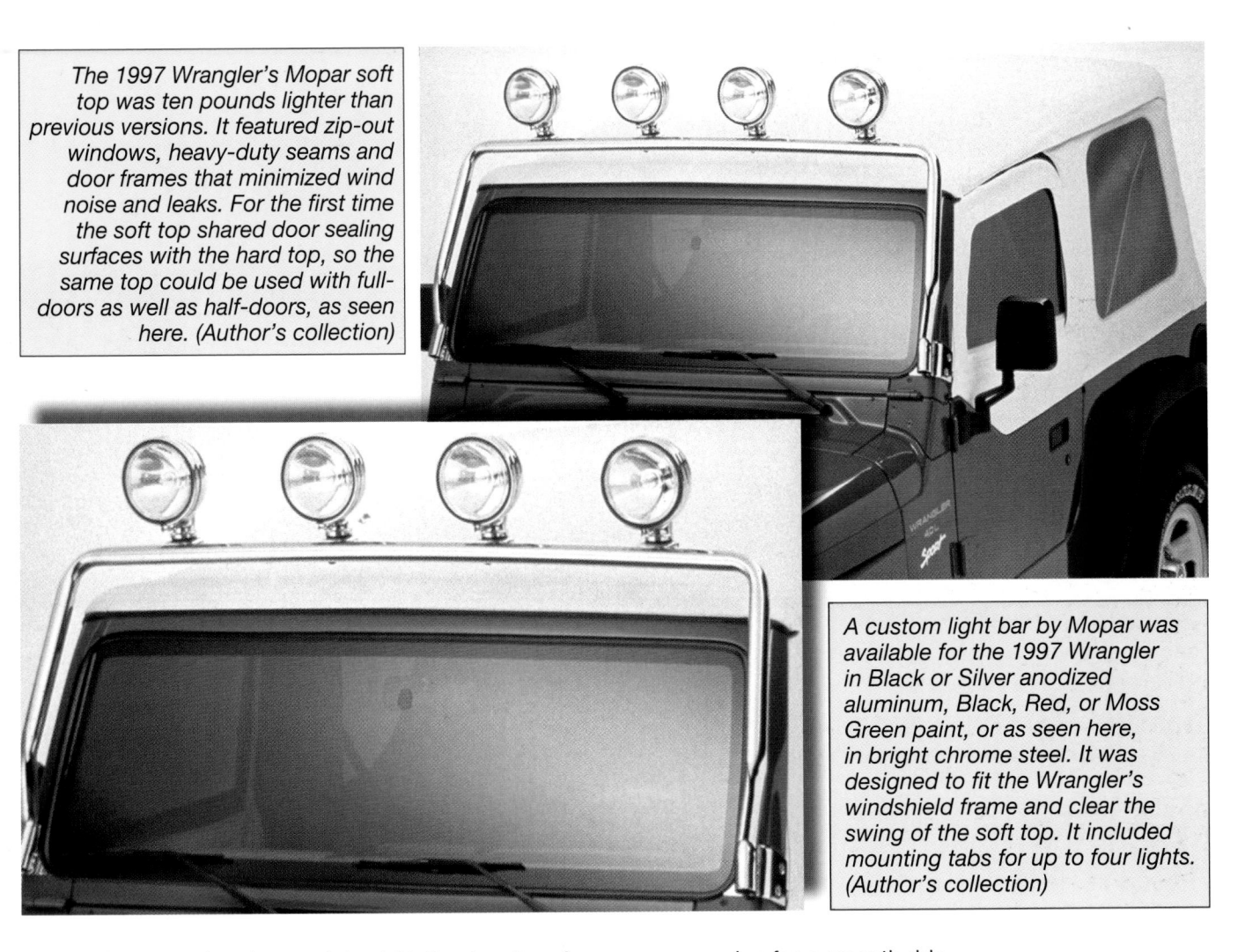

The 1997 Wrangler's Mopar soft top was ten pounds lighter than previous versions. It featured zip-out windows, heavy-duty seams and door frames that minimized wind noise and leaks. For the first time the soft top shared door sealing surfaces with the hard top, so the same top could be used with full-doors as well as half-doors, as seen here. (Author's collection)

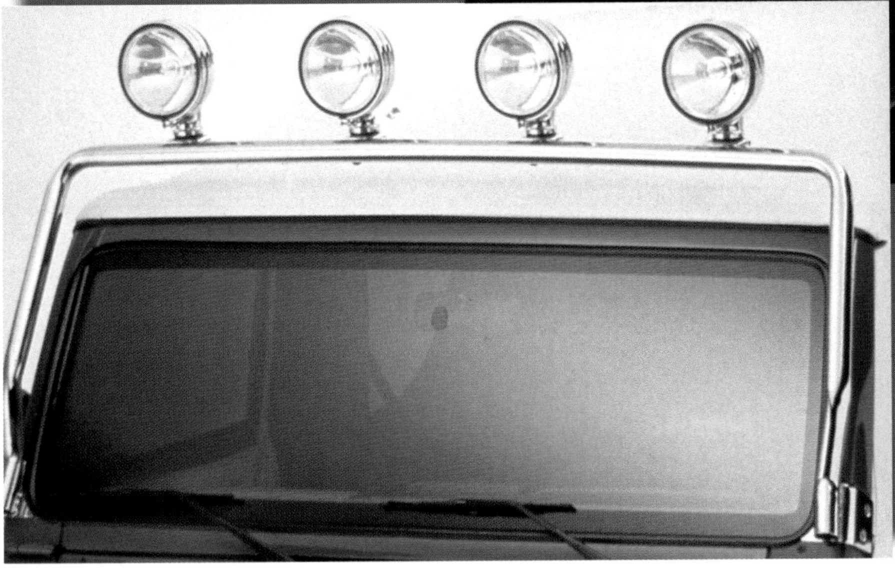

A custom light bar by Mopar was available for the 1997 Wrangler in Black or Silver anodized aluminum, Black, Red, or Moss Green paint, or as seen here, in bright chrome steel. It was designed to fit the Wrangler's windshield frame and clear the swing of the soft top. It included mounting tabs for up to four lights. (Author's collection)

springs because they have minimal friction to allow free articulation and smooth operation. Grand Cherokee, Wrangler's upscale sibling, pioneered this system with excellent results"

Chrysler cited these examples of the Quadra-Coil's benefits for Wrangler buyers:

-More durable and less complex than independent systems
-Less tire wear than independent systems because tire chamber does not change during ride motions
-Excellent ride – comparable to independent systems on the road and far superior to them off the road
-Excellent ride control due to wide-mounted coil springs and shock absorbers
-Ample wheel travel balanced between jounce and rebound for comfort and confidence in off-highway operation
-More dynamic ground clearance than independent systems
-Less friction and a lower rate than a leaf spring suspension for a smooth ride
-Excellent isolation of the passenger compartment from harshness cause by impact bumps
-Excellent diagonal articulation – approximately 7.9in (178mm) more than the current Wrangler – providing off-highway capabilities surpassing those of the legendary Jeep CJ
-Excellent handling characteristics – transient handling response, handling precision, handling linearity, cornering performance, cross wind stability and on-center handling response; equal to or better than its predecessor
-Excellent straight-line tracking – the ability to hold a straight course with minimal steering correction

Both the front and rear springs were computer-selected to maintain the specified ride height and ride frequency regardless of the equipment installed on the Wrangler. The front springs had a conventional single-rate design while variable-rate rear springs were used. Aside from providing a comfortable ride the variable-rate springs helped maintain consistent handling under varying load conditions. This was particularly useful in a vehicle such as the Wrangler where loading was usually concentrated at the rear.

Link-type stabilizer bars were used both front and rear. The front stabilizer bar was mounted above the frame to maintain a steep front ramp angle and to protect the bar from damage. The rear stabilizer bar was mounted atop the axle housing, also to protect it from damage. It was linked to the body forward of the axle.

The standard shock absorbers were of conventional low-pressure gas design with twin tube construction and were equipped with oversize reservoir tubes to help keep the fluid cool. Deflected disc valves were used to control ride motions.

A new front axle differential carrier placed the drive pinion below the axle center line to avoid interference with the floor pan and to reduce universal joint angles for smoother and quieter operation. The pinion was also shorter to further reduce joint angles. Seamless axle tubes provided increased strength compared to the welded construction used in 1995. Axle ratio availability was the same as in 1995.

Longitudinal location of the axles was by leading control arms in the front and trailing control arms in the rear. Attachments of lower control arms and shock absorbers brackets to the frame were designed to minimize their vulnerability in off-highway situations. Long cross-vehicle front and rear track bars provided lateral location with only minor angle change during suspension travel.

The jounce bumpers were of a progressive, dual-rate, micro-cellular design. Use of urethane provided internal damping that prevented suspension spring-back from a compressed condition. It had the added benefit of a nearly constant rate regardless of temperature, a major factor in maintaining ride quality in all weather conditions.

Summing up the impact of the new chassis and suspension, Craig Winn, said it gave the Wrangler "the best 'out-of-the-box' off-highway capability of any of its predecessors or the competition, for that matter". The Chrysler Corporation asserted that the new Wrangler's suspension was equal to, or better than, its predecessors in such key areas as transient handling response, cornering performance, cross wind stability and on-center handling response. With no changes made in the Wrangler's brakes for 1997, it was equipped with 11 x 0.94in front-vented disc brakes with single piston sliding calipers and 9 x 2.5in drums at the rear. Respective front and rear swept area was 198.5in^2 and 141.4in^2.

Customer expectations for compactness and excellent maneuverability mandated that the Wrangler's exterior dimensions remain unchanged. A comparison of the interior and exterior dimensions of the 1995 and 1997 Wranglers indicates the scope of the changes made:

Model:	**1995**	**1997**
Interior dimensions (in inches)		
Headroom, front/rear:		
Soft top:	41.4/40.3	42.3/40.6
Hard top:	40.2/40.6	40.9/39.4
Leg room, front/rear:	39.4/35.0	41.1/34.9
Shoulder room, front/ rear:	57.5/47.0	51.9/57.3
Hip room, front/rear:	53.6/34.5	51.0/43.5
Cargo volume (cubic feet)		
Rear seat up:	5.31	11.3/10.9*
Rear seat folded:	16.57	36.9/35.7*
Rear seat removed:	22.14	55.2/53.5*
*Soft top/hard top		
Exterior dimensions (in inches)		
Wheelbase:	93.4	93.4
Overall length (to spare tire):	151.9	151.8
Overall length (to bumper):	unknown/ omit	147.7
Overhang, front/rear:	23.9/34.7*	24.1/33.7
*With P215 spare tire; 35.7in with P225 spare tire		

Track, front/rear:	58.0/58.0	58.0/58.0
Overall width:	66.0	66.7
Height (at curb weight)		
Soft top:	71.9	70.0
Hard top:	69.5	68.9
Ground clearance		
Front axle (min/max):	7.5/8.4	8.0/9.6
Rear axle (min/max);	8.4/8.6	7.9/9.5
Minimum running clearance:	10.0	9.7
Angle of approach/ departure:	33.2°/36.1°	42.5°/30.5°
Breakover angle:	26.7°	25.5°
Frontal area:	25.5ft^2	28.2ft^2
Drag Coefficient:		
Hard top:	0.63	0.55
Soft top:	0.65	0.58

Replacing the S, Rio Grande, SE, Sport and Sahara models of 1995 were just three Wranglers for 1997; the SE, Sport and Sahara. The SE corresponded to the 1995 Wrangler S, and the Sport was equivalent to the SE. The status of the Sahara was unchanged.

Modest variations in weight existed between the three Wranglers:

Model:	SE	Sport	Sahara
Curb weight (approx)	3092lb	3229lb	3229lb
GVRW:	4360lb	4380lb	4380lb
Weight distribution (F/R):	49/51	51/49	51/49

More significant were the various tire and wheel combinations available for the SE, Sport and Sahara Wranglers.

A – available *NA – not available* *S – standard* **Tires**	SE	Sport	Sahara
Goodyear Wrangler RT/S P205/ 75R15 BSW A/T:	S	NA	NA
Goodyear Wrangler GS-A P215/ 75R15 BSW A/T:	NA	S	NA
Goodyear Wrangler GS-A P225/ 75R15 OWL A/T:	NA	A	S
Goodyear Wrangler RT/S P215/ 75R15 OWL A/T:	A	A	NA
Goodyear Wrangler GS/A P225/ R15 OWL A/T:	A	A	NA
Goodyear Wrangler GS-A 30 x 9.5 x 15 OWL:	NA	A	A
Wheels			
15 x 6in styled disc:	X	NA	NA
15 x 7in full-face steel:	A	S	NA
15 x 7 cast-aluminum:	NA	A	S
15 x 8in cast-aluminum:	NA	A	A

Two new all-terrain tire designs, the Goodyear Wrangler RT/S and Goodyear Wrangler GS-A, were used for the new Wrangler. Their construction and compounding were refined in conjunction with the suspension tuning to fit the Wrangler's ride and handling. Both tires had proprietary names, but featured rubber compounding and carcass construction engineered specifically for the 1997 Wrangler and fine-tuned in conjunction with its suspension system. These tire's development focused on minimizing rolling resistance, providing a smooth ride and maintenance of a high level of adhesiveness on wet and dry pavement.

The Wrangler was the first Jeep vehicle to use the Wrangler RT/S tire. The use of new rubber compounds and a higher inflation pressure gave the RT/S tires twenty-five per cent less rolling resistance than the tires used in 1995. Tire pressure was 33psi (9228kPa) for most sizes. Compared to its predecessor, the RT/S had a longer tread life and greater snow traction. The RT/S had unique sidewall graphics, either black sidewall or Outline White Letter designs.

The GS-A tire was new to the Wrangler but had previously been available for the Grand Cherokee. They had an asymmetrical tread design that improved paved-road steering and handling without sacrificing off-highway traction. On pavement they provided better on-center steering response, improved handling control and less tread noise than strictly off-road tires. The inboard tread pattern was open and designed to provide the traction needed for off-road operation. The outboard tread, with a more open pattern, was similar to a passenger car's tire, providing additional rubber on the road for good response and handling. Its pattern also reduced tread noise on the road. The appearance of the GS-A was enhanced by its Outline White Letter sidewall design.

A set of five new 15 x 7in, 'Grizzly', five-spoke, cast-aluminum wheels was standard with Sahara equipment and optional with Sport equipment. A set of five 15 x 8in aluminum wheels were included with the 30in tires. Continued for 1997 were the previously available Argent, slotted, 15 x 6in steel wheels with black hub covers

A 1997 Wrangler equipped with a chrome grille/brush guard. This accessory did not interfere with federally mandated headlight, or parking light visibility patterns. It had also been impact-tested by Jeep engineering to ensure proper air bag operation. (Author's collection)

(standard for the SE), and the 15 x 7in full-face Argent steel wheels with argent hub covers that were standard for the Sport and optional for the SE.

Carried over from 1995 were updated versions of the Wrangler's 2.5-liter, 4-cylinder and 4.0-liter, 6-cylinder engines along with the previously available 5-speed manual and 3-speed automatic transmissions. These changes resulted in this model/power train availability for 1997:

As noted in the previous chapter, both Wrangler engines had been modified in 1996 for quieter and smoother operation. For 1997 the 4.0-liter engine's power rating differed slightly from their previous levels:

A – available *NA – not available* *S – standard* **Engine/Transmission**	**SE**	**Sport**	**Sahara**
2.5-liter/5-speed manual	S	NA	NA
2.5-liter/3-speed automatic	A	NA	NA
4.0-liter/5-speed manual	NA	S	S
4.0-liter/3-speed manual	NA	A	A

The 2.5-liter engine's compression ratio was also changed from 9.1:1 in 1995/6 to 9.2:1 for 1997.

	1995/6	**1997**
Horsepower:	180 @ 4750rpm	181 @ 4600rpm
Torque:	220lb-ft @ 4000rpm	222lb-ft @ 2800rpm

The 2.4-liter engine's ratings were also revised:

	1995/6	**1997**
Horsepower:	123 @ 5250rpm	120 @ 5400rpm
Torque:	139lb-ft @ 3250rpm	140lb-ft @ 3500rpm

For 1997 the Wrangler engines shared the JTEC power train module with other Jeep and Dodge truck engines. It provided both engine and automatic transmission controls functions as well as the sensing and functional analysis capabilities required by the ORB II diagnostic system. JTEC also included new fuel injection ignition timing and idle speed control software that resulted in better driveability and reduced emissions.

New, larger Group 34 batteries with up to 20 per cent higher cold cranking capacity than in 1995 were used for 1996. Two ratings were available: 500 CCA (Cold Cranking Amperes) and 600 CCA.

The 500 CCA battery was standard for the SE and Sport. The Sahara had the 600 CCA as standard. Both the SE and Sport could be ordered with the Heavy-Duty Electrical Package which included the 600 CCA battery.

The Wrangler's exhaust pipe was routed under the oil pan forward of the sump to provide increased ground clearance. Compared to the arrangement on the 1995

This adjustable cargo tray for the 1997 Wrangler was designed for organizing storage and to help protect the rear cargo area. It was made of high-density polyethylene and had a 5in wall to help contain stored material and help keep spills off the floor carpet. It also had a molded-in Jeep logo and two adjustable dividers to help keep cargo from shifting over rough, uneven terrain. (Author's collection)

Wrangler, the pipe was 3.2 inches higher. As in 1995, the exhaust system used all stainless steel materials and included an under-floor catalytic converter and a rear-mounted muffler. The muffler was 18 per cent larger than in 1995 and was tuned to provide what Chrysler described as a 'beefier' sound with no increase in overall noise level.

The Wrangler's NV231 Command-Trac transfer case was functionally unchanged for 1997. In 4WD low range, the transfer case multiplied transmission torque output by 2.72 times. This gave the 4-cylinder Wrangler sufficient torque to start from a standstill on a 30° slope and easily climb an 18° slope (32 per cent grade) in third gear.

The transfer case's sealing integrity was enhanced for 1997 by eliminating the extension housing for the rear yoke. A lip seal at the rear of the main housing now experienced only rotary motion of the output. Plunging motion of the yoke relative to the output shaft due to suspension action now occurred inside a convoluted rubber boot that rotated with the driveshaft.

The same 5-speed manual transmission used in 1995 was retained for 1997. A new torque converter providing more torque multiplication at low speed was coupled to the 4.0-liter engine. A redesign of both the stator and impeller blades provided a 14 per cent stall torque increase and a substantial reduction in slippage, which helped fuel economy and reduced engine 'flare' at launch.

Chrysler reported that compared to 1995, highway fuel economy of the 4.0-liter Wrangler improved by three miles per-gallon with manual transmission and one mile per-gallon with automatic due to lower wind and rolling resistance. City fuel economy was also two miles per-gallon better with manual transmission compared to 1995.

Highway fuel economy with the 2.5-liter engine improved by one mile per-gallon with both manual and automatic transmission.

The Wrangler's 1997 EPA Fuel Economy ratings were as follows:

Engine	**2.5-liter**	**4.0-liter**
EPA Fuel Economy		
Mpg City/Hwy (manual transmission):	19/21mpg	17/21mpg
Mpg City/Hwy (automatic transmission):	17/19mpg	15/18mpg

As had been the case with previous Wranglers, there were numerous features, subtleties and easy-to-identify features that gave the SE, Sport and Sahara separate and unique personalities.

The standard front bumper for the SE was taller, light and stronger than in 1995. The bumper's increased strength was due to the use of a higher tensile strength steel and use of a 'C' shaped cross-section in place of an open channel. A rear bumper, optional on the SE and standard on the Sport and Sahara, was of the same construction as the front bumper. It replaced the bumperettes used previously. Molded rear bumper end black caps with a grained finish were standard equipment for the Sport and Sahara and were included on the SE when the rear bumper was added.

All three had new removable frame-mounted side steps that were lower, longer and wider than the former sill-mounted steps provided easier entry and exit. To minimize intrusion, the steps tucked under the body sill. They were available alone on the SE and Sport; on the Sahara they were combined with lower body side-moldings. New body color sill moldings for the Sahara were coordinated with larger fender flares.

Two new, more robust, molded plastic fender flare designs with deeper cross sections were used for 1997. Influencing their shape was the availability of the 30in tires on the Sport and Sahara Wranglers. The flares on the SE and Sport retained their previous molded-in-black color but now had a scuff-resistant grain finish. They were also wider than those on earlier models, at 3.5in (90mm), for better tire coverage. Both the SE and Sport Wranglers had standard mud guards mounted behind the front fender flares. They were longer than those used in 1995.

The Sahara's flares were body color, had a smooth finish and were, relative to those found on the SE and Sport, taller and had a 4.25in (110mm) width. They connected with new body-color sill moldings to provide added splash protection. The fender flares on all three models had contoured front side marker lights recessed into their forward top corners.

High-pressure monotube shock absorbers were standard on the Sahara and included with the new optional 30 x 9.5in tire and wheel package for the Sport and Sahara. These shock absorbers were similar to the monotube shocks offered in 1995. However, compared to 1995, their mounting was inverted, placing the shock body lower in the air stream for better cooling, enhancing durability and fade resistance.

As in 1995, four-wheel Teves Mark 20 anti-lock brakes were available (only for the Sport and Sahara Wrangler equipped with the 4.0-liter engine). The system's hydraulic unit was smaller and quieter than the previous unit. To minimize noise transmission from the hydraulic unit into the Wrangler interior, two layers of insulation were provided – between the unit and its bracket, and between the bracket and the body. Performance characteristics and diagnostic functions were unchanged from 1995.

Replacing the previously used center link steering system was a Haltenberger steering linkage similar to that used on the Grand Cherokee. A constant ratio 14:1 recirculating ball, power steering gear superseded the variable ratio gear of 1995. Power steering was standard on the Sport and Sahara and optional for the SE Wrangler which had standard recirculating ball, manual steering with a ratio of 24:1. The power steering pump mounted directly to the intake manifold, reducing weight. The reservoir was integral with the pump on the 4.0-liter engine and remotely mounted on the fan shroud with the 2.5-liter engine.

All models had a new steering wheel and column system ergonomically located for height and reach. The two-spoke steering wheel had a magnesium armature and a steel rim and hub. Magnesium's weight, much lighter than steel's, helped minimize steering wheel shake.

New linkage for the brake pedal resulted in a more refined operation due to lower pedal position and less pedal travel. The hydraulically controlled clutch also had a new pedal linkage that facilitated easier pedal modulation for smooth engagement. Chrysler reported that use of a new accelerator pedal and linkage gave the Wrangler "best-in class accelerator pedal effort and travel".

A new loop-pile carpeting was 20 per cent thicker than prior carpet material. Front floor carpeting was standard for the SE. Full carpeting for front floor, rear floor, rear wheelhouses and cargo floor was standard for the Sport and Sahara. The Sahara also had separate pieces of carpet with a semi-rigid backing covering the cowl sides, side sills and the rear body sides forward of the wheelhouses.

New vinyl-covered sun visors had swivel hinges for side window coverage. Two weather-resistant spare tire covers were offered. With Sahara equipment the cover included a new Sahara logo. A cover with Jeep logo was available with Sport and SE equipment. The color and material of the cover carried over from 1995.

At mid-year, a new, stronger rear axle, the Dana 44 was available for the Sport and Sahara models. It replaced the Dana 44-3 unit and was standard for high altitude use and optional elsewhere. It included a 3.55:1 gear ratio and

Trac-Lok differential as well as larger ring and pinion gears and larger axle shafts than the standard axle. It also had unit bearing construction that provided a higher lateral load capacity.

A new Fusion vinyl seat fabric was standard for both the SE and Sport models. It had a pebble-grain texture and a printed surface. Both Pueblo cloth, optional for the SE and Sport was carried over as was the Trailcloth feature for the Sahara.

The new Wranglers were available with this array of standard and optional equipment:

A – available
NA – not available
S – standard

Feature	**SE**	**Sport**	**Sahara**
Dual air bags:	S	S	S
Passenger assist handle:	S	S	S
Black body side steps:	A	A	S
Anti-lock 4-wheel brakes[1]:	NA	A	A
Black front bumper:	S	S	S
Black rear bumper:	A	S	S
Black front and rear bumper end caps[2]:	A	S	S
Air conditioning[3]:	A	A	A
Heater with instrument panel ventilation:	S	S	S
Electronic digital clock[4]:	A	S	S
Convenience Group[5]:	A	A	S
Rear window defroster[6]:	A	A	A
Trac-Lok rear differential[7]:	A	A	A
4.11:1 axle ratio (standard with 5-speed manual transmission):	S	NA	NA
3.73:1 axle ratio (standard with 5-speed manual transmission):	A	NA	NA
3.07:1 axle ratio:	NA	S	S
3.55:1 (standard with Dana 44-3 rear axle High Altitude Requirement or when both Trac-Lok and ABS are ordered):	NA	A	A
Dana 44-3 rear axle (required Trac-Lok, not available with ABS):	NA	A	A
Full steel doors with roll-up windows and tinted glass:	A	A	A
Half steel door with side curtains:	S	S	S
Engine block heater:	A	A	A
4.0-liter decal on upper cowl side:	NA	S	S
Sahara decal cowl side:	NA	NA	S
Sport decal on upper cowl side:	NA	S	NA
Black fender flares[8]:	S	S	NA
Premium body color fender flares[9]:	NA	NA	S
Body color grille:	S	S	S
Chrome-plated headlight bezels:	S	S	S
Spare tire cover with Sahara logo[10]:	NA	NA	S
Black vinyl spare tire cover:	A	A	NA
15-gallon fuel tank with tethered cap:	S	S	NA
19-gallon fuel tank with tethered cap:	A	A	S
Halogen fog lamps[11]:	NA	A	S
Tinted windshield:	S	S	S
Deep Tint hard top rear quarter and lift gate windows:	A	A	S

Two hood cover designs featuring Jeep logos were available for the 1997 Wrangler. Seen here is the traditional style. (Author's collection)

The new 'T'-style hood cover for the 1997 Wrangler. Like the traditional version, it was made of black vinyl with 22oz floss and had turned-over-and-sewn edges for extra strength. (Author's collection)

Tinted hard top rear quarter and lift gate windows:	S	S	NA
Heavy-Duty Electrical Package[12]:	A	A	S
Color-keyed front floor 10oz carpeting:	S	S	S
Color-keyed carpeting for rear foot well, wheelhouse and cargo floor[13]:	A	S	S
Cargo area net[13]:	S	S	S
Cargo tie down loops (4):	S	S	S
Door trim panels with map pockets:	S	S	S
Carpeted front floor mats:	A	A	S
Mini console with cup holder and storage tray:	S	S	NA
Full Sports bar padding:	NA	S	S
Sports bar padding for side and rear only:	S	NA	NA
Fold and swing sun visors (2):	S	S	S
Footwell courtesy and driver side interior lamps:	S	S	S
Dual exterior swing-away black mirrors:	S	S	S
AM/FM stereo ETR radio with two speakers:	A	S	NA
AM/FM stereo ETR radio with seek, cassette, instrument panel speakers (2), Sports bar speakers (2) and dome lamp[14]:	A	A	S
Sound Bar speakers (2) and Dome lamp for standard radio:	NA	A	NA
Sound Package[15]:	A	NA	NA
Fusion vinyl seat fabric:	S	S	NA
Pueblo cloth:	A	A	NA
Trailcloth:	NA	NA	S
Front reclining High-Back bucket seats with passenger-side easy entry:	S	S	S
Rear Fold & Tumble rear bench seat:	A	S	S
High pressure gas charged shock absorbers[16]:	A	A	S
Fuel tank and transfer case skid plates:	S	S	S
Body color Sports bar with removable front extension:	S	S	S
Power steering:	A	S	S
Low-pivot tilt steering column:	A	A	S
Soft-feel two-spoke steering wheel:	S	S	NA
Leather-wrapped two-spoke steering wheel:	A	A	S
Add-A-Trunk[17]:	A	A	A
Locking bin-type glove compartment:	S	S	S
Seat back map pockets:	NA	NA	S
Tire and Wheel Package – 30in[18]:	NA	A	A
Compact spare tire with steel wheel:	S	S	N
Conventional spare tire with steel wheel[19]:	A	A	S
Soft top with soft windows:	S	S	S
Hard top[20]:	A	A	A
Front tow hooks (2):	A	A	S
Argent styled steel wheels with black hub covers (4):	S	NA	NA
Argent full-face steel wheels with Argent hubs (4)[21]:	A	S	NA
Grizzly five-spoke cast-aluminum wheels (5):	NA	A	S
2-speed windshield wipers and washers:	S	S	NA
2-speed intermittent wipers and washers[22]:	A	A	S

[1]Available with 4.0-liter engine only
[2]Included with rear bumper on SE
[3]Requires power steering
[4]Included only with radio
[5]Included engine compartment light, passenger's side footwell courtesy light, full console with lockable storage,dual cup holders, coin hold and storage tray
[6]Available for hard top only, requires Heavy-Duty Electrical Package
[7]Required full-size spare tire, available on SE only with manual transmission
[8]Front flares included mud guards
[9]Included sill moldings and mud guards
[10]Deleted with 30in Tire and Wheel Package
[11]Required Heavy-Duty Electrical Package
[12]Included 117amp generator and 600 amp battery
[13]Included on SE only with rear seat
[14]Included full Sports bar padding on SE
[15]Included AM/FM stereo ETR radio, Instrument panel speakers (2), Sound Bar (with 2 speakers), dome lamp and full Sports bar padding
[16]SE must have P215 or larger tires
[17]SE must have rear seat
[18]Included 30 x 9.50R15 Wrangler GS-A tires (5),

high pressure gas shock absorbers, 15 x 8in 5-hole aluminum wheels, and conventional spare tire
[19]Included with optional tires and/or aluminum wheels
[20]Included full steel doors with roll-up windows, rear window wiper and washer, and rear cargo lamp
[21]SE must have P215 or larger tires (5 wheels on SE)
[22]Available only with tilt steering wheel

A – available
NA – not available

Color	SE	Sport	Sahara
Lapis Blue:	A	A	NA
Black:	A	A	A
Citron Pearlcoat:	A	A	NA
Moss Green Pearlcoat:	A	A	A
Dark Blue Pearlcoat:	A	A	NA
Flame Red:	A	A	NA
Stone White:	A	A	A
Bright Jade Satin Glow:	A	A	NA
Gunmetal Pearlcoat*:	A	A	NA
Emerald Green Pearlcoat:	A	A	NA

*Late availability

The available soft and hard top colors for the 1997 Wrangler were Black, Stone White and Spice. The Fusion vinyl seats of the SE and Sport were offered in Mist Gray or Saddle. An optional Pueblo cloth trim for the SE and Sport was available in Mist Gray or Saddle. The Sahara's standard Trailcloth seats were finished in Saddle/Moss Green.

1997 Jeep Wrangler prices

Model	MSRP*
Wrangler SE with soft top:	$13,495
Wrangler Sport with soft top:	$17,192
Wrangler Sahara with soft top:	$19,263

*Included $510 destination charge

Option	Price
3-speed automatic transmission:	$624
Add-A-Trunk Lockable Storage[1]:	$125
Air conditioning[2]:	$878
Trac-Loc differential[3]:	$278
Rear black bumper:	$73
Convenience Group:	$162
Anti-lock brakes (not available for SE):	$599
Rear window defroster for hard top[4]:	$164
Full-doors with roll-up windows[5]:	$125
Heavy-duty electrical system:	$135
Front floor mats:	$18
Extra capacity,19-gallon fuel tank:	$62
Sunscreen glass (rear quarter windows and liftgate) for hard top:	$168
Engine block heater:	$31
AM/FM radio with 2 speakers:	$270
AM/FM radio with cassette (includes sound bar and sports bar padding):	$713
Sound Group[6]:	$533
Power steering[7]:	$300
Leather-wrapped steering wheel:	$48
Black bodyside steps:	$73
Tilt steering wheel[8]:	$193
High pressure gas shock absorber suspension[9]:	$90
P215/75 OWL A/T tires[10]:	$272
P225/75R OWL A/T tires[10]:	$463
Conventional spare tire:	$111
Black vinyl spare tire cover[11]:	$46
Two front tow hooks:	$40
Five-spoke full-face steel wheels[12]:	$230
Emissions: Calif, Mass, NY:	$128
Non-federal emissions:	$128
Fusion vinyl bucket seats[13]:	$592
Pueblo cloth bucket seats[14]:	$699
Hard top (Sport and SE):	$755
Hard top (Sahara):	$923
30in tire and wheel package (Sport and Sahara only)[15]:	$113

[1]Required rear seat on SE.
[2]Requires power steering.
[3]Not available with automatic transmission. Requires conventional spare.
[4]Required hardtop and Heavy-Duty Electrical Package.
[5]Late availability with soft top; included with hard top.
[6]Not available with Sport or Sahara.
[7]Mandatory option on early production.
[8]Includes intermittent windshield wipers.
[9]Standard for Sahara.
[10]Standard for Sahara.
[11]Not available with full-size spare.
[12]Optional for SE.
[13]Reclining, with rear seat.
[14]Reclining, with rear seat. If ordered in place of Fusion vinyl seats, the price was $107.
[15]Deletes spare tire cover.

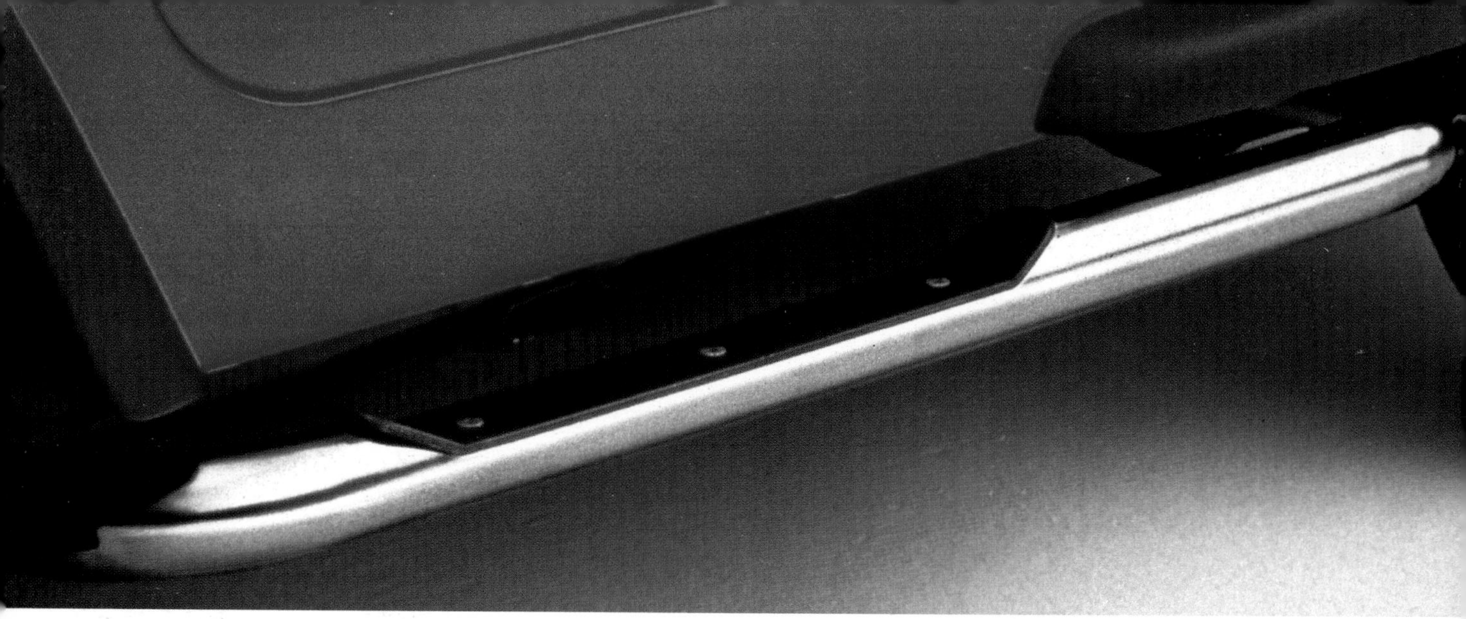

The tubular side steps for the 1997 Wrangler had 24in skid resistant step surfaces. They were designed to blend in with the Wrangler's fender lines for a clean, consistent appearance and were available in the same selection of colors as the grille/brush guard and tubular rear bumpers. (Author's collection)

In addition to those factory options, 1997 Wrangler owners had access to a large number of dealer-installed accessories from Chrysler's Mopar Parts Division. Referring to previous models, Larry Baker, General Manager of the Mopar Parts Division, said that "on a per-vehicle basis, Wrangler is Chrysler's most accessorized vehicle. So it's fitting that during its development, accessories were designed and engineered concurrently with the vehicle itself to create an all-new line of rugged accessories worthy of the Wrangler name."

Referring to Chrysler's new trend-setting and time-saving approach to vehicle design, Baker explained that "Mopar is now a full-participant in Chrysler's Platform Team approach to designing and developing new vehicles. All Wrangler accessories were designed specifically for this vehicle only."

In his view, this policy directly benefited Wrangler owners: "When accessories are designed to fit more than one vehicle, inherent sacrifices in quality and appearance are common. That's not the case with the items Mopar has developed for the Wrangler.

"For Wrangler owners that means accessory items such as grille guards and rear bumpers will not interfere with Federally mandated headlight and tail-light beam patterns. Grille guards will also fit correctly and blend more effectively with the vehicle's appearance. And because Mopar's hood and front end covers are designed and engineered specifically for the 1997 Wrangler, owners are assured of a tight, snug fit and outstanding performance and durability. Furthermore, because Mopar tubular bumpers and grille and brush guards are designed and developed specifically for the Wrangler, they do not obstruct air flow to the engine compartment or interfere with proper air bag operation."

In total, Mopar offered over sixty manufacturer-engineered accessories for the Wrangler that had been developed simultaneously with its development.

Among the most popular was the bike and ski carrier in either a spare-tire or hitch-mount configuration. The spare-tire-mounted carriers attached directly to the exterior spare tire and held two bikes or four pairs of skis. Cables and tabs were included to lock bike and skis to the carrier and the carrier to the vehicle.

The hitch-mount carriers were adaptable to any 1.25in standard receiver and were also designed to carry two bikes or four pairs of skis. A fold-down feature allowed the lift gate to be opened without removing the bikes or skis.

Mopar also offered off-road and fog lights in sets of two that included protective covers with a Mopar logo. The light bar for the off-road lights was custom-designed to fit the Wrangler's windshield frame. It included mounting tabs for up to four lights and was pre-wired for convenient installation.

Grille and brush-guards for the Wrangler were available in a variety of colors and material combinations. For example, those with a chrome finish had a ductile nickel base coating covered by a semi-bright nickel seat coat topped with hexavalent chrome plating for a bright, smooth finish. The Mopar's tubular bumpers for the Wrangler had true mandrel bends for a clean, finished appearance. They included Luron ASA plastic end caps that were resistant to shrinking, expanding and cracking. All tubular accessories such as the bumpers and grille/brush guards were impact tested during their development.

The tubular rear bumper available for the 1997 Wrangler is seen here in red. It was also offered in the same choice of colors and finishes as the grille/brush guard. (Author's collection)

All chrome-finished accessories such as the side steps, bumpers and grille/brush guards successfully passed a 44-hour Copper Accelerated Acidic Spray Test (CAST) that ensured their durability and resistance to corrosion.

Two hood covers, one a traditional style the other a new 'T' type offered protection from road debris. Both were made of black vinyl with 22-ounce floss backing and featured a turned-under-and-sewn edge for a finished appearance. They also had Jeep logos.

Mopar developed all-new step bumpers for the 1997 Wrangler. They provided easier access and were offered in either Original Equipment (OE) or tubular style. The OE steps were molded in durable plastic and were designed to blend with the fender lines. The steps used collapsible nuts for installation and no drilling was required.

The Add-A-Trunk accessory which had a capacity of 2.5 cubic feet of lockable store space (down from 3 cubic feet in 1995) was joined by several other Mopar cargo-handling accessories for the Wrangler. They included a new color-keyed and lockable front console and an easily attached tailgate storage pouch.

For music fans, Mopar offered a full range of audio systems from AM/FM stereo cassette models to units featuring CD players and five-band graphic equalizers.

The familiar open-air driving accessories popular with generations of Jeep enthusiasts were offered for the newest Wrangler. Mopar sun bonnets protected front seat occupants from the sun and fastened easily to the Original Equipment attaching points. A windscreen could be installed behind the front seats to reduce wind turbulence when the Wrangler was in motion. A tonneau cover was offered that shielded the rear seats and cargo area from the elements and kept the contents out of sight. All of these accessories were constructed using the cotton-polyester blend used for the Wrangler's soft-top and were available in matching colors for a coordinated appearance.

Perhaps the new Wrangler would have been a sales success even if its manufacturer hadn't spent a dime on publicity but Chrysler wasn't about to take that chance and the latest edition of the Jeep was the subject of an ambitious advertising campaign using a 'Jeep – There's Only One' theme to demonstrate the Wrangler's improved capability and uncompromised position as the icon of the Jeep brand.

This effort, created by the Detroit office of the Bozell Worldwide advertising agency, portrayed the Wrangler as having plenty of fun-to-drive attributes as well as a rugged off-road capability and contemporary safety features. The advertising, consisting of television and print presentations, began on April 3, 1996. Included in the television portion were spots on NBC's *Friends*, ABC's *The Drew Carey Show*, and CBS' *Late Night With David Letterman*.

"This advertising campaign establishes, without a doubt, that Wrangler has evolved," said Mary Meyers, Advertising Executive for Jeep. "The 1997 Wrangler is new and improved without losing sight of its original Jeep heritage. Wrangler is still the authentic Jeep vehicle and makes that statement through ads that clearly define its rugged, no-compromise character."

The introductory commercial, entitled *Ice Fishing*, opened on a remote, frozen pond. With his Wrangler parked nearby, an ice fisherman patiently waits for a tug on his line. As time passes, the scene shifted to below the

This Combo Kit for the 1997 Wrangler included a sun bonnet, windscreen and tonneau cover. Wrangler owners received a 36-month/36,000-mile warranty on all accessories installed prior to vehicle delivery and 12-month/12,000-mile coverage on products installed after delivery. (Author's collection)

Opposite: The Jeep Icon was depicted by Chrysler as a "Jeep for the next Millennium". It had a Steel Blue Metallic body and 8 x 19in, cast-aluminum wheels with 245 6DR-19 Rock Climber tires. Its interior featured Olive and Gunmetal Gray leather upholstery with Anodized Magenta accents. (DaimlerChrysler Media Services)

icy surface, where a school of fish were seen admiring the new Wrangler, while ignoring the fisherman's lure. After touting the new Jeep's improvements, the voice-over added, "It's the changes beneath the surface that will really get your attention."

The second advertisement used a children's puzzle book to demonstrate the Wrangler's off-highway capability and what was depicted as its 'go anywhere, do anything attitude'. When a young boy is challenged to "help the rocket get back to earth", he attempts to solve the maze by routinely guiding the lost space ship through the puzzle's established paths. When he is asked to "help the Jeep Wrangler find the fishing hole", his face lights up as he accepts the challenge and draws a line straight across the page, over three mountain ranges and a pit of quicksand. The ad concludes with: "Jeep Wrangler. It's even more fun than you imagined."

The final television ad, *The Rookie*, emphasized the Wrangler's competitive price. The commercial opened showing a man who had recently learned to appreciate the wonders of nature. He is seen shouting into a canyon. As the Wrangler's dual air bags and other improvements are listed, his frenzied behavior continues and he begin to yodel. Another man, seen in the canyon below, turns to his companion and says, "Must be his first Jeep." To which she replies, "Rookie."

Evaluating the effectiveness of these advertisements, Bill Morden, Managing Partner, Creative Director at Bozell, said, "This campaign helps us establish that the Wrangler is new from the ground up without compromising its premium Jeep status. Consumers are turned on to the Jeep experience and our advertising conveys that fun, adventurous attitude that only a Jeep can promise and deliver."

In addition to the television commercials, the campaign included a series of print advertisements touting the Wrangler's improvements and amenities. These ads ran in the May/June issues of numerous magazines including *4-Wheel & Off-Road*, *Backpacker*, *Four Wheeler*, *Mountain Bike*, *Rolling Stone*, *Summit* and *WIndsurfing*.

The new Wrangler was used by Chrysler as the basis for two concept vehicles: the Icon and the Dakar. Their debut at the 1997 North American International Auto Show in Detroit on January 5, 1997 gave Jeep enthusiasts a glimpse into what the future held for the Jeep marque.

Referring to the Icon, John E Herlitz, Chrysler Corporation's Vice President of Product Design, said it was "a creative exploration for a next-generation Jeep Wrangler ... it's solid, stable, built like a rock and its capabilities have been further enhanced."

Clearly aware that any redesign of the Wrangler at some point in the twenty-first century would not be any less daunting than the creation of the 1997 Wrangler, Trevor Creed, Chrysler Corporation's Design Director, said, "We have a responsibility as caretakers of one of the world's most recognized brands. Sooner or later we will be challenged with freshening Jeep Wrangler's appearance without sacrificing its distinctive image and instantly recognizable characteristics."

A stated goal of the Icon's designers was to give it a compact, muscular appearance. In practice this was achieved by giving it, relative to the 1997 Wrangler, a larger bumper, tires and wheel arches. "Our objective," explained Creed, "was to give Icon a trim, poised look while keeping much of Jeep Wrangler's unique character. However, we widened Wrangler's track, reduced its length by 5in (137mm), its overhang by 2in (51mm), and increased its wheel travel from 8in (203mm) to 10in (254mm)."

The Icon's technical specifications were as follows:

Dimensions	
Overall length:	142.0in (36,707mm)
Overall width:	67.7in (1720mm)
Overall height:	70.1in (1781mm)
Wheelbase:	93.4in (2372mm)
Front track:	59.2in (1504mm)
Rear track:	61.6in (15,675mm)
Wheels:	8 x 19in cast-aluminum
Tires:	Goodyear 245 6DR-19 Rock Climber
Engine:	4-cylinder, 2.4-liter
Transmission:	5-speed manual
Suspension:	Double wishbone (front and rear)
Wheel travel:	10in (254mm)
Brakes:	ABS 4-wheel disc
Exterior color:	Steel Blue Metallic
Interior color:	Olive and Gunmetal Gray leather upholstery with Anodized Magenta accents

Inherent in the creation of the Icon was the redefining and updating for the next century of many traditional Jeep Wrangler design cues such as its long dash-to-axle proportions, classic front end, exposed hinges, folding windshield and roll cage. "We wanted to capture the essence of practical product design which fits the Jeep image," explained Trevor Creed. "We kept the familiar grille, but made it shorter and wider. We also kept the exposed hinges, bold bumpers, exposed door handles and fuel cap which were designed to give the vehicle more of a mechanical, industrial design feel, and at the same time add a lot of intrinsic value." Comparing the Icon to the current Wrangler, Creed explained that "where the vehicle differs the most is that it is designed as a unibody construction with an integrated aluminum roll cage."

Icon designer. Robert Lasler explained that this did not compromise Icon's off-road capability: "Just like top-of-the-line mountain bikes and our current line-up of Jeep sport-utility vehicles. Icon was built to go anywhere. Its parts are high-quality, lightweight and purpose-built. To communicate the quality of each part, we branded our Jeep logo on Icon's hinges, door-handles, wheels and bumpers."

It was left to Creed to have the final say on the Icon: "As we move closer and closer to the next century," he said, "Jeep enthusiasts will be happy to know their Jeep will still look like a Jeep."

The second concept Jeep at the show, the Dakar, with a Desert Sand exterior and a Saddle Tan interior with woven leather seats, also broke with a major element of Jeep Wrangler heritage by having a four-door body configuration. "People will definitely look twice when they see Dakar," said John E Herlitz. "Compared to our 1997 Jeep Wrangler, Dakar comes complete with twice as many doors, and is prepared for twice the adventure."

To make room for its additional set of doors, the Dakar's wheelbase measured 108.5in (2756mm), nearly 15in (381mm) longer than the Wrangler's. Trevor Creed explained the consequences of this extended wheelbase: "With a longer wheelbase we are able to offer additional space for passengers and their gear. We are also able to further improve the ride by positioning backseat passengers in front of the rear axle as opposed to directly on top of it."

The Dakar had these major dimensions and specifications:

Overall length:	166.6in (4229mm)
Overall width:	72.0in (1829mm)
Overall height:	75.0in 1905mm)
Wheelbase:	108.5in (2756mm)
Wheels:	15 x 7in cast-aluminum
Tires:	Goodyear 31 x 10.5in Wrangler AT
Engine:	4.0-liter
Transmission:	4-speed automatic
Suspension:	Wrangler

In reality, the Dakar, rather than signaling an impending change in the Wranglers, served as a look ahead to the 2002 Jeep Liberty. Anticipating the popularity of the Liberty and its distinctive appearance, Creed added: "At a time when many sport utility vehicles look the same, Dakar is in a class by itself. No one will mistake the identity of Jeep Dakar as it is an authentic, instantly recognizable design execution that opens up new opportunities for one of the world's most recognized brands."

Jeep enthusiasts who, while preferring the unadulterated lines of the Wrangler, didn't object to the appearance of 'hot' Wranglers were likely to be pleased with the Wrangler Tabasco concept. "What do you get," asked Chrysler, "when you cross a legendary go-anywhere vehicle with the legendary, eye-watering, tongue-tingling hot sauce?" Without beating around the bush, Chrysler provided the answer: "What else – Wrangler Tabasco."

This concept Jeep, which Chrysler – clearly enjoying the moment – explained was "currently adding a lot of heat to auto shows and special events around the country", began when the Jeep Division was approached by the McIlhenny Company, the makers of Tabasco products, to jointly create a promotional Jeep vehicle that would feature its Tabasco logo.

For the Jeep design team assigned to this project this was just the beginning as they "couldn't", said Chrysler, "resist adding a dash more spice and create a special edition Wrangler Jeep that's literally built to blaze new trials."

Supporting these sizzling statements were the Tabasco's primary features:

- -Unique Red-Hot Chili Pepper/White Pearl paint scheme
- -Five-spoke wheels engraved with red chili peppers
- -Goodyear tires with 'hand-cut' chili pepper tread pattern
- -Mopar Power Tech performance camshaft, premium fuel calibration engine computer and dual catalyst with dual exhaust
- -NOS nitrous system for extra power disguised as a Tabasco bottle
- -Functional hood scoop
- -Red-tinted windshield
- -Unique Agate interior with custom fabrics and red leather sports-bar covers

The Wrangler Tabasco concept vehicle had a unique Chili Pepper Candy Red paint scheme that blended to White Pearl at the rear. Seen here on the spare is the special 'hand cut' chili pepper tread pattern of its tires. (DaimlerChrysler media services)

Welcoming the RHD Wrangler, which was unveiled on the company's stand at the International Motor Show in Birmingham on October 15, 1996 to the UK market, Richard MacKay, Managing Director of Chrysler Jeep Imports UK, said, "Looking at the 1997 Wrangler is like looking at an old friend. The shape and design cues are familiar but over three quarters of the parts have been redesigned to enhance the overall package.

"The signature Jeep grille and round headlights, famous from earlier Jeep models, still give the Wrangler a traditional front end. The Jeep is an American icon and you tamper with it at your peril. I think our customers will be pleased that we have made these improvements but at the same time have left its heritage intact."

Chrysler Jeep was celebrating its fourth anniversary in the UK with the introduction of the right-hand drive Wrangler. After the formation of a new Dover-based company in 1992, Wranglers converted to RHD by Chrysler Jeep Imports UK were displayed at the 1992 Birmingham Motor Show along with factory-built RHD Jeep Cherokees. The Cherokee had been the first volume production vehicle to be built with right-hand drive for export to the UK by a North American car manufacturer. Sales of the RHD Cherokee in the UK began on January 15, 1993. Shortly thereafter, sales of RHD Wranglers began. At that time the Wrangler was priced at £12,495.

Richard MacKay was optimistic about the Jeep's UK future: "The return of the rejuvenated Chrysler, through its world renowned Jeep products, is the most significant arrival on the four-wheel drive market for many years.

"Sales of 4x4 vehicles have been booming, even without the biggest name in four-wheel drive, Jeep. That sector is going to increase and we are now contributing to that growth with aggressively priced and superbly equipped Jeep Wrangler and Jeep Cherokee models.

"These will provide tough opposition for other 4x4 marques and we know from the staggering reaction we experienced at the Motor Show, and more recently to our new advertising campaign, that the British public just can't wait to get their hands on a new Jeep.

"There is no other 4x4 vehicle with the heritage to match that of Jeep – which began the whole four-wheel drive movement back in 1941 with those famous general purpose military vehicles. Jeep has had 50 glorious years – now it's going to have a great future in the UK."

In 1995 the line-up of RHD Jeeps for sale in the UK was completed when the Jeep Grand Cherokee, produced in Graz, Austria, was introduced. Looking back at events leading to the RHD Wrangler, Jeep UK said that "the company's pioneering work in converting the Jeep Wrangler from left- to right-hand drive at its UK headquarters, and then experimental work on converting a Jeep Grand Cherokee to right-hand drive were said to be instrumental in persuading Chrysler Corporation of the viability for other right-hand drive applications for its vehicles in export markets all over the world."

Initially, on January 2, 1997 three models of the latest Wrangler were announced for the UK market: the 2.5-liter Wrangler, Wrangler 4.0 and Wrangler 4.0 Limited, priced from £12,495 to £14,395.

As it traveled around the US, the Wrangler Tabasco was part of the Jeep Health and Fitness Tour. "While you might not be able to take it on the trail anytime soon," said Chrysler, "it's fun to imagine what a vehicle with red-hot power, capability and natural gusto could accomplish if it were ever set free." (DaimlerChrysler Media Services)

When the Wrangler went on sale in March 1997 its model range had this composition:

Model	Price
Jeep Wrangler 2.5 Sport:	£13,995
Jeep Wrangler 4.0 Sport:	£15,495
Jeep Wrangler 4.0 Sahara:	£17,650
Jeep Wrangler 4.0 Sahara Automatic:	£18,250

The Wrangler's starting price of £13,995 was £455 less than that of the comparable model of 1996.

All three Wranglers had a Trac-Lok rear differential and hard top as standard equipment. Chrysler Jeep Imports UK reported these performance figures for the 2.5 and 4.0-liter engines which had slightly lower horsepower ratings* than the US versions:

Engine/ Horsepower	0-60mph Time	Max. Speed
117hp/2.5-liter:	13.6sec	92mph
174hp/4.0-liter (manual trans):	8.8sec	112mph
174hp/4.0-liter (auto trans):	9.5sec	109mph

*Jeep UK Media also listed the horsepower of the 2.5 and 4.0-liter engines as 123 and 184, respectively

A summary of Wrangler sales in the UK from 1993 through 1997 indicates that the availability of the RHD version impacted favorably upon sales:

Year:	1993	1994	1995	1996	1997
Sales:	498	422	309	110	840

In Australia, where Jeeps had been commonplace during WWII, the new Wrangler went on sale in October 1996. In November 1997, when an all-time monthly record of 216 Wranglers were sold, Bill Needle, Director-General Manager of Chrysler Jeep Australia, commented on the Wrangler's Australian heritage: "Jeep Wrangler carries on the tradition that started with the original World War II Jeep – and it has fallen into favor with a growing number of Australians."

"There is no doubt Wrangler has become a cult vehicle in Australia," added Bronwyn Humphrey, National Marketing Director for Chrysler Jeep Australia, "whether you live in the outback, on the beach, or in the inner-city suburbs." For the full year Wrangler set a new record of 1458 units, a total not exceeded until 2005.

Summing up the attributes of the 1997 Wrangler and the efforts of those who participated in its development, Craig Winn said, "This is a package that the entire Jeep team is very proud of. We improved Wrangler's capability and function; added safety features, improved the on-road ride and handling; we developed a new Wrangler that is still a Wrangler, and all this for a relatively low $260 million."

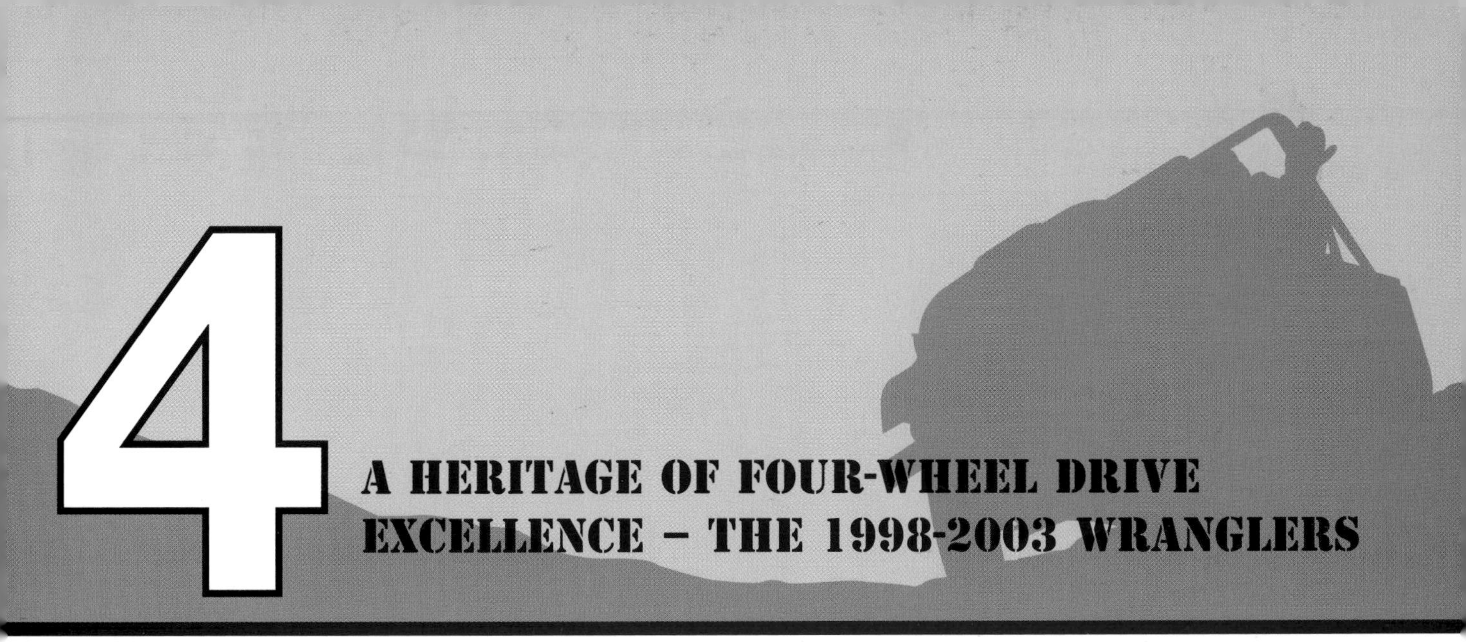

4 A HERITAGE OF FOUR-WHEEL DRIVE EXCELLENCE – THE 1998-2003 WRANGLERS

The Wrangler had entered the 1997 model year with the dominant share of what the auto industry described as the 'mini sport-utility segment' of the automotive market:

Vehicle	Per cent of market
Jeep Wrangler:	37.0
Toyota RAV4:	29.3*
Geo Tracker:	16.2*
Suzuki Sidekick:	9.5
Other:	8.0

*Sales included both two- and four-door models

The Wrangler's customer profile (listed below) indicates that its sales leadership was based on an appeal that was broad and diverse:

-Thirty-five years old median age
-Fifty-two per cent married
-$55,000 median household income
-Thirty-two per cent female
-Forty-nine per cent college graduates
-Forty-seven per cent professional/managerial positions

When the 1998 version debuted it was riding the crest of the second generation Wrangler's popularity as indicated by its strong sales.

1997 model year	
Total US vehicle market:	15,376,935
Total US small utility segment:	142,679
Wrangler sales:	84,270
Wrangler segment market share:	59.1 per cent

Adding to the Wrangler's favorable public image were the many positive evaluations it received from the media, including recognition as 4x4 of the Year from *Peterson's 4-Wheel & Off-Road* magazine.

On the basis of its 1997 model year sales, Chrysler updated the Wrangler's demographic profile which now had this form:

Median age:	36
Annual household income:	$53,500
Female/male buyers:	38/62 per cent

Surveys also indicated that fifty per cent of Wrangler owners took their vehicles off highway, far more than owners of any other vehicle.

The Wrangler's popularity as an off-road, recreational vehicle did not sway Chrysler from promoting the Wrangler's practical aspects, particularly in export markets. An example was the introduction on May 30, 1998 of a two-seater version for sale in Australia. This Wrangler, available on special order from all Jeep dealers in Australia, could be purchased tax-exempt for agricultural use. Except for its seating, this Wrangler was identical to the four-seater and was offered in either soft or hard top form.

Demonstrations of the Wrangler's ability to function under difficult conditions had been a major element of a popular weekly television series, *Outback Adventures*. A Jeep Australia spokesperson noted that the show's host, Troy Dann, "gives his Jeep Wrangler a beating every Thursday". For his part, Mr Dann said, "My Wrangler really works hard out here. It's a great vehicle in the bush and as tough as a scrub bull. The Wrangler is equally happy whether it is picking a track through dry creek beds or flying along a dirt road in the Territory."

The positioning of this dramatic photo of a 1946 CJ-2A on the inside cover of Jeep's full-line 1998 sales brochure, *The Jeep Book 1999*, reminded prospective owners of a new Wrangler that they would be acquiring a vehicle with a pedigree unlike that of any of its contemporaries. (Author's collection)

15"x6" *Styled steel* (*Standard*: SE)

15"x7" *Full-face steel* (*Standard*: *Sport*, *Optional*: SE)

15"x7" *Grizzly cast aluminum* (*Standard*: *Sahara*, *Optional*: *Sport*)

15"x8" 5-Hole *cast aluminum* (*Optional*: *Sport*, *Sahara*)

The 1998 Wrangler's standard and optional wheels consisted of these steel and aluminum variations.

For her part, Bronwyn Humphrey, Chrysler Jeep Australia General Manager – Marketing, added, "There's no doubt that Australia needs tough 4WD vehicles and the Jeep Wrangler is certainly that. And now, with the two-seat version offering tax advantages for the primary producer, it is more affordable than ever."

New for 1998 were standard front bumper guards for all Wranglers. Replacing Citron Pearlcoat and Dark Blue Pearlcoat in the 1998 exterior color selection were Chili Pepper Pearlcoat and Deep Amethyst Pearlcoat.

The major interior change was a 'toning down' of the Pueblo seat-cloth design.

Continued from its spring 1997 introduction was the dual top option enabling customers to order both a hard top and a soft top directly from the factory. Aside from eliminating the need for Wrangler owners to later purchase after-market tops, this option was more affordable than purchasing the two tops separately. It included full-doors with roll-up windows.

Another option, originally available at mid-1997 model year that remained available for Wranglers with cloth seats, was an EZ Access driver's seat. By allowing the seat to be folded and pivoted forward, it provided easy access to the rear seat from the driver's side. This seat did not slide like the tip-and-slide front-passenger seat.

A major technical upgrade was the use of 'next generation' air bags that were certified to new federal regulations allowing less forceful air bags. They helped provide extra safety for the driver and front passenger in the event of a severe frontal collision. Prior to their

Along with a 1998 Jeep Cherokee Classic and 1998 Jeep Grand Cherokee, this Flame Red 1998 Wrangler SE was photographed on the Moab Rim Trail in Utah. It was fitted with optional 15 x 7in, full-face wheels. (Author's collection)

use in the Wrangler, they had been tested to minimize unintended deployment under severe off-highway conditions. The unit's module was waterproof to help protect its components from the elements. In May 1998, a passenger air bag cut-off switch was added to this system.

Optional on the Wrangler for the first time was automatic speed control and a Smart Key Immobilizer theft deterrent system. The speed control option was offered for all Wrangler models and included steering wheel switches and a leather-wrapped steering wheel on the SE and Sport.

The Smart Key Immobilizer (also identified as the Sentry Key Theft Deterrent System), had a November 1997 availability and used the Wrangler's on-board electronics and a small integrated circuit chip in the key to prevent the engine from running without a valid ignition key. When an attempt was made to start the vehicle without the Smart Key, the system cut off the fuel supply. This option was supplied with two keys. Additional keys were obtainable only through Chrysler Corporation dealerships.

Power steering was now standard for all Wranglers. In 1997 it had been optional for the SE and standard for the Sport and Sahara. For 1998 the steering was more responsive due to a new gear ratio that varied from 15:1 on center to 13:1 at the extremes of travel. In 1997 the power steering had an overall ratio of 14:1. Chrysler asserted that the lower on-center ratio improved steering feel, while the higher ratio at the extremes of travel maintained overall maneuverability.

Replacing the 3.55:1 axle ratio option of 1997 offered with the Dana 44-3 rear axle with Trac-Lok and the 4.0-liter engine, was a 3.73:1 ratio. For 1998 this option required a full-size spare tire and was not available with ABS. In addition, the clutch-starter interlock jumper wire was replaced with a fuse, making it easier to use the starter without the use of the clutch for 'key starts' in four-wheel drive, low range situations.

The prices of the 1998 Wranglers and their options were as follows:

Model	
Wrangler SE with soft top:	$14,615
Wrangler Sport with soft top:	$18,030
Wrangler Sahara with soft top:	$20,101
Option	**Price**
Emission equipment:	$170
3-speed automatic transmission[1]:	$625
SE Quick Order Package[2]:	$865
Convenience Group[3]:	$165
Heavy Duty Electrical Group[4]:	$135
Sound Group[5]:	$265
Air conditioning:	$895
Rear Trac Lok differential[6]:	$285

This view of a 1998 Wrangler Sahara highlights its standard Black body side steps, body-color fender flares, round halogen fog lamps and 15 x 7in Grizzly cast-aluminum wheels. (DaimlerChrysler Media Services)

Anti-lock braking system with 3.73:1 axle ratio (Sport and Sahara only):	$600
3.73:1 axle ratio:	NC
Rear window defroster for hard top (SE and Sport)[7]:	$165
Hard full-doors[8]:	$125
Front floor mats (SE and Sport):	$30
Fog lights (Sport only):	$120
19-gallon fuel tank (SE and Sport):	$65
Deep tinted rear quarter and lift gate glass (SE and Sport):	$405
Engine block heater:	$35
AM/FM stereo radio[9] (SE):	$270
AM/FM stereo radio with cassette[10]:	$445
Sound Bar (Sport only):	$245
Hard top (SE and Sport)[11]:	$755
Dual tops (SE and Sport)[12]:	$1395
Cloth high-back bucket seats[13] (SE):	$150
High pressure gas shock absorbers[14]:	$90
Spare tire cover (SE and Sport)[15]:	$50
Speed control (SE and Sport)[16]:	$300
Leather-wrapped steering wheel (SE and Sport)[17]:	$50
Tilt steering wheel (SE and Sport)[18]:	$195
Body side steps (SE and Sport)[19]:	$75
Lockable storage trunk[20]:	$125
Sentry key theft deterrent system:	$75
Tow hooks (SE and Sport)[21]:	$40
Cast-aluminum wheels (Sport):	$265
Sport Quick Order Package[22]:	$540
30in tire and wheel group (Sport)[23]:	$785
Tires	
P215/75R15 All Terrain OWL (Sport)[24]:	$235
P225/75R15 All Terrain OWL (Sport)[25]:	$425
Conventional spare tire:	$115

[1]Includes 3.73:1 axle ratio.
[2]Not available for Sport or Sahara. Includes AM/FM stereo radio with two speakers, high-back bucket seats, rear carpet and rear seat.
[3]Available for SE and Sport, standard for Sahara. Included engine compartment light, full-length console with storage and two cup holders.
[4]Available for SE and Sport, standard for Sahara and for vehicles with air conditioning. Included heavy duty 600amp battery and heavy duty 117amp alternator.
[5]Price listed was for vehicles with Quick Order Package. For Wranglers without that option the price was $535.00. This package included AM/FM stereo radio, two instrument-panel-mounted speakers, overhead sound bar with two speakers, dome light (significantly brighter than the previous lamp), and additional sports bar padding. Not available for Sport and Sahara.
[6]Standard with rear Dana 44 axle (Sport and Sahara only). Required regular size spare tire. Not available with automatic transmission on SE. Included 3.73:1 axle ratio on Sport and Sahara.
[7]Standard on Saharas built after January 5, 1998.

A 1998 Wrangler Sport with standard 15 x 7in, full-face, steel wheels and optional OWL tires. The full padding of its Sport Bar was standard. (DaimlerChrysler media Services)

Required air conditioning or Electrical Group. Standard on SE and Sport equipped with deep tinted glass for rear quarter and tailgate.

[8]Standard with hard top. Included windup windows.

[9]Included digital clock.

[10]Price listed was for SE equipped with Quick Order Package. Price for SE not fitted with this option was $715.00. Price for Sport was $425.00. Option included digital clock and Sound Bar with four speakers.

[11]Included rear quarter glass, hard full-doors, rear window wiper/washer, cargo department light.

[12]Included 775lb payload, hard top, soft top, full-doors with roll up windows, rear wiper/washer, rear cargo light, light tinted door, rear quarter and lift gate glass (deep tint on Sahara).

[13]Price listed was for SE fitted with Quick Order Package. Includes LH walk-in device, cargo net, rear carpeting, and folding rear seat. Price for SE not fitted with this option was $745.00.

[14]Standard on Sahara before January 5, 1998. Available for SE, Sport and Sahara after that date.

[15]Not available for Sahara after January 5, 1998; standard for Sahara prior to that date. Not available with 30in Tire and Wheel Package.

[16]Included leather-wrapped steering wheel.

[17]Standard for Sahara.

[18]Standard for Sahara. Included intermittent windshield wipers.

[19]Standard for Sahara.

[20]Required either cloth or vinyl high-back bucket seats on SE.

[21]Standard for Sahara.

[22]Included Convenience Group, tilt steering wheel, 19-gallon fuel tank and conventional spare tire.

[23]Price when ordered with Quick Order Package was $670.00. Package included high pressure, gas-charged shock absorbers, 3.73:1 axle ratio (with manual transmission), 30 x 9.5R15 All Terrain OWL tires and 5-hole cast-aluminum wheels (five).

[24]Not available for SE or Sahara. Not available for 30in Tire and Wheel Package. Price was $120.00 when ordered with option package consisting of Convenience Group, 19-gallon fuel tank, and conventional spare tire.

[25]Not available for SE or Sahara. Not available for 30in Tire and Wheel Package. Price was $310.00 when ordered with option package consisting of Convenience Group, 19-gallon fuel tank, and conventional spare tire.

This 1998 Flame Red Wrangler S has a number of Mopar accessories, including tubular front and rear bumpers, tubular light bar, winch and aluminum wheels. (Author's collection)

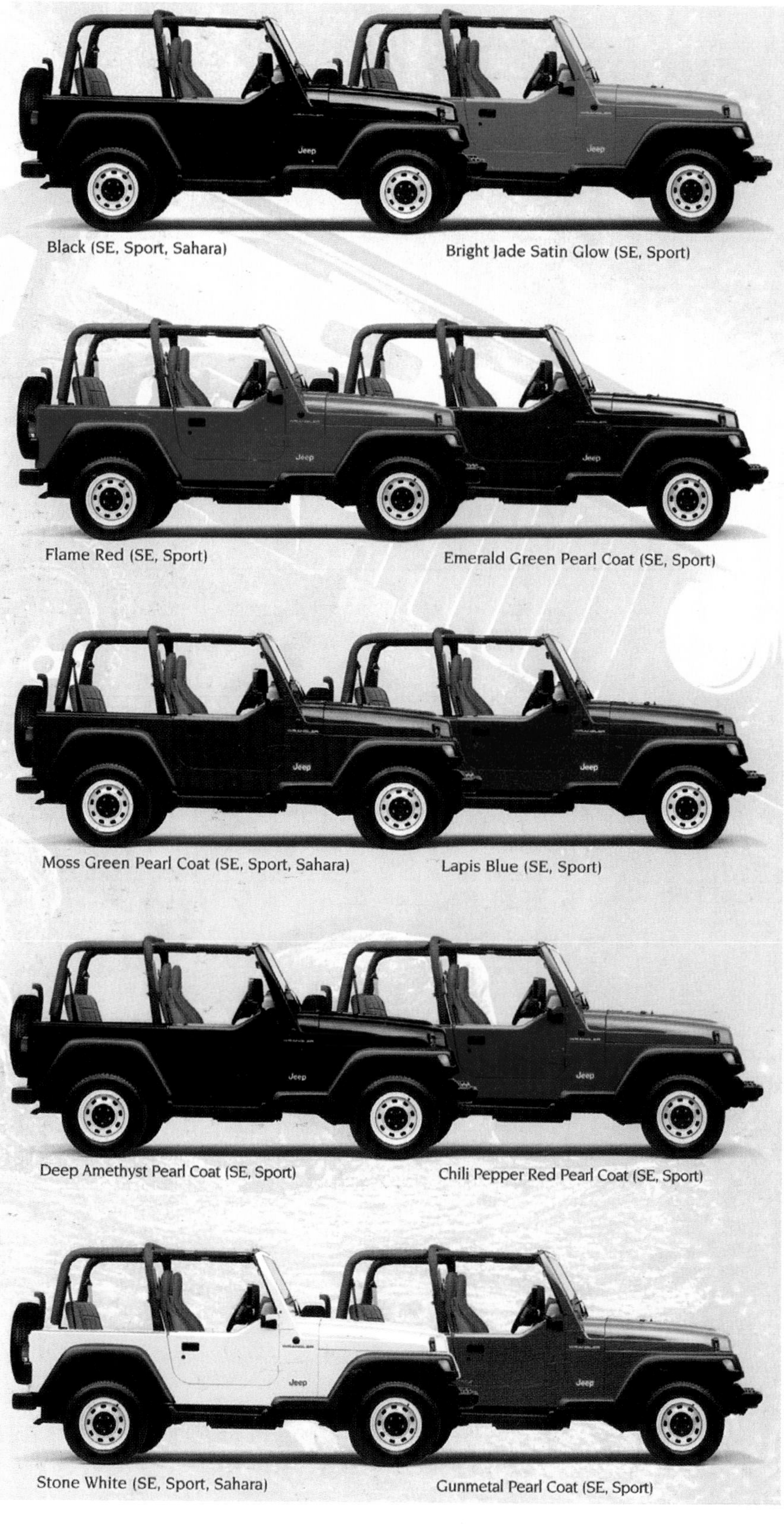

A time-honored Jeep tradition maintained by the Wrangler was the ease with which owners could clean its interior. Thanks to the Wrangler's removable carpet, floor drain plugs and water resistant seat fabrics, all the job required was a garden hose and decent water pressure. (Author's collection)

Seen here on a 1998 Sahara is the Wrangler's standard tip-and-slide front-passenger seat. (Author's collection)

This gathering of ten Wrangler SE models illustrates the colors available for 1998. (Author's collection)

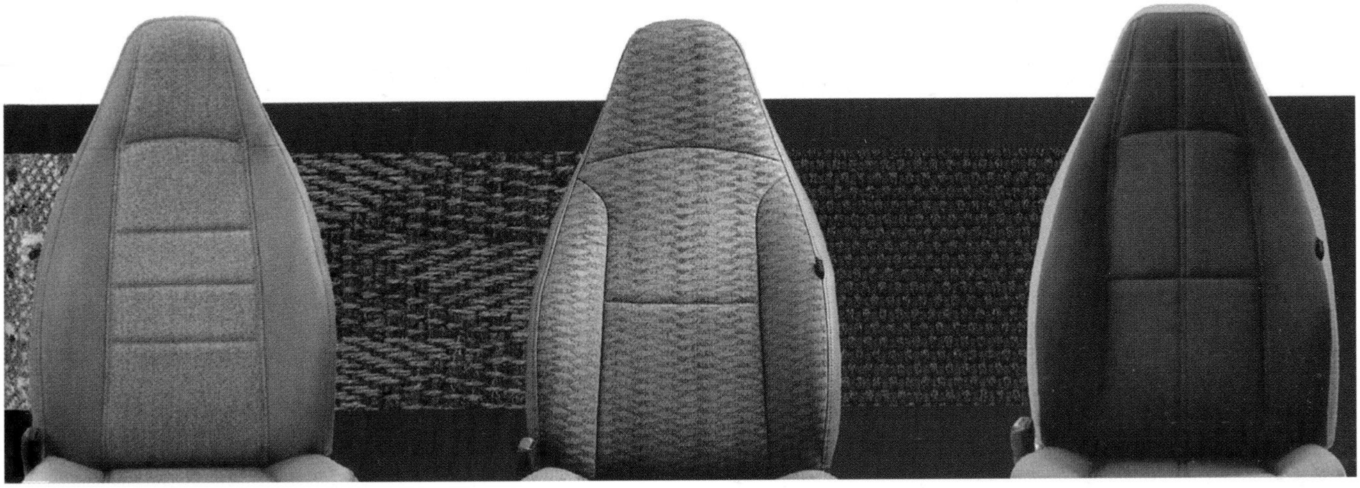

Left to right: the Fusion vinyl seat, standard for the SE and Sport in Saddle; the Pueblo seat option for the SE and Sport in Mist Gray; followed by the Sahara's standard Pueblo cloth seat in Saddle/Moss Green. (Author's collection)

The Ultimate Rescue Jeep was based on the 1998 Wrangler Sport. Prototype Mopar Performance parts included a higher performance camshaft, stainless steel exhaust headers, lower restriction exhaust and upgraded engine computer-controls. These components increased its 4.0-liter engine output to 206hp and 247lb-ft of torque @ 2800rpm. Other Ultimate Rescue features included Goodyear 'Rock Climber' 31in tires and Centerline 'convo' 15 x 12in wheels. Its tubular styling theme included bumpers storing 150psi rescue air-supply tanks to inflate the tires when needed, a Mitsubishi satellite phone system, Alpine Voice Guidance Navigation System, and a Prince Corp Autolink overhead console. (DaimlerChrysler Media Services)

The Wrangler line-up for 1999 – again consisting of the SE, Sport and Sahara soft top models – had these prices:

Wrangler SE:	$14,345
Wrangler Sport:	$17,905
Wrangler Sahara:	$20,135
The Destination Charge for all models was an additional $535.	

Replacing the previous slider-control system were new rotary heating, ventilation and air conditioning controls. These were intended to both improve feel over the previous slider-controlled system and be operated with a gloved hand. A redesign of the Wrangler's frame resulted in a weight reduction of 16lb (7.3kg). The SE's standard 2.5-liter engine now met TLEV (Transitional Low Emission Vehicle) requirements in the California, New York, Maine and New England Trading Region States.

All power trains had new engine sensors, a new JTEC+ engine controller and a new catalyst for reduced emissions, improved reliability and increased durability.

The replacement of Lapis Blue, Bright Jade Satin Glow, Emerald Green Pearlcoat, and Moss Green Pearlcoat by Medium Fern, Forest Green, Intense Blue and Desert Sand provided these exterior color choices for 1999:

A – available *NA – not available* **Color**	SE	Sport	Sahara
Black:	A	A	A
Flame Red:	A	A	NA
Stone White:	A	A	A
Forest Green Pearlcoat:	A	A	A
Chili Pepper Red Pearlcoat:	A	A	NA
Desert Sand Pearlcoat:	A	A	A
Intense Blue Pearlcoat:	A	A	NA
Deep Amethyst Pearlcoat:	A	A	NA
Gunmetal Pearlcoat:	A	A	NA
Medium Fern Green Pearlcoat:	A	A	NA

Left: A 1999 Wrangler Sahara in Desert Sand Pearlcoat. In 1923, Ned Jordan created his famous 'Somewhere West of Laramie' advertisement for his Jordan Playboy; instead of focusing on the practical nature of an automobile, it appealed to the viewer's imagination and the emotional bond owners could establish with certain vehicles. Such machines were few and far between but the Wrangler was one of them. "Out there somewhere," said Jeep, "is a slice of paradise you've seen only in your dreams. Access is limited – only to those who own a Jeep Wrangler." (DaimlerChrysler Media Services)

The 1999 Wrangler Sahara was only offered with Trailcloth seats in Dark Green/Camel. (Author's collection)

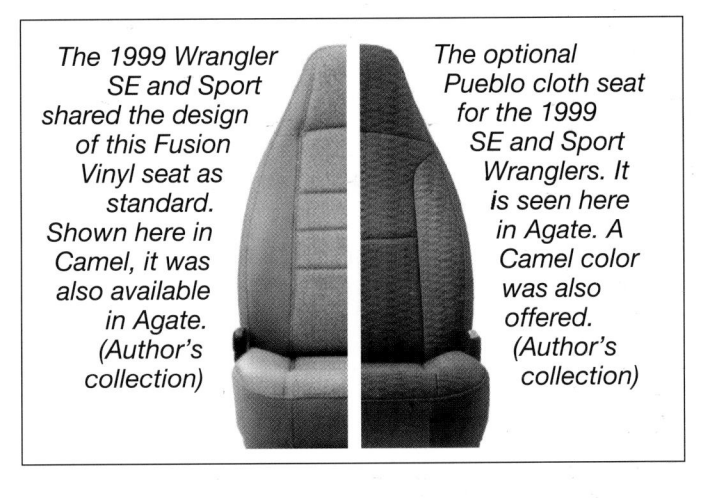

The 1999 Wrangler SE and Sport shared the design of this Fusion Vinyl seat as standard. Shown here in Camel, it was also available in Agate. (Author's collection)

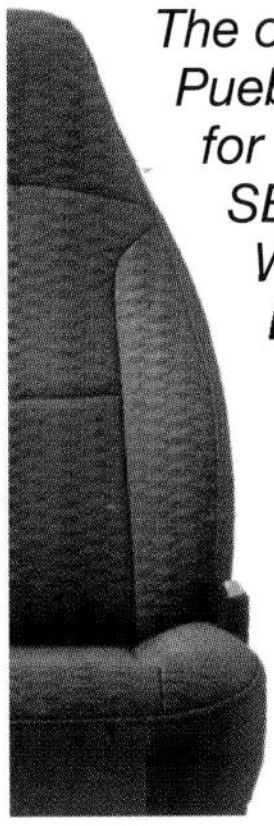

The optional Pueblo cloth seat for the 1999 SE and Sport Wranglers. It is seen here in Agate. A Camel color was also offered. (Author's collection)

Joining this revision were new Camel and Agate interior colors. New for the Sahara was a Camel and Dark Green seat trim. Both the soft and hard tops were available in a new Dark Tan as well as Stone White or Black. A mid-year addition to the Wrangler's options was an AM/FM stereo radio with a CD player.

Wrangler sales for both the model and calendar year set new records in 1999. On October 1, 1999 DaimlerChrysler announced that 88,908 had been sold in the 1999 model year, up eight per cent from the old record set in 1998. By mid-December 1999, a total of 85,188 had been sold, easily surpassing the old calendar year high mark of 83,861, also set in 1998.

Among the numerous factors behind the Wrangler's popularity was Jeep's support of programs, such as Camp Jeep, Jeep 101 and Jeep Jamboree, that assembled Jeep owners to participate in activities designed to increase owner loyalty and enhance what was regarded as the 'Jeep Lifestyle'.

Among the most popular and best attended of these gatherings was the annual Camp Jeep, the first of which took place at Camp Hale, Colorado in 1995. It continued to operate at that location until August 6-8, 1999 when, celebrating its 5th anniversary, Camp Jeep moved to Oak Ridge Estate, located in the foothills of the Blue Ridge Mountains of Virgina's Nelson County.

Martin Levine, Vice President of the Chrysler/Plymouth/Jeep Division, regarded Camp Jeep as the pinnacle of the Jeep Marketing Program. "We're thrilled to bring Camp Jeep for 1999 east of the Mississippi and provide participants with an all-new outdoor playground," he said. "Acres of sublime scenery combined with Virginia's historical characteristics make Oak Ridge Estate, close to the Wintergreen Resort, an ideal location for Jeep owners, their families and friends to enjoy a spectacular vacation experience that includes Jeep 101 courses and miles and miles of surrounding trails."

Jeep 101, held in cities across the US, was a spin-off of Camp Jeep. On the eve of the 1999 season, Lou Bitonti, Senior Manager Jeep Director Marketing discussed the early days of Jeep 101. "The Jeep 101 concept originated at Camp Jeep five years ago," he said. "It was so successful with both beginners and expert off-road drivers that we decided to take the canyon to the city for our owners and prospects."

Jeep 101 was intended to simulate difficult trail conditions in the wilderness, and featured a number of off-highway driving challenges, allowing thousands of Jeep owners and prospective owners to encounter steep downhill grades, log crossings, and sand banks close to their homes. Paired with an experienced guide they learned basic skills of safe, yet adventurous, off-road driving as well as the essential techniques successful drivers use when encountering large rocks, logs and other off-road obstacles.

Owners were then able to put their new or enhanced

A 2000 Wrangler Sahara in the new Solar Yellow color. (DaimlerChrysler Media Services)

Also with the Solar Yellow exterior, this 2000 Wrangler Sport has the optional 15 x 7in, Grizzly, aluminum wheels, fog lamps and hard top. In addition to Black, as seen here, the top was also offered in Dark Tan or Stone White. (DaimlerChrysler Media Services)

skills to use with their own vehicles on a variety of nearby off-road trails, rated according to their level of difficulty.

Offering both a mini-history of Camp Jeep and its benefits, Levine explained that "in total, more than 15,000 people from 48 states have gathered for the past four years for this unique vacation get-away. As a result, participants leave as safer and more environmentally-conscious drivers of four-wheel drive vehicles, and have a stronger tie to the Jeep family."

In 1999, the cost for the three-day Camp Jeep gathering was $225 per vehicle, which included participation in all activities, exhibits and a Saturday night concert. There was no per-person charge. Over 8000 people from 46 states attended Camp Jeep, making it the largest 'city' in rural Nelson County.

On November 18, 1999, DaimlerChrysler announced that Camp Jeep 2000 would be expanded to three full days and would be returning to the Oak Ridge Estate. Lou Bitonti, discussing the momentum generated by the previous Camp Jeep gatherings, had no doubt about their impact on Camp Jeep's future: "We place a great emphasis upon building one-to-one relationships with our customers in unique and interactive ways. The enthusiastic response to Camp Jeep demonstrates that Jeep vehicles mean much more to people than just a mode of transportation. People from all over the country come to this 'summer camp' for Jeep owners not only to learn more about what their vehicles can do, but to meet with other owners, Jeep representatives and enjoy a wide variety of adventurous outdoor activities."

Camp Jeep 1999 had sold-out months in advance and even a price increase to $275 per vehicle didn't prevent a similar response to Camp Jeep 2000.

For 2000, the updated Power-Tech 6-cylinder that had been introduced in the all-new 1999 Jeep Grand Cherokee was available for the Wrangler. This engine gave the Wrangler a more refined level of performance and a reduced noise level. Key elements of its redesign included a revised cylinder head, new exhaust manifolds, a rail-coil distributorless ignition system, and enabling its compliance with US low emission vehicle (LEV) requirements, dual, close-coupled, mini-catalytic converters. The 4.0-liter engine's torque and horsepower remained unchanged from 1999 levels.

As in 1999, this was the standard engine for the Sport and Sahara Wranglers and was coupled to an all-new standard NVG 3550 5-speed overdrive manual transmission. With a synchronized reverse gear improving shift quality, this gearbox had these ratios:

Amanda Zamora of Lennox, California, was the winner of a Jeep Wrangler given away by the United Auto Workers and DaimlerChrysler in conjunction with the Democratic National Convention. The UAW and DaimlerChrysler were partners in a display at the Petersen Automotive Museum in Los Angeles during the week of the convention. Ms Zamora visited the museum on Sunday, August 13, 2000 with her husband, Claudio, to celebrate his birthday. (DaimlerChrysler Media Services)

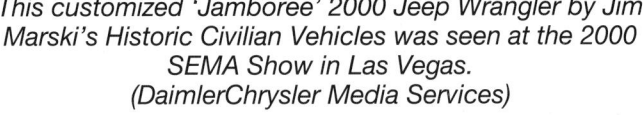

This customized 'Jamboree' 2000 Jeep Wrangler by Jim Marski's Historic Civilian Vehicles was seen at the 2000 SEMA Show in Las Vegas. (DaimlerChrysler Media Services)

First:	4.04:1
Second:	2.32:1
Third:	1.38:1
Fourth:	1.00:1
Fifth:	0.78:1
Axle:	3.07 (3.73 optional)
Overall top gear:	2.39 (2.90 with optional axle ratio)

The SE's 2.5-liter engine now met both the Euro Stage III emissions and the US LEV requirements in California, Maine, Massachusetts, New York, Vermont and the Northeast Trading Region states.

All Wranglers for 2000 had the previously optional 19-gallon fuel tank as standard. Included with the rear seat (standard for the Sport and Sahara, and available as a package option for the SE) were child seat tether anchorages. Now standard for the Wrangler Sport was a radio/cassette combination with four speakers. The Sahara's audio upgrade consisted of a radio/CD unit. Two of the speakers in these systems were located in the overhead sports bar, the others were positioned in the dashboard, "dramatically enhancing the sound quality," said Chrysler.

Three new exterior colors – Solar Yellow, Patriot Blue Pearlcoat and Silverstone Metallic – were offered for 2000. Carried over from 1999 were Flame Red, Desert Sand Pearlcoat, Medium Fern Green Pearlcoat, Forest Green Pearlcoat, Black and Stone White. The entire exterior color selection was offered for all three Wrangler models.

In its August 2000 issue, Petersen Publishing's *Four Wheeler* magazine ranked the Wrangler as best in the 'Removable Top 4x4'. category. Paying tribute to the Wrangler's reputation, *Four Wheeler* said, "Long known as one of the most capable out-of-the-box four-wheel drive vehicles around and, and certainly one of the most popular choices on tougher trail rides, the Jeep Wrangler has been a consistent breath of fresh air in a world polluted with all-wheel drive pretenders." *Four Wheeler* also rated the Jeep Cherokee tops in the 'Compact Four-Door' category.

In response, Craig R Love, Vice President – Jeep Platform Engineering, said, "We are very proud to be recognized in this fashion. Jeep vehicles stand on the promise to deliver rugged, versatile vehicles with authentic four-wheel drive capability, It's great to see a publication with the off-road credibility of *Four Wheeler* agrees with us."

Leading the Wrangler's list of refinements for 2001 was its soft top that was reengineered, said DaimlerChrysler, "for enhanced quietness and increased durability". The top's thicker four-ply design provided a two-decibel noise reduction. For the first time the soft top was available with optional rear quarter, and rear deep tint, windows. The introduction of three new exterior colors – Amber Fire

A 2001 Wrangler Sport in Solar Yellow Clearcoat. (DaimlerChrysler Media Services)

The interior of a 2001 Wrangler Sport. A new instrument cluster included a fog lamp telltale. (DaimlerChrysler Media Services)

Pearlcoat, Steel Blue Pearlcoat, and Sienna Pearlcoat provided these color combinations for 2001:

Color	SE	Sport	Sahara
Flame Red:	A	A	NA
Amber Fire Pearlcoat:	A	A	NA
Steel Blue Pearlcoat:	A	A	NA

A 2001 Wrangler Sahara in Stone White. DaimlerChrysler reported that "as the 4WD leader, the Jeep Wrangler is not only fully capable, but fun to drive and affordable. The unique and distinctive design of the Wrangler allows it to be both personalized and customized to fit a broad, but distinct range of buyers. (DaimlerChrysler Media Services)

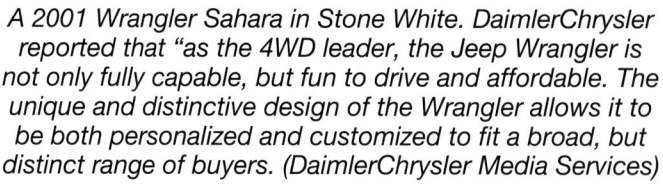

Patriot Blue Pearlcoat:	A	A	NA
Solar Yellow Clearcoat:	A	A	NA
Silverstone Metallic:	A	A	NA
Sierra Pearlcoat:	A	A	A
Black:	A	A	A
Stone White:	A	A	A
Forest Green Pearlcoat:	A	A	A

The seats in the SE and Sport models had a new standard Sutton vinyl seat material. Also new were their optional Nomad cloth seats (Nomad cloth was used for the rear seat, rear foot well, wheelhouse and cargo carpet on the SE). Trailcloth remained the Sahara's standard interior.

Added to the Sahara's standard equipment and optional for the SE and Sport was a sub woofer. It was located in a new center console with rear cup holders. The standard color-keyed mini console with dual cup holders for the SE and Sport models was redesigned. Available for all Wranglers was a new injection molded Add-A-Trunk option. Its top had a detente in the up position for use with objects too large to fit inside. The lid's underside had drink holders with a tray that could be used when the rear seat back was tipped forward. In addition, thumbscrews in the side of the Add-A-Trunk allowed it to be either slid forward or removed from the Jeep.

A new steering wheel tilt mechanism providing lower effort and an increased range of finer adjustments was standard for the Sahara and optional for the SE and Sport.

Jim Holden, DaimlerChrysler President, at a 2001 press conference in Toledo, Ohio, explaining a new technology used to make lightweight, low-cost, recyclable parts. Its first application was in 2001 Wrangler hard tops that were 23 pounds lighter than their predecessor. (DaimlerChrysler Media Services)

A view of the production of the 2001 Wrangler's new lightweight hard top. (DaimlerChrysler Media Services)

This highly modified 2001 Wrangler was displayed at the SEMA Show in Las Vegas in October 2001. It was constructed by Warn Off-Road Products as a showcase for its winches, body armor and skid plates. (DaimlerChrysler Media Services)

"And, of course, we continue to sell Wranglers to off-road enthusiasts, the opinion leaders that recognize there is no substitute for the original," – Martin R Levine, Vice President Chrysler-Plymouth – Jeep Division, speaking of the 2001 Wrangler. (DaimlerChrysler UK Media Services)

All three Wranglers had a new multi-function steering column switch combining headlamp, fog lamp, turn signal and windshield functions. Also standard across the line were intermittent windshield wipers and a wider rearview interior mirror. A revised instrument panel cluster included fog lamp and door-open telltales, 'Parade Mode' lighting, and battery-saver control of interior lighting and odometer display.

Joining a redesigned on/off switch for the front passenger air bag as important safety elements were user-ready child seat tether anchors installed on the Wrangler's rear floor fan.

Improving the Wrangler's off-road performance was the adoption of a standard thicker fuel tank skid plate.

For the really off-road, off-road experiences the 2001 Wrangler was made to order. It was, said Jeep UK, "The authentic 4x4, ready and willing to take you just as far as you want to go, an off-roader that is meant to be used off-road, not just puttering to the supermarket." (DaimlerChrysler UK Media Services)

This back-to-basics Jeep Willys concept vehicle was first displayed at the 2001 North American International Auto Show in Detroit in January, (DaimlerChrysler Media Services)

Enhancing the driver's efficiency were the Wrangler's new standard intermittent windshield wipers and a larger interior rearview mirror.

Additional improvements for 2001 included a quarter-turn fuel-filler cap, a new anti-lock brake system, quick-removal sidesteps, a long life, environmentally friendly, 100,000 mile engine coolant, and molded key heads with 'Jeep' identification.

Adding another layer of luster to the Wrangler's public image was its recognition by Edmund's.com as number one in its 'Most Wanted Specialty SUV' category.

Evoking memories of the original Willys Jeep was the Jeep Willys concept vehicle exhibited at the 2001 North American International Auto Show in Detroit. "The Willys," said DaimlerChrysler, "creates a fresh, ultra-modern interpretation of the legendary Jeep brand. Confidence-inspiring shapes such as the seven-slot grille, the uniquely executed wheel arches, the extremely short rear and the vehicle's athletic stance maintain true Jeep character."

Jordan Meadows, Product Designer at DaimlerChrysler's Pacifica Design Center in Carlsbad, California, who was responsible for the Jeep Willys, had this to say about its design. "The Jeep Willys design was inspired by American culture. Individualism and free thinking are pure American values as well as Jeep brand elements. My 'pure American' design philosophy for the Jeep Willys led me to the very clean, precise and mechanical appearance. However, it still shows traditional Jeep design cues such as the trademark grille and wheel arches and its commanding feel on the road as well as off the beaten path."

The Jeep Willys' interior had a light palette of colors and materials combining brushed aluminum, and aqua and grey leather with Starlite Silver accents. For Jeep watchers constantly on the alert for clues from DaimlerChrysler about the Wrangler's future, Meadows' comments about its interior were noteworthy. "In detailing Willys' interior with an honest look and feel," he said, "we reinforced

DaimlerChrysler Vice President, Product Design, Trevor Creed, highlighted styling cues of the Jeep Willys for his audience at the Detroit show. (DaimlerChrysler Media Services)

The Jeep Willys was driven to center stage for its world debut in Detroit on January 9, 2001. (DaimlerChrysler Media Services)

DaimlerChrysler said the Jeep Willys was "designed with a sense of adventure to create a fresh, ultra-modern interpretation of the legendary Jeep brand". (DaimlerChrysler Media Services)

Trevor Creed, DaimlerChrysler's Senior Vice-President of Design, said the Jeep Willys was intended to be "perfectly suited for the rigors of an active lifestyle". (DaimlerChrysler Media Services)

The Jeep Willys had a decidedly athletic stance. (DaimlerChrysler Media Services)

This view of the Jeep Willys shows its extremely short rear overhang. (DaimlerChrysler Media Services)

The use of molded-in-color plastic permitted designers to create shapes with crisp, rigid lines that gave the Jeep Willys a high-tech, machined finish. (DaimlerChrysler Media Services)

Commenting on the Jeep Willys interior, designer Jordan Meadows said that it was detailed with "an honest look and feel". (DaimlerChrysler Media Services)

The Jeep Willys retained many traditional Jeep design cues including the trademark grille and wheel arches. (DaimlerChrysler Media Services)

This limited edition 60th anniversary Wrangler was available through the 97 dealers of the UK Jeep network. Simon Elliott, Director of Chrysler and Jeep UK, noted that "this new commemorative model will bring even more customer appeal to the popular Wrangler range." (DaimlerChrysler UK Media Services)

the versatile Jeep lineage. The Jeep Willys is a prime example of a vehicle embracing its past while looking to its future."

While the Jeep Willys remained true to the marque's legendary capacity, it was, in many ways, a radical approach to Jeep design. "We designed this concept vehicle," explained Trevor Creed, Senior Vice President – Product Design, "with the self-expressive, free-thinker in mind. The Jeep Willys' usefulness and versatility were developed to exist in ecological harmony with nature while being perfectly suited for the rigors of an active lifestyle."

The Willys body was made of carbon fiber to simulate the weight savings that could be achieved with an injection-molded plastic body. Used on several other contemporary Chrysler Group concept cars, this type of construction saved approximately fifty per cent in weight and manufacturing costs. The body was also nearly one-hundred per cent recyclable. In addition, its molded-in-plastic color enabled designers to create shapes such as the Willys' crisp, rigid lines that were not feasible with stamped steel.

The one-piece body was molded to an aluminum frame by the use of frame-web technology, similar to that used in contemporary top-performance sports and military equipment. This gave the Willys, said DaimlerChrysler, "industry-leading rigidity".

Powering the Jeep Willys was a supercharged 1.6-liter, in-line 4-cylinder engine rated at 160hp and 155lb-ft of torque. A 4-speed automatic transmission was coupled to a shift-on-the-fly transfer case with full-time four-wheel drive and low-range modes. Estimated performance figures included a 0-60mph time of 10.2sec and a top speed of nearly 90mph (140kph).

The suspension consisted of an independent, custom-built, short-and-long arm front and multi-link solid rear axle arrangements with coil-over-shock set-up and 22in wheels with P235/840R560 PAX tires.

Additional specifications included the following:

Wheelbase:	95in (2413mm)
Front/rear track:	58.9in (1496mm)/59.4in (1509mm)
Curb weight:	2900lb (1315kg)
Weight-to-power ratio:	15:1

Summing up the attributes of the Jeep Willys, Creed remarked, "the custom suspension and supercharged power train were engineered to preserve the rugged capabilities that the Jeep brand is known for. We wanted the DNA of the Willys to speak to the heritage of its ancestors. We were looking for the most efficient yet stylish way to capture the spirit of classic Jeep vehicles enhanced with modern technology. Marrying 21st century innovation with 20th century tradition, the pure American Willys captures the bare essence of the Jeep brand."

In late June 2001, the Chrysler Group was the only automotive manufacturer to receive Gold Awards in the 2001 Industrial Design Excellence competition, an annual event co-sponsored by the Industrial Designers Society of America (IDSA), and *Business Week* magazine. The awards were presented to Chrysler for the Chrysler PT Cruiser and the Jeep Willys.

A jury of 18 non-affiliated designers reviewed 1250 entries during two and a half days of evaluation and debate. Only 44 designs received the Gold Award. In regard to the Jeep Willys, Chris Bangle, IDSA judge and the head of design at BMW said, "Nice details, such as extending the wheel's spokes into the tires, and an appropriate and innovative interior combine to make a significant concept vehicle, one that expands our narrow range of thought about what it means to be a Jeep."

Previously, in mid-June 2001, Chrysler UK had

A 2002 Wrangler Sahara for the UK market. The Wrangler was 4x4 magazine's '4x4 of the Year'. (DaimlerChrysler UK Media Services)

introduced a limited edition Wrangler 60th Anniversary model commemorating six decades of 4x4 heritage. Its debut followed the Jeep Cherokee 60th Anniversary commemorative model.

Major features of the Wrangler version included body-colored wheel-arch flares, 16in Icon alloy wheels, 225/16 All Terrain tires and 60th Anniversary badging. Two exterior colors, Silverstone and Black, were offered. Included in the commemorative model's £15,995 price were unique embroidered floor mats with a 60th anniversary theme.

Tom Marinelli, Vice President, Chrysler/Jeep Division Global Brand Center, took advantage of the introduction of the 2002 Wranglers to offer his perspective on the Wrangler's enduring popularity. "The Wrangler offers a lot of fun to a very diverse group of customers," he said. "Not only does the vehicle appeal to younger buyers for whom the Wrangler is their only vehicle, but we also see older buyers making a long-term wish come true – they've always wanted one. For them, Wrangler is a second or even third vehicle in their garage."

DaimlerChrysler added additional depth to the Wrangler's competitiveness by strengthening its line-up with a new X model. The strategy that it represented was, if not original, one that had been highly effective for many manufacturers – the offering of an attractively-priced/affordable model equipped with a powerful engine. In the case of the Wrangler X, its engine was the 4.0-liter, 6-cylinder developing 190hp and 235lb-ft of torque that was also standard for the Sport and Sahara models.

Standard for the Sahara, and optional for the other Wranglers, was a premium sound system combining two instrument panel tweeters with the center console-positioned sub woofer. Also added to the Sahara's standard equipment was the 30in Tire and Wheel Group, full steel doors with roll-up windows, rear window wiper/washer and cargo lamp, speed control and sentry key.

"These items," said DaimlerChrysler, "will truly complement our premium model."

The Sport model had a new look for 2002, resulting from the inclusion of the hard doors with full roll-up windows, fog lamps and tow hooks to its standard content.

All models had modified heating, ventilating and air conditioning (HVAC) controls for increased air flow. As well as being quieter than the previous version, this system was also five pounds lighter.

Added to the wheel and tire line-up for the SE, Sport and X models was the Ecco Wheel and Tire Group consisting of Ecco cast-aluminum wheels and P225/75R15 OWL tires. This combination was also available for the X as part of an option package that included a CD player and the premium sound system.

During the 2001 model year, cash rebates had been offered on Jeeps and, as explained by a company representative, "rolling the 2001 model $2000 cash rebates into the 2002 pricing allows Jeep vehicles better internet price positioning versus the competition. Customers have access to the true transaction price without seeking incentives. This pricing action will also allow moderation of the aggressive incentive programs pursued in the 2001 model year."

The retail prices of the four Wranglers were:

Model	**MSRP***
Wrangler SE:	$15,815
Wrangler X:	$18,995
Wrangler Sport:	$20,665
Wrangler Sahara:	$24,035
*Includes $585 destination charge	

The replacement of Forest Green by Shale Green Metallic resulted in this exterior color selection for 2002:

A – available
NA – not available

Model	SE	X	Sport	Sahara
Flame Red:	A	A	A	NA
Amber Fire Pearlcoat:	A	A	A	NA
Steel Blue Pearlcoat:	A	A	A	NA
Patriot Blue Pearlcoat:	A	A	A	NA
Silverstone Metallic:	A	A	A	NA
Solar Yellow:	A	A	A	NA
Sienna Pearlcoat:	A	A	A	A
Stone White:	A	A	A	A
Shale Green Metallic:	A	A	A	A

At the start of the 2002 model year the most popular Wrangler color was Solar Yellow which had been introduced in 2000.

The introduction of the X model resulted in this line-up of models, standard and optional equipment for 2002:

A – available
NA – not available
P – included in option package
S – Standard

Model	SE	X	Sport	Sahara
Black body side steps:	NA	NA	A	S
Full steel doors with roll-up windows and tinted glass:	A	A	S	S
Half steel doors with soft windows:	S	S	A	NA
Black fender flares with front mud guards:	S	S	S	NA
Premium fender flares with sill moldings and mud guards:	NA	NA	NA	S
Fog lamps:	NA	NA	S	S
Tinted windshield glass:	S	S	S	S
Tinted rear quarter and back windows (requires hard top):	S	S	S	NA
Deep tint rear quarter and lift gate windows:	NA	A	A	S
Body color grille:	S	S	S	S
Chrome-plated headlamp bezels:	S	S	S	S
Dual black swingaway mirrors:	S	S	S	S
Body color Sport Bar:	S	S	S	S
Black vinyl spare tire cover[a]:	A	A	A	NA
Black, Dark Tan tire cover (top colors):	A	A	A	A
Soft top with soft windows:	S	S	S	S
Hard top (includes full steel doors with roll-up windows, rear window wiper and defroster:	A	A	A	A
2-speed, variable-delay intermittent windshield wipers:	S	S	S	S
Add-A-Trunk:	A	A	A	A
Front floor color-keyed carpeting:	S	S	S	S
Rear footwell, wheelhouse and cargo floor color-keyed carpeting[b]:	P	S	S	S
Air conditioning:	A	A	A	A
Heater with instrument panel ventilation:	S	S	S	S
Electric rear window defroster for hard top:	A	A	A	A
Color-keyed door trim panels:	S	S	S	S
Color-keyed carpeted front floor mats:	A	A	A	S
Locking glove compartment:	S	S	S	S
Footwell, courtesy, driver's side interior lights:	S	S	S	S
Color-keyed mini console with dual cup holders:	S	S	S	NA
AM/FM radio with cassette:	A	S	S	S
AM/FM radio with CD:	A	P	A	A
Four speakers and Sound Bar (includes dome lamp on Sound Bar):	A	S	S	S
Seven speakers in five locations (includes amplifier sub woofer in console and dome lamp on Sound Bar):	NA	P	A	A
Sutton vinyl seat fabric:	S	NA	NA	NA
Nomad cloth seat fabric:	S[b]	S	S	A
Trailcloth:	NA	NA	NA	S
High-back reclining bucket seats with passenger side easy-access:	S	S	S	S
Seat back map pockets:	NA	NA	NA	S
Fold and tumble rear seats:	P	S	S	S

Speed control with leather-wrapped steering wheel on SE and Sport:	A	A	A	S
Sport Bar padding (full):	NA	S	S	S
Sport Bar padding (side and rear only):	S	NA	NA	NA
Low-pivot tilt steering column:	A	A	A	S
Soft-feel, two-spoke steering wheel:	S	NA	S	NA
Leather-wrapped, two-spoke steering wheel:	A	A	A	S
Color-keyed fold and swing sun visors:	S	S	S	S
2.5-liter engine/5-speed manual transmission:	S	NA	NA	NA
2.5-liter engine/3-speed automatic transmission:	A	NA	NA	NA
4.0-liter engine/5-speed manual transmission:	NA	S	S	S
4.0-liter engine/3-speed automatic transmission:	NA	A	A	A
[4]wheel anti-lock brakes:	NA	NA	A	A
Trac-Lok rear differential[c]:	NA	NA	A	A
Engine block heater:	A	A	A	A
Dana 30 front axle:	S	S	S	S
Dana 35 rear axle:	S	S	S	S
Dana 44 rear axle[d]:	NA	NA	A	A
Suspension – Normal Duty:	S	S	S	NA
High-pressure gas charged shock absorbers:	NA	NA	P	S
Full size, restricted use spare tire:	S	S	S	NA
Full-size with matching wheel:	A	A	A	S
P205/75R15 Goodyear Wrangler RT/S BSW, All-Terrain tires:	S	NA	NA	NA
P215/75R15 Goodyear Wrangler RT/S raised black letter All-Terrain tires:	NA	S	S	NA
P225/75R15 Goodyear Wrangler GS-A OWL All-Terrain tires:	A	P	P	S
15 x 6in styled steel wheels:	S	NA	NA	NA
15 x 7in full-face steel wheels:	P	S	S	NA
15 x 7in Ecco aluminum wheels:	P	P	P	S
Tire and Wheel Group – 30in[e]:	NA	NA	A	S
Tire and Wheel Group – Full-face[f]:	A	A	A	NA
Tire and Wheel Group – Ecco[g]:	A	P	A	NA
Rear three-point seat belts:	A	S	S	S
Convenience Group[h]:	A	A	A	S
Dual top Group (hard top and soft top in matching colors):	NA	NA	A	A

[a]Not available with 30in Tire and Wheel Group.
[b]Included on SE with optional rear seat package. Also used for rear footwell, wheelhouse and cargo carpet.
[c]Requires full-size spare tire.
[d]Requires 4.0-liter engine. Includes Trac-Lok differential with 3.73:1 ratio. Not available with ABS
[e]Includes 30 x 9.5R15 Goodyear Wrangler GS-A All-Terrain tires, high-pressure gas-charged monotube shock absorbers, 15 x 56in Canyon aluminum wheels, includes conventional spare tire and matching wheel. Available only with 3.73:1 axle ratio.
[f]Includes 225/75R15 Goodyear Wrangler GS-A OWL All-Terrain tires, full-size spare tire with matching wheel, 15 x 7in full-face steel wheels.
[g]Includes 225/75R1 Goodyear GS-A OWL All-Terrain tires, full-size spare with matching wheel, 15 x 7in Ecco aluminum wheels.
[h]Includes engine compartment lamp, passenger-side footwell courtesy lamp, full console with lockable storage, dual cup holder, coin holder and storage tray.

In the UK, the 2002 Wrangler was available in three specification levels – Sport, Sahara and Sahara Auto with prices ranging from £15,725 to £18,995. One of the UK's leading off-road magazines, *4x4*, selected the Wrangler as '4x4 of the Year, 2002'. It was also recognized as the class winner in the 'Hard Core' category. In regard to these two honors, David Sutherland, Editor of *4x4* said, "With big grunt from its 4.0-liter engine, excellent approach and departure angles, and brilliant visibility from the driver's seat, the Wrangler has everything a serious off-roader needs. But it has more too; style and charisma sufficient to make every journey made in the American icon an adventure."

Responding to these awards, Simon Elliott, Managing Director of Chrysler Jeep in the UK, said; "We are absolutely delighted. Not only have we received the highest accolade awarded to a 4x4 vehicle in the UK, but to receive another two accolades for the Jeep brand is fantastic." Elliot was also acknowledging the selection of the Grand Cherokee V-8 Limited by *4x4* as the winner in its 'Luxury' category.

Following these recognitions, the Wrangler's UK

Jordan Meadows (left) and Trevor Creed presenting the Jeep Willys2 at the 2001 Tokyo Auto Show, October 2001. (DaimlerChrysler Media Services)

model range was expanded in the summer of 2002 with the arrival (Chrysler Media said it was "unleashed" of a special edition 'Grizzly' model, priced at £16,795 and equipped with 16in Icon alloy wheels, 225/70R16 AT tires, a spare tire cover and special 'paw-print' badging.

Simon Elliot remarked that "with its lusty 4.0-liter engine, brutish good looks and open topped capability, we expect the Grizzly to appeal to current Wrangler owners as well as a new breed of buyers who are looking for the ultimate style accessory this summer."

Earlier, in October 2001, less than a year after taking the wraps off the Jeep Willys concept model at the 2001 North American International Auto Show, Trevor Creed introduced its successor, the Jeep Willys2, at the 2001 Tokyo Auto Show. This was the first time the Chrysler Group had scheduled the world premier of a design study at the Tokyo Show. Jordan Meadows who, as Product Designer at Chrysler's Pacifica Advanced Design Center, was primarily responsible for the Jeep Willys2 was also on hand for its debut. "Willys2," he said, "embodies the Jeep brand's core values of fun, freedom and legendary capability, generating interest from the young and young at heart."

"We call it the pure American," added Creed. "The Jeep Willys2's usefulness and versatility were developed to exist in ecological harmony with nature, while being perfectly suited for the rigors of an active lifestyle."

Like its predecessor, the Willys2 had a one-piece carbon fiber body on an aluminum frame. Its removable hard top was constructed of carbon fiber and was equipped with a roof rack featuring a full-size spare tire holder, an integrated luggage carrier, and bindings for securing a wide range of outdoor gear. Mounted at the rack's front were three auxiliary fog and search lamps. Both the body and the hard top were finished in Action Green metallic paint.

Typifying its 'go anywhere and do anything at any time' capability was the Willys2's 12in ground clearance. Exemplifying its 'easy-on-the-environment' design was the nearly 100 per cent recyclable content of its body.

Except for some minor changes noted below, the Jeep Willys2, essentially a hard top version of the Jeep Willys, had the same basic specifications as its predecessor.

Concept Vehicle	Jeep Willys	Jeep Willys2
Wheels:	22in	21in
Tire size:	P235/840R560	P235/65R21
Curb weight:	2900lb	3000lb

By 2002, Camp Jeep was in its 8th year and, as a three-day, family-oriented outing, provided plenty of action-packed activities. There were also engineering round table discussions enabling Jeep owners to meet with engineers who developed their vehicles, ask questions and have them answered. In this give-and-take environment, engineers also obtained valuable feedback from Jeep owners.

Added to the Camp Jeep program in 2002 were new extreme sport activities, additional popular lifestyle-family activities and daily live performances by top musicians, including a patriotic concert and a fireworks display.

Approximately 10,0000 people attended Camp Jeep 2002, held in the Ozark Mountains near Branson, Missouri.

The Jeep Willys2 interior blended Aqua and Silver colors with translucent plastics for a new approach to Jeep design that remained true to the marque's traditional versatility. "You can still take a water hose to this interior and clean it out," said Jordan Meadows. (DaimlerChrysler Media Services)

The Jeep Willys2 front end design was dominated by an ultra-modern interpretation of Jeep's noble seven-slot grille. (DaimlerChrysler Media Services)

DaimlerChrysler emphasized that the Jeep Willys2 was a concept vehicle with no imminent production plans. (DaimlerChrysler Media Services)

This profile view of the Jeep Willys2 shows its trapezoidal wheel arches linking it with the first civilian CJ-2A Jeeps The stylized 'Willys2' identification adds a nice contemporary touch. (DaimlerChrysler Media Services)

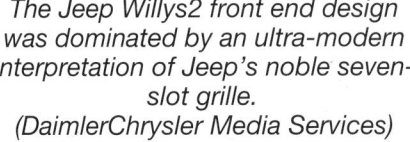

Seen here are details of the Jeep Willys2 spare tire holder and an example of the ease with which a variety of recreational items could be safety secured in the luggage rack. (DaimlerChrysler Media Services)

The Jeep Willys2 was finished in Action Green metallic paint. Its 21 x 7.5in wheels were fitted with P235/65R21 Goodyear tires. (DaimlerChrysler Media Services)

Speaking at the Jeep Willys2's North American debut at the 2002 NAIAS, Jordan Meadows observed that "more than 60 years after the original Willys, Willys2 embodies the Jeep brand's core values of authenticity, freedom and legendary capability, generating interest from the young and young at heart." (DaimlerChrysler Media Services)

The Jeep Willys2's carbon fibre top was removable. (DaimlerChrysler Media Services)

Each day began with opening ceremonies featuring local organizations. The two live outdoor concerts, one by Daryl Hall and John Oates, opened the event, the second, by the Blue Brothers (Dan Aykroyd and Jim Belushi), headlined the 'Jeep Jubilee' grand finale. Family activities included hiking, kayaking, outdoor survival skills, fly casting, children's activities, spa services, yoga, an outdoor gourmet cooking school and numerous arts and crafts.

New for 2002 was the Thrills and Spills Zone, a hybrid sports arena featuring skate boarding, BMX biking and a snow boarding trampoline. Attendees were able to participate as well as watch live demonstrations of Olympic caliber athletics including Robbie Miranda, Kevin Gutierrez and Leigh Donavan.

In December 2002, Camp Jeep was recognized at the Marketing Agency Association (MAA) Worldwide GLOBES Awards, held in Miami, Florida, as the 'Best Program Generating Brand Loyalty'. MMA Worldwide annually honored the best marketing campaigns created by agencies from around the world. Camp Jeep was selected from over 1200 entries from 28 countries.

A month earlier, in October, Camp Jeep had received the same honor at *Promo* magazine's annual PRO Awards for the second consecutive year. In 2001 Camp Jeep was

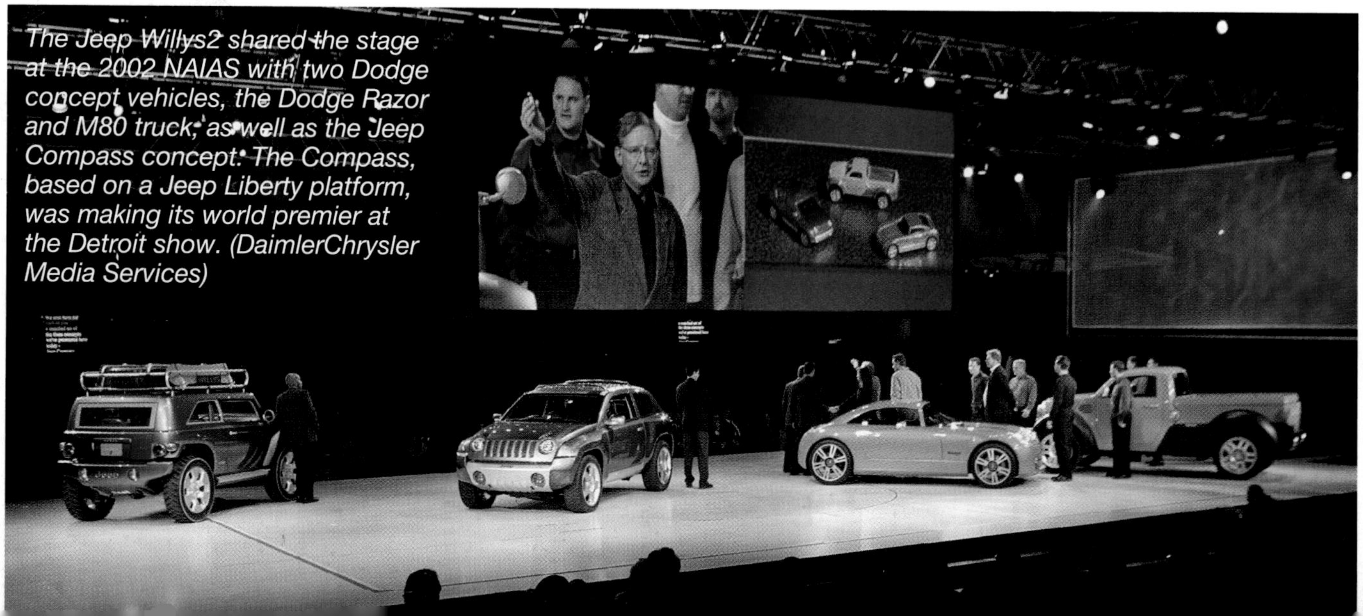

The Jeep Willys2 shared the stage at the 2002 NAIAS with two Dodge concept vehicles, the Dodge Razor and M80 truck, as well as the Jeep Compass concept. The Compass, based on a Jeep Liberty platform, was making its world premier at the Detroit show. (DaimlerChrysler Media Services)

A 2003 Wrangler Sport rendezvousing in the wild with the 2003 Grand Cherokee and Pioneer models. (DaimlerChrysler Media Services)

the first inductee into the PRO Awards Hall of Fame. The Hall of Fame recognized Camp Jeep as "a benchmark for measuring the success of customer relationship marketing events around the world". Previously, Camp Jeep had won PRO Awards for 'Best Copywriting', 'Best Database Management', and 'Best Use of Direct Marketing'.

"It is an honor to receive a GLOBES Award and a PRO Award," said Lou Bitonti, then serving as DaimlerChrysler's Senior Manager of Brand Events. "We have had wonderful support from our Jeep owners and we love having them come back to different locations for Camp Jeep. We're dedicated to raising the bar each year to create an event that reaches above and beyond owners' expectations."

Highlighting the Wrangler's 2003 model year was the introduction of the new Wrangler Rubicon model, use of a new Power Tech 4 engine for the base line Sport models, the availability of a new 4-speed automatic transmission for use with both the 2.4-liter and 4.0-liter engines, (in addition to the standard fuel tank and transfer case skid plates that were carried over from previous years, the automatic transmission was protected by an additional skid plate), a new standard 5-speed manual gearbox for the SE, the availability of four-wheel disc brakes and the Wrangler's availability as a right-hand drive rural mail delivery vehicle.

Taking its name from one of the toughest off-road trails of Jeep history, the Rubicon was considered a limited production extreme off-road model intended for Wrangler owners who customarily utilized after-market components when modifying their vehicles for serious trail work.

Referring to the Rubicon on September 1, 2002, when full details of the Jeep line for 2003 were announced,

A 2003 Wrangler Sport in Flame Red. Its standard 4.0-liter engine could be linked to either a standard 5-speed manual or a new 4-speed automatic transmission. (DaimlerChrysler Media Services)

Along with the all-new Jeep Liberty Renegade and the Jeep Compass concept car, the 2003 Wrangler Rubicon was introduced to the media at the Chicago Auto Show on February 7, 2002 by Dave Bostwick, Chrysler Group Director of Corporate Market Research, (left), Tom Mannelli, Vice President Chrysler/Jeep Global Brand (center), and Craig Love, Vice President of the Jeep Product team (right). (DaimlerChrysler Media Services)

This view of the Inca Gold Pearlcoat Wrangler Rubicon at the Chicago Auto Show shows its hood graphic which DaimlerChrysler said was intended to invoke memories of legendary Jeeps such as the CJ Renegades and Laredos. (DaimlerChrysler Media Services)

the head of the Jeep Product Team, Craig Love, positioned its attributes in the mainstream of Jeep's off-road heritage. "The 2003 Jeep Wrangler Rubicon features an off-road performance as only Jeep can engineer," he said, "allowing serious off-road enthusiasts the opportunity to drive over some of the most extreme trails in the country and then drive it home."

The Rubicon was equipped with air-actuated front and rear Tru-Lok locking differentials that could be driver-actuated when the transfer case was in low range and the Wrangler's speed was below 10mph (16kmh). When engaged, this feature mechanically locked the axle shafts

The 2003 Wrangler Rubicon's standard Wrangler 'Maximum Traction/Reinforced' 31in tires had a 'beefy' tread pattern that wrapped around the sidewall to help grab ledges along the trail. This state-of-the-art tire also had a three-ply sidewall and an advanced silica compound for added durability and puncture resistance. (DaimlerChrysler Media Services)

together to drive all four wheels at the same speed. A dash-mounted rocker switch enabled the driver to lock the rear axle and toggle the front axle lock on/off for improved maneuverability. Unlocked, the rear axle had a torque-slip feature providing better on-road traction and handling.

Heavy-duty Dana Model 44 axles with 4.11:1 ratios were used front and rear. This ratio compared with others offered for 2003 in this way:

Application:	**NV3550**	**42RLE**
Transmission:	5-speed man	4-speed auto
Axle ratio:		
Standard:	3.07	4.56 (2.4 engine), 3.73 (4.0 engine)
Optional	3.73	–
Rubicon:	4.11	4.11

The transfer case, a fixed output NV242 Off-Road unit, had a 4:1 low range that slowed vehicle speed to give the driver more control, while increasing the amount of torque available at the wheels. This unit was engineered specifically for the Wrangler Rubicon and met all durability requirements that were established for intense off-road operation. Also used for this reason were increased torque capacity, heavy-duty drive-shafts and universal joints.

The Wrangler's new 4-wheel disc brakes were standard for the Rubicon (and optional for the Sport and Sahara models). Jeep reported they gave the Wrangler "better brake feel on-road, with decreased stopping distance and reduced brake fade. Off-road, four-wheel disc brakes are self cleaning."

They had these dimensions and specifications:

Front	
Size:	11.0 x 0.94in (280 x 24mm)
Type:	Vented disc with single piston sliding caliper

Critics praised the 2003 Wrangler Rubicon's engineering which combined everyday drivability and reliability with outstanding off-road performance. (DaimlerChrysler Media Services)

A 2003 Wrangler Rubicon with the optional hard top. Heavy gauge, diamond plate sill guards were bolted to the body side to protect the rocker panels from damage in off-road excursions. (DaimlerChrysler Media Services)

This perspective of the 2003 Wrangler Rubicon shows the tread pattern of its 'Maximum Traction' reinforced 31in tire that was designed to provide added stiffness and uniform wear. (DaimlerChrysler Media Services)

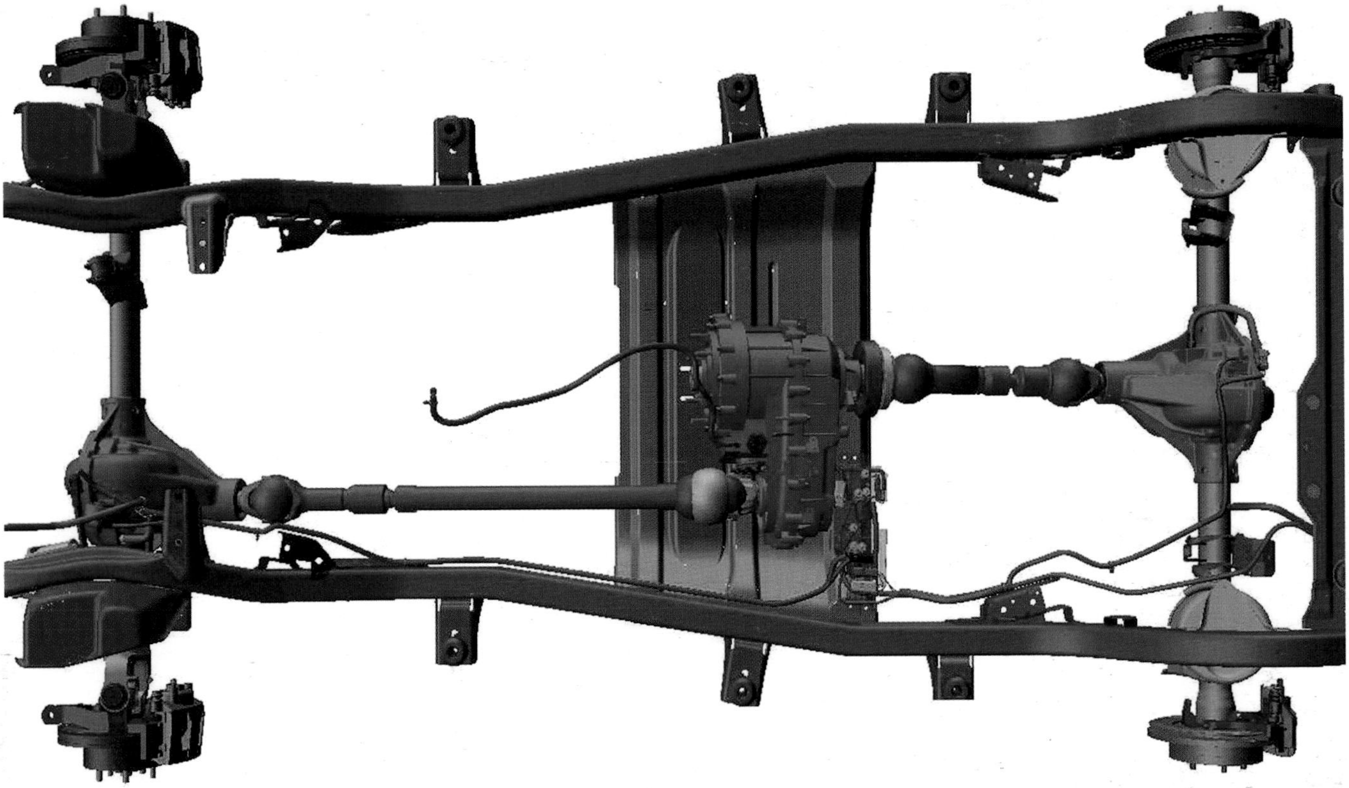

The chassis of the 2003 Wrangler Rubicon showing its locking front and rear differentials and Dana Model 44 axles as well as its 4:1 low range Rock-Trac transfer case. (DaimlerChrysler Media Services)

Swept area:	198.5in^2 (1281cm^2)
Rear	
Size:	11.2 x 0.47in (285 x 12mm)
Type:	Solid disc with single piston sliding caliper
Swept area:	96.8in^2 (625sq cm)

Craig Love wasn't modest when summing up the collective capability of these components: "This combination of what would typically be after-market hardware provides tremendous off-road capability to give our enthusiast owners a rig that is ready for their favorite trails right out of the box."

The use of the Rubicon name put the new Jeep right in the center of the marque's storied off-road history. The original Rubicon Trail Jeep Jamboree had been in existence for some 45 years and by 1998, Jeep Jamborees took place over trails with rating ranging from 1, the least difficult, to 10, the most difficult.

Undoubtedly Love was pleased when Matthew Phenix, of *Automobile* magazine, deemed the Jeep deserving of its name. "The Rubicon Trail," Phenix noted, "meanders some 22 miles through the piney, rock-strewn wilderness that stretches out west of Lake Tahoe ... It's the most storied off-highway pass in America, and an automaker that dares evoke the name must be prepared to put up or shut up. With its new top-spec Wrangler, Jeep has put up." Apparently so did many Rubicon owners as Jeep later reported that 90 per cent of Rubicon owners took them off-road. Quickly becoming one of the most popular Wrangler models, the Rubicon accounting for 20 per cent of Wrangler sales in 2003.

The Rubicon was equipped with Goodyear Wrangler 'Maximum Traction' reinforced 31in tires with a tread pattern that, by wrapping around the sidewall, was intended to provide added traction on ledges confronted along an off-road trail. Increased tread thickness and uniform wear were two benefits of the tire's new tread pattern. These LT245/7R16 tires also provided the Rubicon with an additional 0.5in (13mm) of ground clearance and were the largest tires ever offered from the factory on a Wrangler.

Paired with these tires were 16in, five-spoke aluminum wheels. The dished face of these wheels was intended to prevent them from damage by off-road obstacles

The Rubicon's standard power train was the familiar 4.0-liter, 6-cylinder engine and 5-speed manual transmission. The new 42RTLE 4-speed automatic transmission, with electronic-controlled shifting instead of

American Expedition Vehicles displayed this Jeep Wrangler Scrambler at the November 2002 SEMA Show in Las Vegas. The Wrangler's wheelbase was extended 24 inches to provide the basis for a Jeep with the Rubicon's contemporary off-road capability and a load capacity reminiscent of the CJ-7 based Jeep Scrambler produced from 1981 through 1986. It was powered by the 190hp 4.0-liter Power Tech engine, and had the Rubicon's Dana 44 axles, locking differentials, and disc brakes. (DaimlerChrysler Media Services)

hydraulic controls, was optional for the Rubicon as well as the other 2003 Wranglers.

"This smoother-shifting transmission," said a Jeep representative, "provides better highway fuel efficiency and quieter engine operation at highway speeds compared to the previous 3-speed automatic transmission." The two transmissions had these ratios:

Transmission:	30/32 RH (2002)	42RLE (2003)
Gear ratios		
1st:	2.74	2.84
2nd:	1.54	1.57s
3rd:	1.00	1.00
4th:	–	0.69

DaimlerChrysler made certain that the Rubicon's unique mechanics would be matched by a distinctive exterior. A Rubicon graphic was applied to each side of the hood. Wide riveted fender flares were installed and heavy gauge diamond plate sill guards were bolted to the body side to protect the rocker panels from damage in off-road situations. The Rubicon was available in any of the Wrangler's standard exterior colors.

The American Expedition Vehicles' Jeep Wrangler Scrambler was one of the winners of the Chrysler Group's 2002 Design Excellence Awards. These were presented to companies that, said Chrysler, "express innovation, superior design and brand focus in developing after-market vehicle lifestyle packages for Chrysler, Dodge Truck and Jeep vehicles". The entries were judged by the Chrysler Group's Vehicle Excitement Team consisting of four cross-functional teams representing Engineering Design, Product Planning and Marketing. (DaimlerChrysler Media Services)

The Rubicon joined the Wrangler Sport and Sahara that were sold outside North America in either left- or right-hand drive with the 4.0-liter engine. Wrangler Sport models with the 2.4-liter engine were offered only in left-hand drive form.

The entry level Wrangler SE's new 2.4-liter Power Tech engine and standard 5-speed manual transmission had been introduced in 2002 on the Jeep Liberty SUV. When announced on September 1, 2002, the dual overhead cams, 16 valve Power Tech had estimated power ratings of 150hp @ 5200rpm and 165lb-ft of torque @ 4000rpm, representing a 25 per cent increase in horsepower and an 18 per cent increase in torque when compared to the 2.5-liter engine. Its increased output was achieved using

A 2003 Wrangler Sport in Sienna Pearlcoat. Its fog lamps were standard. (DaimlerChrysler Media Services)

The 2003 Wrangler X had a standard 190hp 4.0-liter engine and 5-speed manual transmission. Evident in this view are the Wrangler's new taller seat backs. (DaimlerChrysler Media Services)

aluminum cross-flow cylinder heads, dual overhead cams and a four-valve-per-cylinder design. Jeep asserted it was quieter, more fuel-efficient and was engineered for longer life and ease of maintenance. It also met the current NLEV (National Low Emission Vehicle) light-duty truck standards and had these final-for-2003 specifications:

Availability:	Standard for Wrangler SE
Type:	4-cylinder, in-line, liquid cooled
Displacement:	148.2cu-in (2429cc)
Bore x stroke:	3.44 x 3.98in (88 x 101cm)
Valve system:	Belt drive, DOHC, 16 valves, stamped steel followers, hydraulic lash adjustment
Fuel injection:	Sequential, multi-port electronic
Construction:	Cast-iron block, cast-iron bed plate, aluminum cylinder head and balance shafts
Compression ratio:	9.5:1
Horsepower:	147 @ 5200rpm:
Torque:	165lb-ft @ 4000rom
Max. engine speed:	6240rpm (electronically limited)
Fuel requirement:	Regular unleaded, 87 octane
Oil capacity:	5qt (5.3L)
Coolant capacity:	10.1qt (9.6L)
Emission controls:	Catalytic converters, oxygen sensors, on-board vapor recovery system, leak detection system
Estimated EPA fuel economy mpg (City/Hwy):	19/20 manual/17/19 automatic

For the Europe market, the 4.0-liter engine had a 172hp rating. The 2.4-liter was rated at 143hp.

Jeep reported that the SE's new 5-speed had several advantages over its predecessor including a synchronized reverse gear and improved shift quality in cold weather. A side-by-side comparison of the two gearboxes also highlights several other points of difference between them:

Transmission:	AS72 (2002)	NV1500 (2003)
Gear ratios:		
1st:	3.93	3.85
2nd:	2.33	2.25
3rd:	1.45	1.48
4th:	1.00	1.00
5th:	0.85	0.80
Axle ratio:	4.10	4.10
Overall top gear:	3.48	3.28

While not losing any of the unique ambiance of a Jeep interior, the Wrangler's was virtually all-new for 2003. New front seats increased rear travel by 0.79in (20mm), enabling drivers to sit a bit further away from the steering wheel, if desired. The seat backs were also taller for a more comfortable seating position. A lever on the right side of the passenger seat provided easier access to the rear.

A new fold-and-tumble rear bench seat (standard for the X, Sport, Sahara and Rubicon, and optional in a package for the SE) could be more easily removed.

Added to the Sahara's interior was a electrochromic rearview mirror with map lights, and a temperature and compass display. This feature was optional for the Sport and Rubicon models. Both the SE and X models had a new Soft-feel vinyl four-spoke steering wheel. A two-spoke version had been used in 2002. A new leather-wrapped steering wheel was used on the Sport, Sahara and Rubicon models.

Common to all Wranglers was an additional power outlet on the dash. Replacing the previously optional Sound Bar, were new corner pods located just behind the B-pillar on both sides of the Jeep, housing interior lights and providing room for optional speakers. Energy-absorbing foam was added to the sport bar and new trim was positioned around the windshield and on the back of the hard top.

The Wrangler's interior conformed to the 2003 federal standard for upper head impact protection as well as meeting the LATCH (Lower Anchors and Tethers for Children) requirement.

Replacing the Agate and Camel colors offered for the 2002 Wrangler interior were two new shades: Dark Slate and Khaki.

All models were equipped with On-Board Refueling Recovery (ORVR) systems. A new exterior mirror design reduced vibration, while increasing stability and durability. A sign of the times was the introduction of a new Smoker's Package consisting of a removable ashtray and a cigar lighter option for all Wranglers. Two new audio options also made their first appearances on the 2003 Wranglers. Both were flush-mounted AM/FM radios, one with a cassette player, the other with a CD player.

Four exterior colors were new for 2003: Intense Blue Pearlcoat, Inca Gold Pearlcoat, Bright Silver Metallic and Light Khaki Metallic. Carried over from 2002 were Stone White, Flame Red, Black, Patriot Blue Pearlcoat, Shale Green Metallic and Sienna Pearlcoat. With the exception of the Sahara, all Wranglers were available in any of these colors. The choice for the Sahara was limited to Patriot Blue Pearlcoat, Shale Green Metallic, Light Khaki Metallic and Sienna Pearlcoat. Black was available for Saharas destined for the European markets. Replacing Tan as a color for the Wrangler's soft and hard top for 2003 was Dark Khaki. Black continued as an alternative.

Commenting on the likely impact of these changes and revisions upon the Wrangler's popularity in Europe, Thomas Hausch, the Chrysler Group's Executive Director of International Sales, predicted that "the new engine and transmission improvements will further expand the appeal of the Jeep brand with power trains particularly well-suited for the European market."

The full range of features for the five Wrangler models for 2003 follows:

A – available *NA – not available* *P – included in option package* *S – Standard* **Feature**	**SE**	**X**	**Sport**	**Sahara**	**Rubicon**
Black body side steps:	NA	NA	A	S	NA
Front and rear bumpers with black end caps and front bumper guards:	S	S	S	S	S
Doors:					
Full, steel with roll-up windows:	A	A	S	S	A
Half steel with soft windows:	S	S	A	A	S
Fender flares:					
Black, mold-in color:	S	S	S	NA	NA
Premium, body color:	NA	NA	NA	S	NA
Premium, Black:	NA	NA	NA	NA	S

This Performance West Surf & Turf Wrangler made its debut at the November 4, 2002 Innovations Day Luncheon at the SEMA show in Las Vegas, Nevada. Its features included KW suspension shock absorbers, stainless steel rear disc brakes and PIAA model 80 racing lights. (Photo by Joe Wilssens, courtesy of DaimlerChrysler Media Services)

Fog lamp:	NA	NA	S	S	S
Glass:					
Tinted windshield:	S	S	S	S	S
Deep tinted sunscreen rear quarter and back light windows:	NA	A	A	S	A
Tinted rear quarter and lift gate windows:	S	S	S	NA	S
Body color grille:	S	S	S	S	S
Chrome-plated headlamp bezels:	S	S	S	S	S
Dual swing-way black mirrors:	S	S	S	S	S
Diamond plate sill guards:	NA	NA	NA	NA	S
Black vinyl spare tire cover[1]:	A	A	A	NA	NA
Tops:					
Soft, easy-folding with soft windows:	S	S	S	S	S
Hard, with full steel doors with roll-up windows, rear window wiper and washer and rear window defroster:	A	A	A	A	A
2-speed wipers with variable-delay intermittent and washers:	S	S	S	S	S
Add-A-Trunk:	A	A	A	A	A

Passenger assist handle:	S	S	S	S	S
Auxiliary 12-volt outlet:	S	S	S	S	S
Color-keyed front carpet:	S	S	S	S	S
Color-keyed rear footwell, rear wheelhouse and cargo floor carpeting[2]:	P	S	S	S	S
Cargo tie down loops (4):	S	S	S	S	S
Air conditioning:	A	A	A	S	A
Mini floor console with dual cupholders:	S	S	NA	NA	NA
Full-length floor console with four cup holders:	NA	NA	S	S	S
Color-keyed molded door trim panels with map pockets and pull handles:	S	S	S	S	S
Color-keyed carpeted front floor mats:	A	A	A	A	A
Locking glove compartment:	S	S	S	S	S
Electrochromic rearview mirror[3]:	NA	NA	A	S	A
Radio delete:	S	NA	NA	NA	NA
AM/FM stereo radio with cassette:	A	S	S	NA	S

The Surf & Turf Wrangler was one of forty new custom vehicles created by SEMA member companies and the Chrysler Group displayed at the November 2002 Las Vegas show. (Photo by Joe Wilssens, courtesy of DaimlerChrysler Media Services)

AM/FM stereo radio with CD:	A	A	A	S	A
Four speakers:	A	S	S	NA	S
Seven speakers[4]:	NA	P	A	S	A
Vinyl seat fabric:	S	A	A	A	A
Cloth seat fabric:	A	S	S	NA	S
Premium cloth:	NA	NA	NA	S	NA
Rear fold-and-tumble seat[5]:	P	S	S	S	S
Full sport bar padding:	S	S	S	S	S
Low-pivot tilt steering wheel:	P	P	S	S	S
Soft-feel, four-spoke steering wheel;	S	S	NA	NA	NA
Leather-wrapped, four-spoke steering wheel:	P	P	S	S	S
2.4-liter Power Tech engine and 5-speed manual trans:	S	NA	NA	NA	NA
2.4-liter Power Tech engine and 4-speed automatic trans:	A	NA	NA	NA	NA
4.0-liter Power tech engine and 5-speed manual trans:	NA	S	S	S	S
4.0-liter Power tech engine and 4-speed automatic trans:	NA	A	A	A	A
Power front disc/rear drum brakes:	S	S	S	S	NA
Four-wheel disc brakes:	NA	NA	A	A	S
Four-wheel anti-lock brakes:	NA	A	A	A	NA
Trac-Lok differential[6]:	NA	A	A	A	NA
Tru-Lok differential[6]:	NA	NA	NA	NA	S
Engine block heater:	A	A	A	A	A
Dana 30 front axle:	S	S	S	S	NA
Dana 44 heavy-duty front axle:	NA	NA	NA	NA	S
Dana 35 rear axle:	S	S	S	S	NA
Dana 44 heavy-duty rear axle:	NA	NA	A	A	S
3.73 axle ratio:	NA	P/A	P/A	P/A	NA
Fuel tank and transfer case skid plates:	S	S	S	S	S
Power steering:	S	S	S	S	S

Gas charged shock absorbers:	S	S	S	NA	NA
High-pressure gas-charged shock absorbers:	NA	NA	P	S	S
Full-size restricted use spare tire:	S	S	NA	NA	NA
Full-size spare tire with matching wheel:	A	A	S	S	S
Tires:					
P205/75R15 Goodyear Wrangler RT/S BSW AT:	S	NA	NA	NA	NA
P215/75R15 Goodyear Wrangler RT/S RBL AT:	NA	S	S	NA	NA
P225/75R15 Goodyear Wrangler GS-A OWL AT:	P	P	P/A	NA	NA
30 x 9.5R15 LT Goodyear Wrangler OWL AT	NA	NA	A	S	NA
LT245/75R16 MTR Goodyear BSW on/off tires:	NA	NA	NA	NA	S
Tow hooks (two, front; one, rear):	A	A	S	S	S
Transfer case:					
Command-Trac, part-time 4WD:	S	S	S	S	NA
Rock-Trac heavy-duty part-time 4WD:	NA	NA	NA	NA	S
Wheels:					
Styled steel 15 x 6in:	S	NA	NA	NA	NA
Full-face steel 15 x 7in:	P	S	S	NA	NA
Ecco 15 x 7in aluminum:	P	P	P	NA	NA
Canyon 15 x 8in aluminum:	NA	NA	P	S	NA
Moah 16 x 8in cast-aluminum:	NA	NA	NA	NA	S
Passenger side air bag on-off switch:	P	NA	NA	NA	NA
Sentry Key anti-theft system:	NA	NA	A	S	A
Convenience Group[7]:	A	A	S	S	S
Smoker's Group:	A	A	A	A	A
Dual Top Group:	A	A	A	A	A
Tire and Wheel Group (Canyon) 30in[8]:	NA	NA	A	S	NA
Tire and Wheel Group (Full-face)[9]:	A	A	NA	NA	NA

The 2003 Wrangler RHD Postal Unit returned Jeep to the market for 4x4 postal vehicles. (DaimlerChrysler Media Services)

Tire and Wheel Group					
(Ecco)[10]:	A	P	A	NA	NA
Wheel Plus Group[11]:	NA	A	NA	NA	NA

[1]Not available with 30in Tire and Wheel Group
[2]Included with rear seat on SE
[3]Included reading lamps, compass and temperature display
[4]Speakers located in five locations; included amplified sub woofer in console. Convenience Group required
[5]Included three-point rear seat belts and rear footwell, rear wheelhouse and cargo floor carpet
[6]Full-size spare tire required
[7]Included passenger-side footwell courtesy lights, under hood lamp, full console with lockable storage, four cup holders, coin holder and storage tray
[8]Included 30 x 9R15 LT Goodyear Wrangler GS-A AT tires, high-pressure gas-charged monotube shock absorbers, 15 x 8in Canyon aluminum wheels (3.73 axle ratio only), matching spare tire and wheel
[9]Included 225/75R15 Goodyear Wrangler GS-OWL AT tires, full-size spare with matching wheel, 15 x 7in full-face steel wheels
[10]Included 225/75R15 Goodyear Wrangler GS-OWL AT tires, full-size spare with matching wheel, 15 x 7in Ecco aluminum wheels
[11]Included Tire and Wheel Group (Ecco), AM/FM radio with CD and changer control, seven speakers including sub woofer and tweeters

Beginning in December 2002, the Wrangler was available in a right-hand-drive 4.0-liter Postal Unit with a standard automatic transmission. The Chrysler Group might have been a bit optimistic by suggesting the Postal Unit might be able to "ease the upcoming holiday mail load", but it was historically correct in referring to the "Postal Jeep's reintroduction ... " Providing modern customers with a concise lesson in the Wrangler's heritage, it added that "Jeep is the ultimate utilitarian vehicle. When Jeep returned from WWII, it went immediately into government, agricultural and postal services."

Specific ancestors of the Wrangler Postal Unit included the first Jeep vehicle built for the US Postal Service based on the Jeep Dispatcher (DJ-3A) manufactured between 1955-1964 and the DJ-5 (1965-1983). Both these vehicles had two-wheel drive, whereas Jeep 4x4 vehicles were favored by rural letter carriers throughout the US prior to the Postal Unit, the last 4x4 Jeep to be sold to the postal segment was the 2001 Jeep Cherokee which was no longer available.

The Wrangler Postal Unit had a standard hard top with full metal doors and roll-up windows. The interior had a removable rear seat to accommodate bulk mail and package, front cloth seats with easy rear access design, an AM/FM radio with cassette player,

A predecessor of the 2003 Wrangler Postal Unit was this 1974 DJ-5 ¼ton postal delivery vehicle, manufactured by American Motors' AM General subsidiary in South Bend, Indiana. (DaimlerChrysler Media Services)

This line of Freedom Edition Jeeps debuted at the 2003 North American Auto Show. Seen here are the Wrangler, Liberty and Grand Cherokee versions. (DaimlerChrysler Media Services)

and four speakers. A Dana 44 heavy-duty rear axle with Trac-Lok was used along with P215/75R15 Wrangler AT tires and full-face steel wheels. A full-size spare tire was provided. The Postal Unit's MSRP was $20,243 plus a $610 destination charge. It was available in any of the ten standard Wrangler colors for 2003.

European specification Wranglers for 2003 were displayed at the Paris Motor Show in late September 2002. On June 27, 2003, the Rubicon made its off-road debut in Europe at the Euro Camp Jeep 2003 meet in La Thuile, Italy. At that time the Chrysler Group announced that the Rubicon was "a limited production vehicle that is available for selected left-hand drive markets across Europe".

When the Rubicon had been introduced in September 2002, Jeep had reported that availability was limited to North America, although, it said, "selected international markets are under consideration".

In its third year, Euro Camp Jeep attracted nearly 350 Jeeps. The Chrysler Group made sure that participants enjoyed a wide range of activities, as well as having the opportunity to check out the latest Jeep models. "Euro Camp Jeep has grown into a 'must-do' event for our owners and enthusiasts in Europe," said Thomas Hausch, the Chrysler Group's Executive Director of International Sales and Marketing.

"Jeep is the only brand to bring this many customers together from all over Europe for one special weekend every year. The fact that customers budget their time and money to attend Euro Jeep Camp is testimony to their passion for the Jeep brand and what it represents.

"In the mountains of Northern Italy, in the Valle d'Aosta region, participants will test the go-anywhere, do-anything capabilities of their vehicles – and themselves – in a unique and scenic environment and share their experiences with other Jeep enthusiasts, all in an unforgettable, convivial atmosphere."

Specifically, for 2003, Euro Camp Jeep offered activities ranging from driving over demanding off-road trails to GPS navigation and survival trials to educational round tables where presentations were made on such topics as the latest developments in Jeep technology and off-road driving techniques. There was also a display of classic Jeeps, a Jeep clothing and merchandise shop, sponsor's exhibitions and live evening concerts

"At Euro Camp Jeep," said Hausch, "our owners are able to live life in a Jeep vehicle like they never before imagined. They can learn more about the amazing capabilities of a Jeep, meet great people and have fun with their families. Most of all, they experience personally, in every aspect, why the Jeep brand way of life has become legendary."

Each day numerous family-focused activities were offered, including quad bike riding, river rafting and cultural drives through the region. Also integrated into the meet was a 'Give Something Back' theme that enhanced the awareness among Jeep owners of the 'Tread Lightly' program promoting careful, considerate and responsible off-road driving and protection of the environment. Also taking place was the planting of 150 trees around La Thuile to replace those lost in an avalanche.

In addition, DaimlerChrysler, in conjunction with local civic organizations, jointly funded a project to replace an important bridge in the surrounding mountains which had provided essential access to the ski runs for emergency

From top to bottom: The limited edition 2003 Jeep Wrangler Rubicon Tomb Raider model debuted in July, 2003 to coincide with the release of the film Lara Croft Tomb Raider: The Cradle of Life. *A customized version of the Wrangler Rubicon is driven in* Tomb Raider *by video game heroine Lara Croft; Unique features of the Rubicon Tomb Raider models were 16in Alcoa forged aluminum wheels, Tomb Raider badging, and a number of Mopar accessories including the light bar, riveted fender flares, tubular grille guard, diamond plate bumper, rock rails and tail lamp guards; From any perspective the Rubicon Tomb Raider's out-of-the-ordinary character attracted attention. (DaimlerChrysler Media Services)*

rescue vehicles that had been destroyed by recent heavy rains and snow melt.

Prior to the start of the weekend's events, Hausch officially dedicated and opened the bridge. "We are delighted," he said, "to bring Euro Camp Jeep to the Valle d'Aosta region, which has the natural setting to make this an unforgettable Jeep experience. We are also pleased to be able to leave something behind that allows others to enjoy this beautiful region in the future through our tree planting and bridge repair program."

At the start of the 2003 calendar year, Jeep had used the 2003 North American International Auto Show in Detroit to debut a limited production line of Freedom Edition models. Along with Liberty and Grand Cherokee versions, the Wrangler Freedom Edition's unique exterior appointments and array of standard equipment made it easy to spot on the Jeep stand.

Speaking in general terms about the origin of the three new Jeeps, Jeff Bell, Vice President of the Jeep Marketing Division, said, "We started with the most award-winning brand of 4x4s to create the Freedom Edition Grand Cherokee, Liberty and Wrangler. And capability is just the beginning of the story. Only from behind the wheel of a capable Jeep can you experience the joy that comes with the freedom to go-anywhere and do-anything. That feeling is what inspired this new line of vehicles with their rugged looks and versatile features."

The Wrangler Freedom was identified by its body-colored fender flares. It was fitted with a soft top with full metal doors, fog lamps, and tow hooks. OWL P225/75R15 Goodyear AT tires were mounted on 15in chrome wheels. Four exterior colors – Red, Silver, Blue and Black – were available.

The interior of the Wrangler Freedom was decked out with air conditioning, the Sentry Key theft-deterrent system, an easy access fold-and-tumble rear seat and a choice of Dark Slate Gray vinyl or cloth seating.

Under the Wrangler's hood was the 4.0-liter Power Tech engine linked to a 5-speed manual transmission, using the Command-Trac part-time four-wheel drive system.

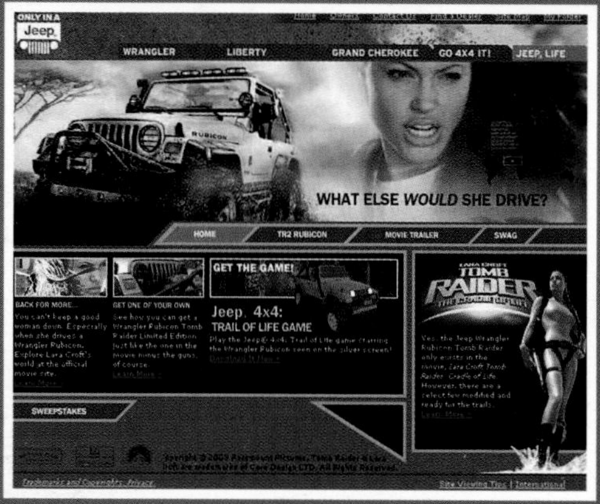

Visitors to www.Jeep.com could virtually drive the Wrangler Rubicon, piloted by Lara Croft in Lara Croft Tomb Raider: The Cradle of Life, *in a game,* Jeep 4x4, Trail of Life, *set in the Mayan jungle. While on the trail, challenges, such as steep inclines and river crossings, must be conquered to earn points. (DaimlerChrysler Media Services)*

Details of the Rubicon Tomb Raider's riveted fender flares. (DaimlerChrysler Media Services)

This view of the Rubicon Tomb Raider shows its diamond plate bumper guard, fog lamp guards and tubular grille guard. (DaimlerChrysler Media Services)

Details of the special edition Tomb Raider badge. (DaimlerChrysler Media Services)

Versions of the Freedom Edition Jeep line were available outside the US as the Rocky Mountain Edition in Canada and the Red River Edition outside North America.

On April 23, 2003, DaimlerChrysler announced that a customized version of the Wrangler Rubicon and actress Angelina Jolie, playing video game heroine Lara Croft, would be showing off their capabilities in a new Paramount movie, *Lara Croft Tomb Raider: The Cradle of Life*.

This was the second *Tomb Raider* movie. In the first film, which had grossed over $47.7 million in its opening weekend (the largest amount ever for a film with a female lead), Lara Croft had driven a Land Rover Defender 90.

From the beginning, both Paramount and Jeep recognized the synergy of the new combination. "We view Jeep as the natural partner in this film," said Lisa DiMarzo, Senior Vice-President of Worldwide Marketing Partnerships, Paramount, "because the brand's attributes are a natural fit with the Lara Croft character. Lara embodies Jeep core values: authenticity, mastery, adventure and freedom."

Trevor Creed, Senior Vice President, Product Design of the Chrysler Group, agreed: "To create the vehicle we took the ultimate off-road machine, a Jeep Wrangler

The Jeep.com web site featured a special section dedicated to Laura Croft Tomb Raider. Imagery including screen savers and computer wallpaper was available for download. Visitors could also view movie clips and acquire information on purchasing the Wrangler Rubicon Tomb Raider model. (DaimlerChrysler Media Services)

Inside the Rubicon Tomb Raider were many unique features including a silver-surround center stack and cluster bezel on the instrument panel, and a Tomb Raider badge with serial number. (DaimlerChrysler Media Services)

Rubicon, and tailored it to fit what aristocratic Lady Lara Croft would need to do her job as a tomb raider."

Jeff Bell offered this perspective on the Tomb Raider venture: "Wrangler is the icon of the Jeep brand and continues to be the original 'go-anywhere, do-anything' freedom vehicle that provides maximum versatility and performance. In the movie, this vehicle will be showcased in many rugged and extreme situations, highlighting key strengths of the brand in a new and exciting way. You'll see the Jeep driving 80mph across harsh desert and jungle terrain without any difficulty. That's real Jeep 4x4 capability and that's Jeep adventure."

The Chrysler Group's Jeep Design Studio team collaborated with Kirk Petruccelli and Graham Kelly from the *Tomb Raider* production team to build Lara Croft's Wrangler. Three Jeeps were eventually built (representing 3677 hours of work), using original Rubicon features, after-market components and what Creed described as "unique, never-before-seen custom features".

Among the array of the Tomb Raider Wrangler's functional modifications were a roll bar with grab bars, a skid plate with simulated HID lighting, and an interior with specially designed gauges, shifters, instrument panel, console and door trim.

Opposite: A Wrangler Sport off-road at Camp Jeep 2003. (DaimlerChrysler Media Services)

The limited edition Wrangler Sport TR2 for the UK market had a production run of just 75 units. (DaimlerChrysler UK Media Services)

The after-market components used to complete the project included Hanson Enterprises front and rear bumpers, Mickey Thompson 35in Baja Claw tires, Classic II wheels with bead locks, Warn winch, Bushwhacker riveted fender flares, and Skyjacker four-inch Rock Ready Long Arm suspension lift.

Many action scenes involving the Rubicon were filmed in Kenya, Africa, and the performance of the Rock Ready suspension in them was a point of pride for its manufacturer, particularly since it was available as an after-market item for the Rubicon. "Lara Croft couldn't be caught in the movie and our competition can't catch us now," declared Lonnie McCurry Jr, Vice President of Skyjacker Suspensions. "We have been blessed to be involved with such a terrific team as the Chrysler Group. The movie came at a perfect time for the appearance of Skyjacker's newly designed suspension system for the Jeep Wrangler Rubicon."

Coinciding with the release of *Lara Croft Tomb Raider* in July 2003, was the debut of the limited edition Jeep Wrangler Rubicon Tomb Raider model. Incorporated into the Tomb Raider's exterior were 16in Alcoa forged aluminum wheels, Tomb Raider badging and a number of Mopar accessories including a light bar, riveted fender flares in graphite, tubular grille guard, diamond plate bumper guard in Black, rock rails, and fog lamp and tail lamp guards.

Inside the Rubicon Tomb Raider were Dark Slate fabric seats with red accent stitching down the center, a silver surround instrument panel bezel, red seat belts

A Solar Yellow Wrangler Rubicon leads a row of Jeeps at Camp Jeep 2003, held at Oak Ridge Estate in the Blue Ridge mountains of Nelson County, Virginia. (DaimlerChrysler Media Services)

and Tomb Raider badge with serial number. As with the custom film version, the Rubicon Tomb Raider model was available only in Bright Silver.

Jeep said this Wrangler was intended to be a collector's vehicle and that just over one thousand would be available. The base price of the Wrangler Rubicon Tomb Raider was $28,815, including destination charge.

Yet another unique Wrangler, well-suited for Jeep enthusiasts in the UK, was the Special Edition Wrangler Sport TR2. Also introduced to coincide with the release of the *Tomb Raider* film, only 75 examples were available for the domestic UK market. Building on images of actress Angelia Jolie driving her modified Wrangler in *Tomb Raider*, Jeep UK asserted that "great looks, the 'go-anywhere' Jeep attitude and the addition of extra equipment should make the new Wrangler Sport TR2 a blockbuster success, just like its big screen partner."

Simon Elliott provided this perspective of the Sport TR2: "Wrangler perfectly sums up the Jeep brand – rugged, reliable, dependable – and the addition of extra equipment that makes the Sport TR2 will only add to its appeal.

"It's fitting that a car like Wrangler should feature in an adventure film and I'm delighted we are able to offer this model which links with *Tomb Raider*.

For £16,750, TR2 purchasers received a Wrangler with special Ecco wheels, 225/75R15 tires, a CD player with seven speakers, special 'SPORT TR2' identification and a choice of either Intense Blue or Light Khaki metallic paint.

These mini Jeep Wranglers were a big attraction for children at the Camp Kid's Village at Camp Jeep 2003. (DaimlerChrysler Media Services)

A procession of Wranglers and other Jeep models at Camp Jeep 2003. (DaimlerChrysler Media Services)

5 THE LEGEND CONTINUES – THE 2004-2006 WRANGLERS

When the 2004 Wranglers, along with the Grand Cherokee and Liberty models, started arriving in Jeep dealerships in late September 2003, they all carried new Trail Rated badges. Jeep Trail Rated was depicted by Jeep as "a new way to communicate to consumers the extensive level of off-road requirements that all Jeep 4x4 vehicles must meet". Asked to provide details of the Jeep Trail Rated program, Jeff Bell explained that it was "an industry-leading methodology to objectively measure and predict off-road performance for all Jeep vehicles. We created 'Jeep Trail Rated' to communicate the legendary Jeep capability that is designed into every Jeep 4x4."

The Jeep Trail Rated program was supported by the Nevada Automotive Test Center (NATC), which had 45 years of off-road vehicle testing experience including the creation of standards for the US military.

In the case of the 2004 Wrangler, its Trail Rated badge indicated that it had been designed to successfully function in five major consumer-oriented performance categories: traction, ground clearance, maneuverability, articulation and water-fording. Jeff Bell offered this perspective of the Trail Rated program's merits to both contemporary and future Jeeps: "Through a combination of natural and controlled field tests, as well as computer-simulated environments, Jeep Trail Rated provides a repeatable and consistent measurement of off-road performance for all Jeep vehicles. As the Jeep brand expands, Trail Rated will help us assure that our legendary 4x4 capability remains a cornerstone of the Jeep brand."

The 2004 Wrangler was described as "the heart and soul of the Jeep brand". (DaimlerChrysler Media Services)

All 2004 Wrangler models had a standard tilt steering wheel. Previously it had been offered as part of a package option for the SE and X models and standard for the Sport, Sahara and Rubicon. A new locking fuel-filler cap was optional. Also standard on Wrangler X, Sport, Sahara and Rubicon models was an AM/FM radio with a single CD player. An AM/FM/CD/cassette radio was optional. The leather-wrapped steering wheel was now packaged with speed control. A spare tire cover with a Sahara logo was added to the Sahara's standard equipment for 2004. A new Ravine aluminum wheel design was standard for the Sahara and was optional on Sport models. A right-hand drive Wrangler model was now available for the US retail market.

Two new colors, Solar Yellow and Electric Lime Green Pearlcoat, were offered for 2004, with Intense Blue Pearlcoat and Inca Gold no longer offered. The following colors were continued from 2003: Flame Red, Bright Silver Metallic, Stone White, Black, Patriot Blue Pearlcoat, Shale Green Metallic, Light Khaki and Sienna Pearlcoat. Except for the Sahara, all ten colors were available for the 2004 Wranglers. The Sahara's choices were Patriot Blue Pearlcoat, Shale Green Metallic, Light Khaki and Sienna Pearlcoat.

The intended purpose of the Jeep Treo concept

An overhead view of a fully-loaded 2004 RHD Wrangler. With its rear seat removed, the soft top Wrangler had a rear cargo capacity of 47.2ft^3. (DaimlerChrysler Media Services)

Regardless of the location of the 2004 Wrangler's steering wheel, its appeal as the icon of the Jeep brand was universal. (DaimlerChrysler Media Services)

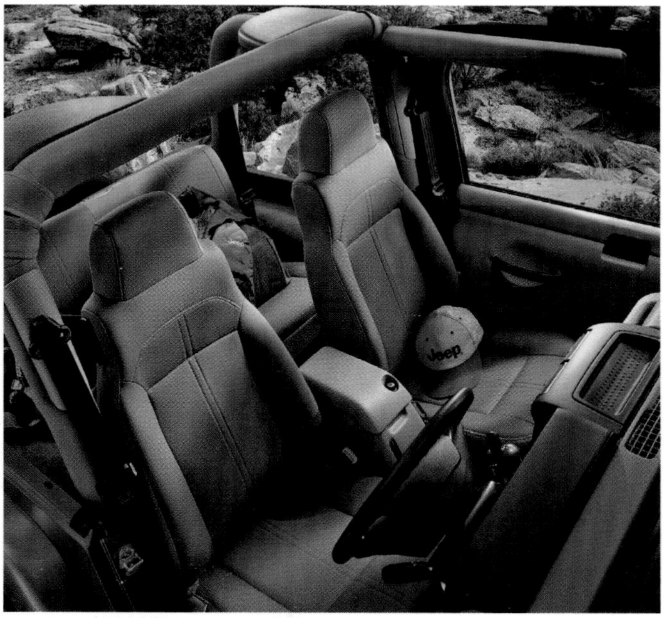

Details of the interior of a 2004 RHD Wrangler. (DaimlerChrysler Media Services)

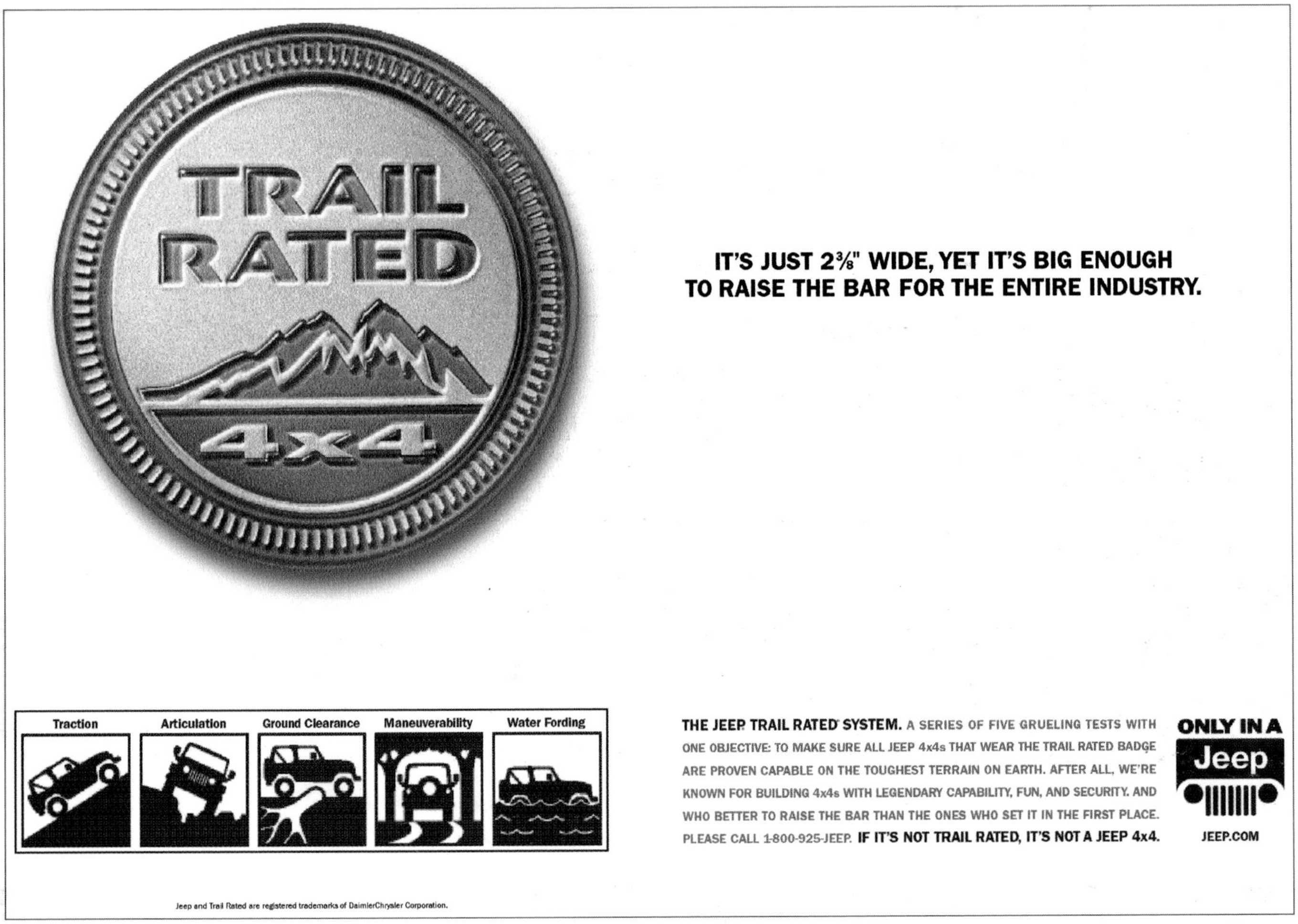
TRAIL RATED
4x4
IT'S JUST 2⅜" WIDE, YET IT'S BIG ENOUGH
TO RAISE THE BAR FOR THE ENTIRE INDUSTRY.
Traction
Articulation
Ground Clearance
Maneuverability
Water Fording
THE JEEP TRAIL RATED SYSTEM. A SERIES OF FIVE GRUELING TESTS WITH ONE OBJECTIVE: TO MAKE SURE ALL JEEP 4x4s THAT WEAR THE TRAIL RATED BADGE ARE PROVEN CAPABLE ON THE TOUGHEST TERRAIN ON EARTH. AFTER ALL, WE'RE KNOWN FOR BUILDING 4x4s WITH LEGENDARY CAPABILITY, FUN, AND SECURITY. AND WHO BETTER TO RAISE THE BAR THAN THE ONES WHO SET IT IN THE FIRST PLACE. PLEASE CALL 1-800-925-JEEP. IF IT'S NOT TRAIL RATED, IT'S NOT A JEEP 4x4.
ONLY IN A
Jeep
JEEP.COM
Jeep and Trail Rated are registered trademarks of DaimlerChrysler Corporation.

This was one of six print advertisements introducing the public to the new Trail Rated badges carried by all 2004 Jeeps. In addition, four television commercials were aired, and Jeep Trail Rated details were also found on Jeep.com. (DaimlerChrysler Media Services)

A 2004 Wrangler Sport in Solar Yellow, a new exterior color for 2004. (DaimlerChrysler Media Services)

A 2004 Wrangler X in Patriot Blue Pearlcoat. Along with the Sport, Sahara and Rubicon, the Wrangler X had a standard CD player for 2004. (DaimlerChrysler Media Services)

A 2004 Wrangler Sport in Sienna Pearlcoat. Beginning in October 2003 all Wranglers had a tilt steering wheel and locking fuel filler cap as standard equipment. (DaimlerChrysler Media Services)

The Treo's name, meaning three in various languages, identified its unique 2+1 seating configuration, which could be changed to accommodate a 2+ gear scenario. (DaimlerChrysler Media Services)

vehicle differed dramatically from that of the Jeep Willys and Jeep Willys2. Whereas they demonstrated the classic Jeep form's viability in the 21st century, the Jeep Treo represented a bold thrust into the future when as yet undeveloped technologies and alternative power sources, as well as demographic trends, might radically alter the automotive landscape. DaimlerChrysler was aware that this environment presented major challenges and opportunities for a marque such as Jeep that took great pride in its ability to blend its rich heritage with the best of modern design and technology.

Its response was to challenge the Treo's designers to look forward a decade or more and extend the Jeep brand's customer base with the creation of an urban mobility vehicle, providing Jeep style and freedom in a compact vehicle at home both in urban environments and at the trail head.

The Chrysler Group's top designer, Trevor Creed, was pleased with the outcome. "The Treo,'' he said, "is a vivid new interpretation of where the Jeep brand could go in the future using the freedom of fuel cell technology. It truly exemplifies the idea of 'fluid imagination' thinking in a stunning, unexpected package.

"Jeep Treo has a form and a presence that challenges the brand's traditional dimensions, but in the end, can still be viewed as being authentically Jeep."

The Treo's world debut took place at the 37th Tokyo Auto Show in October 2003. Its all-new platform was designed to utilize both drive-by-wire technology and a zero-emission fuel cell or other future power plants. As seen in 2003, it was powered by two electric motors driving the front and rear wheels, providing full-time four-wheel drive capability.

The appearance of the Treo reflected these radical concepts, while validating Creed's assertion that it was an authentic Jeep. Its front end was dominated by a see-through, seven-slotted grille, a large windshield and a glass roof that extended over the rear passenger space. Its body tapered front to back in a tear-drop shape and carried two high-mounted rear spar wings that both housed the tail lamps and served as mounts for a pair of Jeep Rubicon mountain bikes. The Treo's ability to accommodate these bikes symbolized the need to provide future Jeeps with the wherewithal to appeal to a new generation of young and active Jeep enthusiasts. Also serving this purpose was the form of Treo's rear hatch, with its large cutout notch providing easy access to the rear storage area.

In addition to its signature seven-slot grille, there were other elements integrated into the Treo's styling connecting it with key elements of production-model Jeeps. The use of flared wheel arches conveyed Jeep ruggedness, while giving its oversized 19 x 6in wheels and 185/65R19 tires plenty of travel room.

Representative of traditional Jeep tenaciousness were the Treo's exposed front tow hooks and front suspension,

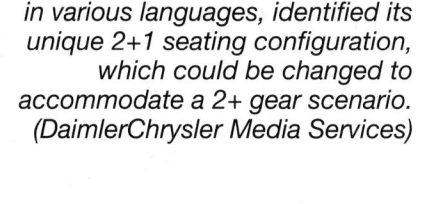

Trevor Creed, with the Jeep Treo Concept at its North American debut during the 2004 North American International Auto Show in Detroit. He described it as a next-generation, urban-activity Jeep. (DaimlerChrysler Media Services, photo by Joe Wilseens)

The two high-mounted spar wings at the rear of the Treo's teardrop-shaped body housed the rear lights as well as serving as mounts for a pair of Rubicon mountain bikes. (DaimlerChrysler Media Services)

The combination of a large windshield, translucent seating material and the modular design of the dash contributed to a sensation of space and openness in the Treo's interior. (DaimlerChrysler Media Services)

The Treo's front end presented a fresh interpretation of the familiar Jeep 'face'. (DaimlerChrysler Media Services)

the 'precision tool' look of its headlights and mirrors, military-style tire tread design, and the hiking boot tread detail of the sill plates.

"The Treo look is rugged," Creed said, "a truly imaginative evolution of the Jeep 'face' with packaging that belies its compact dimensions. It has a real presence in the flesh, one that grows more interesting every time you look at it, from every angle."

The interior of the Treo provided room for three passengers or 'two-plus-gear'. The steering wheel and column, pedals, speedometer and other instruments were housed in a single, sculptured module. The entire unit slid through a slot in the dash for easy adaptability for either left or right-hand drive markets. The radio, global positioning satellite locator and touch-screen-operated climate controls were housed in a second, removable module. Lightweight seats, made of a translucent material, had a strong carbon fiber frame. The rear seat folded flat to increase the Treo's storage capacity. It was also possible to configure the interior to allow the front wheels from the two Rubicon bikes to be removed and mounted in the Treo, enabling a third passenger to ride along.

Elaborating on this aspect of the Treo's design, Creed noted: "Treo's visionary vehicle packaging with its basic three-seat configuration and built-in versatility lends itself to future Jeep activity seekers – at entry-level price positioning. It is rugged and functional in genuine Jeep fashion, but its adaptability is taken to the next level."

Few who saw it would dispute Jeep's assertion that the Treo was a vehicle that explored the limits of the Jeep brand's identity. (DaimlerChrysler Media Services)

Jeep Treo specifications	
Length:	127.4in (3235mm)
Width:	66.1in (1680mm)
Height:	62.4in (1585mm)
Wheelbase:	96.4in (2450mm)
Front and rear track:	59.0in (1499mm)
Ground clearance:	7.8in (200mm)
Front overhang:	13.8in (350mm)
Rear overhang:	16.9in (430mm)
Wheels:	19 x 6in
Tires:	185/65R19
Weight (est):	1800lb (816kg)

In March 2004, six months after the Treo's introduction, the Wrangler Unlimited joined the Jeep line-up as a 2004 ½ model. Veteran Jeep enthusiasts undoubtedly saw a great deal of the CJ-6, introduced nearly a half-century earlier, in 1956, in the design of the new Wrangler Unlimited. With a 103.3in wheelbase, (10in longer than the standard Wrangler's), the Unlimited offered owners more refined on-road comfort and quietness as well as an additional 13 inches of space behind the second row seat compared to the original Wrangler. This added length doubled the Unlimited's cargo capacity. The provision of an additional two inches in the second row provided increased rear passenger leg room (36.7in to the Wrangler's 35.0in). Access to the rear seats was made more convenient by the Unlimited's driver and passenger tip-and-slide seats.

In addition to providing a more refined ride, the Unlimited's longer wheelbase resulted in a best-in-class towing capability of 3500lb, which was 1500lb more than the standard Wrangler's. Elaborating on the origin and implications of these aspects of the Unlimited's design, Jaci Woody, Executive Engineer – Jeep Special Programs Engineering, explained: "We set out to create more space for cargo and passengers, but the increase in wheelbase also improves the on-road ride and towing capability of the Wrangler Unlimited. The added space broadens the appeal of the Wrangler Unlimited to customers who appreciate space and additional towing capability without compromising the character of the Wrangler."

Jeff Bell had much to say about the consequences of changing any major visual or technical aspect of the Wrangler's interpretation of the classic Jeep design. "We hear time and time again that owners don't want us to change a thing on their Jeep vehicles," he said. "But there is also a smaller group of Jeep owners who told us they would love a Jeep Wrangler, but needed more space for their lifestyle. We set out to create a longer wheelbase Wrangler that could give those customers what they really wanted, while maintaining the true fun and freedom of the original Jeep Wrangler."

The Toledo South Assembly line at the Toledo Plant was able to accommodate the longer wheelbase of the Wrangler Unlimited (seen here in Flame Red) without a loss of production of current models by adapting existing equipment and manufacturing processes for the Unlimited. Plant Manager Alberto Gonzalez (left) is shown on May 25, 2004 conducting a briefing for the media on those developments. (DaimlerChrysler Media Services)

Honored on May 25, 2004 for his 60 years of service was Jerome C Wiczynski, an hourly worker at Toledo Assembly Plant. He is pictured in front of a WWII MB Jeep with Plant Manager Gonzalez, (left), and Tom Maxon, the plant's Human Resources Manager (right). Mr. Wiczynski, at age 16, was hired at Toledo Assembly in June 1944 for 80 cents an hour. Except for four years service in the US Navy, he has continually been employed at the Toledo plant where his father worked as an original employee of John North Willys. (DaimlerChrysler Media Services)

Toledo Plant Manager Albert Gonzalez's no-nonsense apparel left no doubt as to his loyalty and appreciation of automotive history. The pickup shown was an early postwar Willys model. He is seen here at the plant as Wranglers move down the assembly line. As a key part of the process that lead to the inclusion of the Unlimited into the assembly process, without a loss of production, workers developed small teams, used new robotics, paint systems and communication technology to make the plant more flexible and efficient. (DaimlerChrysler Media Services)

Stacked like unfinished scale models awaiting their completion by a zealous young Jeep modeling enthusiast, these are, in reality, Wrangler Unlimiteds at the Toledo South Assembly Plant, awaiting – you guessed it – final assembly. (DaimlerChrysler Media Services)

Pictured here are Wrangler Unlimiteds on the final assembly line at the Toledo South Assembly Plant. The changes made at the plant to accommodate production of the Unlimited, while maintaining a high level of quality, enabled Chrysler Group to ship the Unlimited to dealers three weeks ahead of its launch date. (DaimlerChrysler Media Services)

Seen here is Toledo Assembly Plant employee William Grundy installing fluid hoses on a Wrangler Unlimited. (DaimlerChrysler Media Services)

The matter of how much was the right amount to extend the Wrangler's length was an issue carefully considered by the Jeep Special Programs Engineering team that created the Unlimited. Concerns that the new Jeep's off-road performance would suffer as a result of this change were unfounded. Even with its additional wheelbase and increased rear overhang, the Unlimited maintained the 20 degree minimum guideline for off-road driving and earned a Trail Rated designation. "The Jeep Wrangler Unlimited," said Jaci Woody, "stays true to the legendary capability that has made the Wrangler the icon of the brand. The additional 15 inches provided the right

When he presented the 2004 ½ Wrangler Unlimited to the press on January 6, 2004, Joe Eberhardt, the head of the Chrysler Group's Sales, Marketing and Service Organization, offered his audience this often overlooked aspect of its heritage: "Did you know that the Jeep Wrangler boasts the longest-running lineage of any soft top in history? Ever since it was first introduced six decades ago, there has been a Jeep convertible ... on the road ... and off it! Now, our new Jeep Wrangler Unlimited takes over 60 years of tradition and reputation and kicks it up a notch. A big notch!" (DaimlerChrysler Media Services)

The introduction of the Wrangler Unlimited by Joe Eberhardt at the 2004 North American Auto Show on January 6, 2004. This was its world debut.

balance to add more second-row seating comfort and cargo without compromising the Jeep 4x4 capability."

Recalling that the first time Jeep offered both shorter and longer wheelbase versions of the Jeep Universals was 1956, Jeff Bell also reminded Wrangler enthusiasts that "it has been more than two decades since we offered customers a choice in their wheelbase size with the CJ-5 and CJ-6 Universals. We've always listened to our customers by building on the Jeep heritage and giving them truly innovative products that others could never match.

"The Jeep Wrangler Unlimited is an aspirational purchase and will deliver a true emotional connection to its owners. The Jeep Wrangler Unlimited is an extension of the original Wrangler buyer group, and will appeal more broadly to younger buyers and those who select this as their primary, secondary or third vehicle with added versatility."

The Unlimited's standard engine/transmission combination was the 4.0-liter PowerTech 6-cylinder engine (rated at 190hp @ 4600rpm and 235lb-ft of torque @ 3200rom), and a 42RLE 4-speed automatic transmission. Also standard was a Dana 30 front axle, a rear heavy duty Dana 44 axle, 30in tall R15 Goodyear Wrangler GSA tires, 15in Ravine aluminum wheels, high-pressure gas-charged shock absorbers, a 3.73:1 axle ratio, fog lamps, tow hooks,full-steel doors with deep tint windows, padded Sport Bar, air conditioning, AM/FM stereo radio with CD, fold and tumble rear seat, front and rear floor mats, next generation air bags and power steering.

Debuting on the Wrangler Unlimited was a standard Sunrider soft top which included an open-air 'sunroof' feature allowing the top to be folded back over the driver and front passenger, creating a 45 x 23in sunroof opening. The Sunrider's second-row passengers benefited from its large, deep-tinted side windows. The sunroof could be operated from both the exterior or interior of the Unlimited, the latter, cautioned Jeep, only when the vehicle was not in motion. The Unlimited was also available with a new optional hard top with added strength and longer, deep-tint rear windows, rear defroster and a back glass wiper and washer.

Additional optional equipment for the Unlimited included body side steps, electrochromic interior mirror with compass and temperature, engine block heater, locking fuel cap, Sentry Key, seven-speaker sound package, leather-wrapped steering wheel and speed control.

For markets outside North America, a new Wrangler Extreme Sport model was introduced at the 74th Salon International de l'Automobile in Geneva in March 2004. Based on the Wrangler 4.0 Sport (two Wrangler models

The Wrangler Unlimited's Sunrider soft top provided rear passengers with large, deep-tinted side windows. (DaimlerChrysler Media Services)

Compared to the standard Wrangler, the 2004 ½ Unlimited had 15in added to its length, giving it 13in more cargo space and 2in more second-row leg room. (DaimlerChrysler Media Services)

were available in Europe – Sport and Sahara), the Extreme Sport version was fitted with Ecco aluminum alloy wheels and 225/75R15 tires. The wheels were painted graphite and featured a bright machined rim. A choice of Solar Yellow, Black, Flame Red, Patriot Blue, Bright Silver or Stone White was combined with graphite painted wing flares. Completing the package was Extreme Sport badging.

Interior highlights included a silver-painted center stack, a black cluster bezel, two tone cloth seats with embroidered Jeep logo and a seven-speaker stereo system with sub woofer.

The price list for the 2004 Wranglers in the UK was as follows:

Model	On the road price*
Wrangler 4.0 Sport:	£15,750[a]
Wrangler 4.0 Sahara (manual transmission):	£18,620
Wrangler 4.0 Sahara (automatic transmission):	£19,265

*Included 12 months Road Fund License (£160 per annum petrol and £165 diesel). First registration fee (£380) where applicable

[a]Special paint was available for the Sport at £210.

The Rubicon's popularity remained strong in its second year of production. At the start of the 2004 model year, anticipating an increase in demand, Rubicon production was expanded. This action was fully justified. On September 27, 2004, DaimlerChrysler reported that while Wrangler sales had increased 24 per cent year-to date while those of the Rubicon were up more than 30 per cent over 2003.

Even the most experienced and seasoned Camp Jeep and Jeep 101 participants suspected Jeep was up to something new, different and perhaps even a bit out of the ordinary, when DaimlerChrysler announced on April 1, 2004 that "Jeep brings the adventures of off-road driving to the heart of New York with Camp Jeep New York at the New York Auto Show."

What Jeep accomplished at the Show, which was held at the Jacob K Javits Convention Center on 11th Avenue between 34th and 35th Streets, was not merely a static display of muddy veterans of off-road excursions or a computer simulation of a top-rated, class ten trail run, but the opportunity for showgoers to have a legitimate, real-time, off-road experience in a Jeep.

At the show's conclusion, few of those who attended were likely to challenge Jeep's assertion that Camp Jeep New York had created a ground-breaking experimental auto show exhibit by transforming the entire North Pavilion of the Javits Center into a 45,000sq-ft off-road driving course.

As the first-ever Jeep 101 indoor driving course, it comprised several obstacles representative of the Trail Rated criteria that all Jeeps must meet. Six different surfaces comprised the course: dirt, gravel, rocks, water, wood and asphalt. Despite being indoors the course encompassed obstacles found outdoors, including a 20ft vertical climb (through the Javits Center ceiling), a two-foot deep, 15 x 20ft water test and a 15ft section of terrain replicating the surface of fallen logs measuring 18in in diameter.

Included in this line-up of historic military vehicles at Euro Jeep Camp 2004 were, left-to-right, a Willys MB Jeep and an M38. At the far right an M38A1 was parked. The third vehicle is a Kaiser M715. (DaimlerChrysler Media Services)

Joe Eberhardt, Executive Vice President, Global Sales, Marketing and Service, Chrysler Group, began the 2004 Euro Camp Jeep with a welcome ceremony. (DaimlerChrysler Media Services)

"Jeep created this course," explained Jeff Bell, Vice President – Marketing Communications, Chrysler Group, "because we know if a picture is worth one thousand words, then a physical experience is worth one thousand pictures. Jeep is taking the auto show experience to the same level as Camp Jeep and Jeep Jamborees. Our legendary capability is best lived first-hand."

To maintain the trail's integrity, dirt, rocks and other recyclable course materials were transported from Staten Island each evening. Over 4000 cubic yards of dirt, the equal of over 200 truckloads, was required to construct the course. All the dirt was recycled and returned to its original source. Over five tons of rocks, boulders and gravel were used.

To provide the power needed for illumination and display operations, more than 15,000ft of electric cable was needed. Construction of the course took eight days and when it was completed it was possible for eleven vehicles to be on the course at one time. To drive through the course required ten minutes.

To keep participants happy while waiting for their turn to drive through the course, Jeep provided live music as part of the kick-off of a new Jeep Music Trax program that was part of the 2004 Camp Jeep program. It featured live performances by established and emerging musicians.

Camp Jeep at the Javits Center also featured a Jeep Kidz safe area, where visitors could have digital photos taken of their children and receive complimentary Home Organizer software that included a MILK (Managing Information on Lost Kids) digital ID kit.

The Director of the Northeast Business Center, Mark Engelsdofer, was pleased with Jeep's high profile presence at the show. "Jeep continues to be the sport-utility sales leader in the Northeast," he said. "The Jeep brand has a long history with the New York Auto Show and we are proud that the brand is conducting the world premier of three new vehicles in New York." He was referring to the debuts of the 2005 Jeep Grand Cherokee, the 2005 Jeep Liberty Renegade and the 2005 Liberty CRD Diesel.

Also on hand at the show was SoBe Beverages which was entering into a marketing arrangement with Jeep. A special Sobe Jeep Wrangler was displayed and free beverages were available. SoBe Director of Integrated Marketing, Mike Joyce, explained his company's approach to this venture with Jeep. "SoBe is very careful," he noted, "when considering marketing partners. We look

A Commando Station wagon (based on the second-generation Jeepster), a 1985 Scrambler pickup equipped with a Renegade package, a CJ-5 model and a 1950 CJ-3A on display at 2004 Euro Camp Jeep. (DaimlerChrysler Media Services)

Jeep and DaimlerChrysler made a donation for every Jeep that drove over the 2004 Euro Camp Jeep trails to the 'Bear Mile' project, designed to encourage the local European Brown Bear population to return to its original habitat in the Alps of Austria. (DaimlerChrysler Media Services)

for credible, authentic companies that are relevant to our customers, as opposed to brands trying to 'buy cool' by aligning with SoBe. The Jeep brand embraces SoBe's creativity and personality, and demonstrates a similar passion for their consumers that we have for our fans. It's a great fit, and we look forward to offering our fans the benefits of a fun, relevant partnership between two powerful brands."

Jeff Bell, equally enthusiastic, offered Jeep's perspective on the link up with SoBe. "The relationship makes perfect sense. Along with sharing a target market, our brands share common values," he said. "Both are passionate about active lifestyles, music, gaming and action sports. Together we are able to leverage our resources. events and promotions to reach more customers. We look forward to working with the creative, energetic crew at SoBe, and see this partnership extending well beyond traditional marketing."

The Fourth Euro Camp Jeep (June 25-27, 2004). was centered at the Finkenstein Castle on the edge of the southern Austrian Alps. This historic castle was located in the resort area of Faaker See Lake, close to the point where the corners of Austria, Italy and Slovenia meet. Approximately 850 Jeep customers and enthusiasts and 370 vehicles came from over twenty countries, including for the first time individuals from Egypt, Romania, Ukraine, and the US

On the eve of the 2004 Camp's opening, Joe Eberhardt, looking back at Euro Camp Jeep's first three gatherings, said, "Euro Camp Jeep has grown over the past four years into an essential weekend for Jeep customers and enthusiasts in Europe. The ever-increasing participation of people from so many countries is testimony to the passion our customers have for the Jeep brand, its values and the Jeep lifestyle. We expect this year's Euro Camp Jeep in Carinthia, to set yet another attendance record."

For many, the motoring highlight of the meet was the 'Jeep Road Tour', in which drivers were given special authorization to operate their vehicles through each of the 'three corner' countries on a scenic route that included on-and off-road sections.

For most of the weekend, participants used their

A group of historic military M-38A1 Jeeps, made possible by Chrysler Austria, challenged the off-road courses at 2004 Euro Camp Jeep. (DaimlerChrysler Media Services)

Rain didn't stop activities at Euro Camp Jeep. (DaimlerChrysler Media Services)

The special Jeep Wrangler Rubicon driven by the character Lara Croft in the film Lara Croft Tomb Raider: The Cradle of Life *was on display at the 2004 Euro Camp Jeep. (DaimlerChrysler Media Services)*

own vehicles but a collection of historic military Jeeps were available for driving under the guidance of special instructors acting as leaders through a predesignated course. Other classic Jeeps were also displayed. One of the most viewed and most popular Jeeps on hand was the special Jeep Wrangler Rubicon from the *Lara Croft Tomb Raider: The Cradle of Life* film.

Included in the tradition of Euro Camp Jeep was a contribution by DaimlerChrysler to an important environmental project in the region hosting the Camp. For 2004, this took the form both of leaving a legacy in the area as well as encouraging the 'Tread lightly' program for responsible off-road driving and protection of the environment. This was accomplished by the company making a donation for every Jeep that drove on the Euro Camp Jeep trails during the weekend. The proceeds were used to purchase a piece of land known as the 'Bear Mile' adjacent to a new bridge designed to encourage the local European Brown Bear population to disperse from current concentrations in Slovenia back to their original habitat in the Alps of Austria.

Thomas Hausch, once again on hand with his family to take part in the weekend, said in regard to this accomplishment: "We are extremely pleased to bring Euro Camp Jeep to the Carinthia region of Austria, and true to the Jeep brand, we are equally pleased to leave behind

The evocative logo for Camp Jeep California, held August 19-21, 2004. (DaimlerChrysler Media Services)

something that will protect and enhance the natural environment for many years to come."

Camp Jeep made its initial visit to the West Coast in 2004. The first-ever Camp Jeep California, with more than 4000 participants and 1000 vehicles on hand, was held in the Santa Ynez Mountains in Santa Barbara County, August 19-21.

"Camp Jeep has been so successful and attracted so many participants over the past ten years that it was time for the program to expand its reach to the West Coast," said Jeff Bell. ."Camp Jeep is a wonderful opportunity for families from all over to gather and celebrate the utility and versatility of their Jeep products."

Unique to Camp Jeep California was its Californiano Heritage Area that provided campers with the opportunity to experience Hispanic heritage through music, food, history and art. A mariachi band provided live entertainment on Friday evening.

Other musical attractions included Los Lobos, playing a blend of rock, folk, blues R&B, country and Tex-Mex; and the rock band Live, which capped off Camp Jeep California on Sunday night.

Replicas of Diego Rivera paintings were displayed throughout the duration of the Camp until its final day when they were raffled off.

DaimlerChrysler described the limited-production (approximately 1000 were available) 2004 Jeep Wrangler Willys as "the Jeep brand's spirited tribute to a military legend".

For collectors of limited edition Jeeps, its introduction was an opportunity to acquire an eye-catching Wrangler whose World-War-II-inspired features underscored both its heritage and bloodline.

If it had possessed a lesser lineage, Jeep's description of the Wrangler Willys would have been excessive and boastful but such was not the case: "It's the stuff of legend. With World War II looming, the US Army requested a vehicle – and drove off in a hero. The Willys MB, its spirit

The 2004 Jeep Wrangler Willys. When this volume was published, a graphic portrayal of this Wrangler was available at Jeep.com. (Bill Fredette)

Jeep advised owners of the Wrangler Willys to "be sure to follow all instructions in Owner's Manual for removal of top and doors". They were also advised that "driving with doors off is for off-road use only". (Bill Fredette)

forged by the fire of combat and honed in the heat of battle, seared its way into the hearts of warriors fighting for freedom. Fierce emotional bonds often developed between a soldier and his Jeep 4x4. The faithful MB earned a place in every GI's heart, in every area of combat, in every conceivable role ... The legacy continues today with the introduction of the limited-edition 2004 Jeep Wrangler Willys. Reminiscent of the soldier's experiences with the original Willys MB during WWII, today's collectors, veterans, outdoor enthusiasts and adventurers will find themselves establishing a powerful bond with their faithful new Jeep Wrangler Willys."

The Wrangler Willys (officially Option Package ASY), with a $21,700 MSRP, was available in only one exterior

This 'Willys' decal was positioned on the Wrangler Willys' cowl. (Bill Fredette)

The Wrangler Willys' water-resistant camouflaged seats, weather-resistant electronics and floor drain holes were intended to handle rough use. "If your tough 4x4 gets covered in muck while navigating a muddy two-track," said Jeep, "that's okay ... just wash it out!" (Bill Fredette)

color scheme consisting of an exclusive Moss Green body with styled steel wheels painted Dark Green with Black inserts. The Wrangler Willys standard Dark Green soft top was equipped with deep-tint windows in the rear and side panels. The front bucket and rear bench seat had a water-resistance camouflage covering.

Additional standard features consisted of these items:

- -Cowl-mounted 'Willys' decals
- -Diamond-plate sill guards painted Dark Green (these were the same units as used on the Wrangler Rubicon)
- -Body-color fender flares.
- -AM/FM radio with CD player and seven speakers with sub woofer positioned in center console
- -4.0-liter Tech I-6 engine
- -5-speed manual transmission
- -Quadra-Coil suspension
- -Command-Trac 4WD system
- -Tow hooks
- -Fog lamps
- -Full-size spare with matching wheel
- -Lockable full-center console with four cup holders
- -Removable half-doors and fold-down windshield

A limited-availability, $127.00 Willys Accessory Package by Mopar gave the Wrangler Willys an added measure of nostalgia. This dealer-installed item consisted of an authentic, stenciled military-style star for the hood,

A Dark Green soft top was standard for the Wrangler Willys. (Bill Fredette)

These five items comprised the dealer-installed Willys Accessory Package offered for the Wrangler Willys. From left to right: military style hood decal, ID decals for hood sides, fuel decal located above fuel-filler cap, mesh cover for fog lamps and guards for tail lamps. (Bill Fredette)

The 2005 Jeep Wrangler Unlimited Rubicon combined the capability of the Rubicon with the Unlimited's versatility. (DaimlerChrysler Media Services)

ID decals (41MB-04TJ) for both sides of the hood, a 'Fuel' decal positioned just above the fuel filer cap, Mopar Fog Light mesh covers and Mopar Tail Lamp guards.

For 2005 a new model, the Wrangler Unlimited Rubicon, represented what many Jeep owners regarded as the best of two worlds, a Wrangler with the Rubicon's off-road performance possessing the Unlimited model's cargo-carrying capacity. In announcing the newest Wrangler on September 27, 2004, Jeff Bell said, "Jeep Wrangler Rubicon Unlimited aggressively expands the Wrangler line-up, delivering customers extreme off-road capability in a package that provides improved comfort and convenience.

"By marrying Wrangler Rubicon's capability with Wrangler Unlimited versatility, Jeep attracts a broad range of customers who want to tackle the toughest off-road trails, and have the ability to bring along family, friends and cargo.

"Jeep Wrangler Unlimited Rubicon's unique factory off-road system is another chapter in the Wrangler value story. Jeep Wrangler Unlimited Rubicon offers extreme off-road capability at approximately half the price of modifying the vehicle with after-market hardware. Combine that with Jeep engineering, testing on the world's most demanding trails, Jeep's 7-year/70,000-mile Power Train Unlimited Warranty and significantly more space, and it's clear the all-new Jeep Wrangler Unlimited Rubicon delivers the ultimate combination of capability, versatility and value."

Just in case anyone failed to get the drift of Bell's comments, DaimlerChrysler explained that the Unlimited Rubicon allowed 'hard core' Wrangler Unlimited owners to 'Go Anywhere, Do Anything and Bring Everything'.

A new Premium Package was optional for the 2005 Wrangler Unlimited. It included new and unique cloth

Both the 2005 Rubicon and Rubicon Unlimited had unique exterior design cues including heavy-gauge diamond-plate sill guards, 16in, five-spoke, aluminum wheels and a 'Rubicon' graphic placed on each side of the hood. (DaimlerChrysler Media Services)

The 2005 Rubicons had a Rock-Trac transfer case with a 4:1 low range that slowed the Jeep's speed to give the driver more control, while increasing the amount of torque available to the wheels. (DaimlerChrysler Media Services)

seats, a silver painted center stack and instrument cluster bezels, bright grille and body color fender flares. Scheduled for late availability in the model year was an optional six-disc, in-dash CD changer system.

Jeff Bell had plenty to say about the virtues of the latest Wranglers, their place in Jeep history and their appeal to past, present and future Jeep owners. He began by asserting that "the Jeep Wrangler and the Wrangler Unlimited are the heart and soul of the Jeep brand. We have expanded the rugged appeal of the standard Wrangler to a whole new group of Jeep enthusiasts with the Wrangler Unlimited and now the Wrangler Unlimited Rubicon. The Wrangler Unlimited builds on the unique elements of the original Wrangler and continues to deliver a true emotional connection to Jeep customers. But with the Unlimited, Wrangler now appeals to a broader range of core customers who require more space."

Daniel Tardella, Jeep Marketing Senior Manager, elaborating on this point, said that people "told us they love it [the Rubicon], 'but you know, it would be nice if we had more room for some gear or more room in the back seat'." He added that people also said, "I would consider it, but I need more room."

As a result, Tardella concluded, "We expect to attract a broader range of buyers from people who want extreme capability and a lot more room to carry their gear, to people who want the ultimate show piece of Jeep Wrangler."

Jeff Bell did not attempt to portray the Unlimited Rubicon as equaling the off-road prowess of the original Rubicon. "The Wrangler Rubicon was too popular with Jeep owners not to expand it to the successful Wrangler Unlimited," he said. "The standard wheelbase Wrangler Rubicon continues as the ultimate off-road Wrangler, but both are rigs that are ready for serious off-road trails ..."

Just in case there were any lingering doubts about the loyalty of the latest Wranglers to Jeep tradition, DaimlerChrysler made certain that each one carried the Jeep Trail Rated badge.

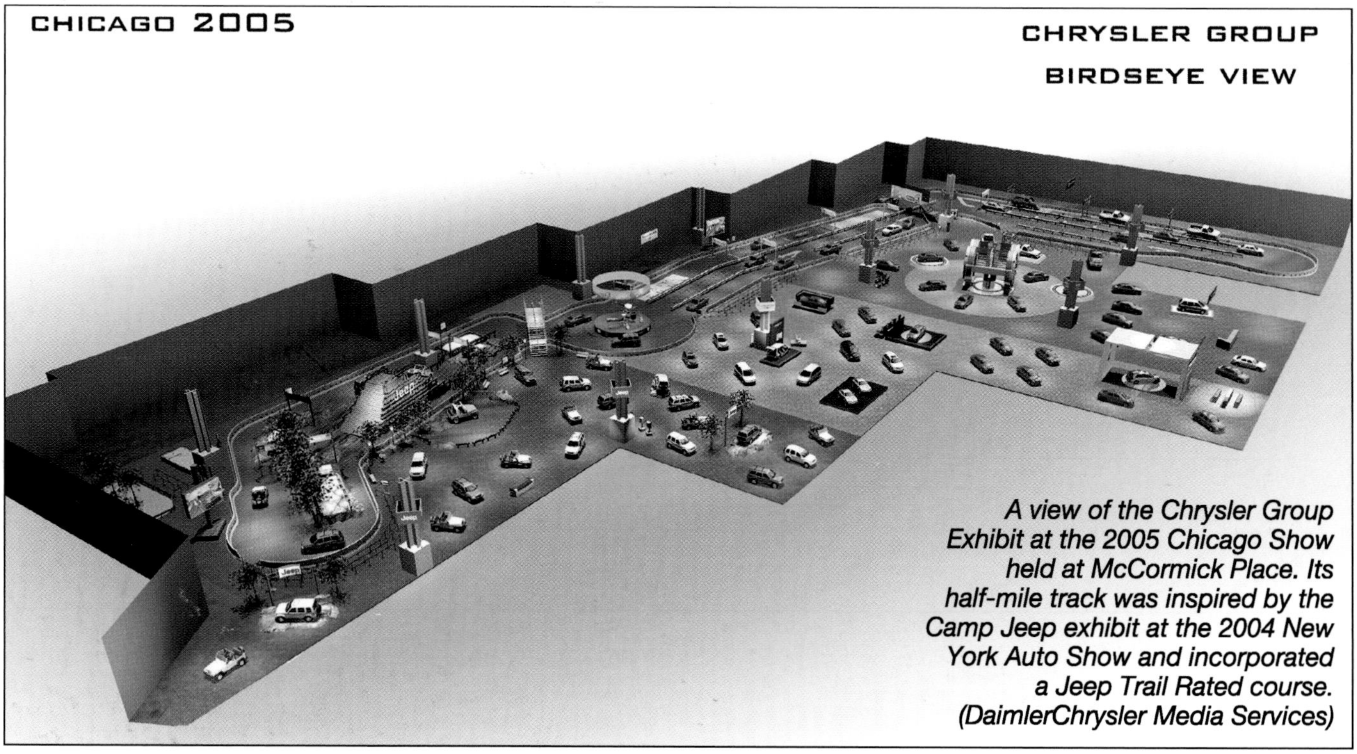

A view of the Chrysler Group Exhibit at the 2005 Chicago Show held at McCormick Place. Its half-mile track was inspired by the Camp Jeep exhibit at the 2004 New York Auto Show and incorporated a Jeep Trail Rated course. (DaimlerChrysler Media Services)

The Wrangler X, Sport, Unlimited and Rubicon models had, as standard equipment, the 4.0-liter Power Tech 6-cylinder engine joined to a new-for-2005 6-speed NSG 370 manual transmission. This transmission had hard-finished gears for improved gear change quality. Other improvements included a lower first gear for brisker acceleration plus a higher top gear for quieter and more economical highway cruising with reduced engine revs.

Its ratios, as compared to the 5-speed manual transmissions it replaced were these:

Transmission:	NV1500	NV3550 (4.0)	NSG 370
Gear Ratios	(2004 – 2.4-liter)	(2004 – 4-liter)	(2005 – all)
1st:	3.85	4.04	4.459
2nd:	2.75	2.33	2.614
3rd:	1.48	1.38	1.723
4th:	1.0	1.0	1.0
5th:	0.80	0.78	0.838
6th:	–	–	0.80

The 42RLE 4-speed automatic was optional. The Wrangler SE was again powered by the 2.4-liter Power Tech 4-cylinder. This engine was only available with the 6-speed manual transmission, but for the first time, the SE could be ordered with the 4.0-liter engine.

All 2005 Wranglers had, as standard equipment, a full-size spare tire. Full-face steel wheels were made standard on the SE, X and Sport Wranglers. Deep tint glass became part of the hard top option for the Sport and Rubicon models. Those two Wranglers were also equipped with standard air conditioning for 2005.

Neutral density fender flares replaced the Premium Black units used in 2004 on the Rubicon. The fender flares, Black in 2004 on the SE, X and Sport were now Medium Gray or Dark Khaki. These colors were also the choice for the Wrangler's top. In 2004 the selection had been Black or Dark Khaki.

The Convenience Group, consisting of passenger-side footwell courtesy lamps, under hood lamp, full console with lockable storage, four cup holders, coin holder and storage tray was made standard for the Wrangler X. As in 2004, it was also standard for the Sport and Rubicon. Its content was unchanged from 2004.

Enhancing the sound quality of the radios of the Sport and Rubicon models was their new standard seven-speaker systems. Scheduled as a late availability option for all Wranglers except the SE was a six-disc, in-dash CD changer.This changer and the seven-speaker system, along with an amplified sub woofer mounted in the console was packaged as a new Premium Audio Group option for the Wrangler X.

An aerial view of the Camp Jeep course at the New York International Auto Show, March 2005. (DaimlerChrysler Media Services)

The floor plan of the Jeep exhibit and the layout of the Trail Rated test track at the 2005 New York International Auto Show. (DaimlerChrysler Media Services)

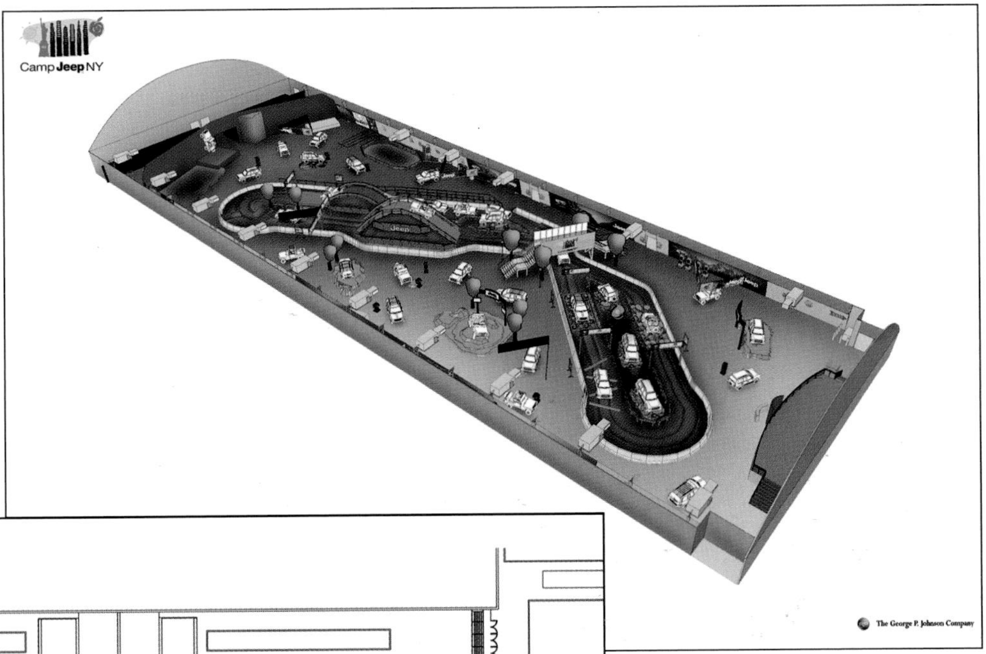

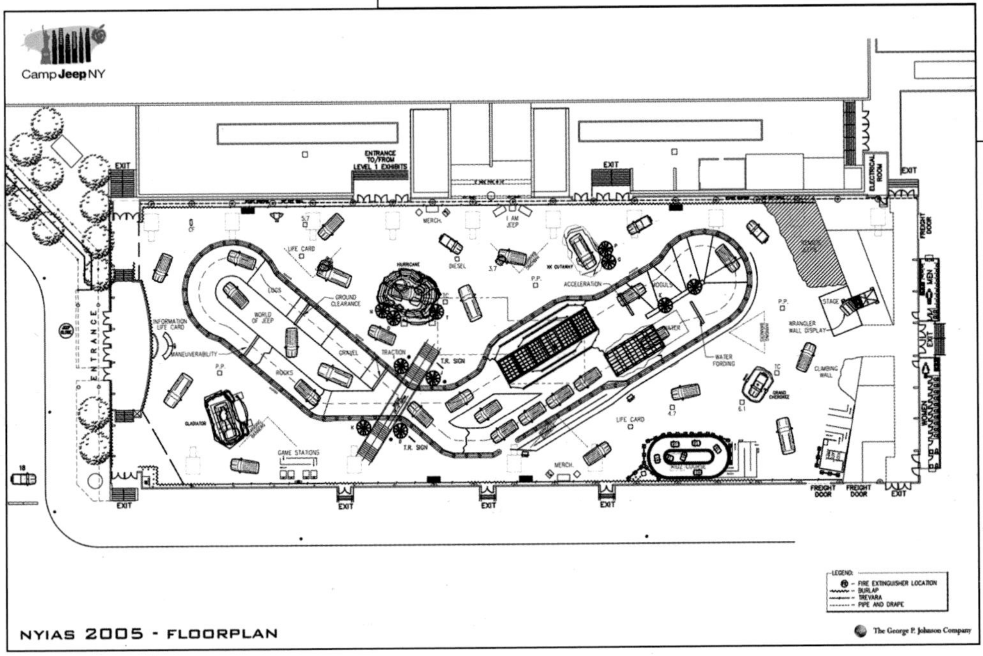

Added to the options for the Sport and Rubicon models was the Security Group, consisting of an electrochromic, auto-dimming rearview mirror and a Sentry Key theft-deterrent system. Standard for the Rubicon and optional for Sport Wranglers was a new Brake and Traction Group containing four-wheel disc brakes and the Trac-Lok differential. Tru-Lok replaced Trac-Lok on the Rubicon. The Sport Wranglers were required to be equipped with the 30in Tire and Wheel Group to be eligible for this option.

The Dana 44 rear axle was now packaged with the 30in tire option.

Wrangler Unlimiteds were also available with a new Premium Package with such features as cloth seats, silver painted center stack and instrument panel bezels, bright grille and body color fender flares. All Unlimited Wranglers had a new dash pad, hood pad and thicker carpet padding resulting in a 30 per cent quieter ride. Other highlights included an additional power outlet on the dash.

The Wrangler Sport was available in RHD form in North American market for use in rural postal delivery and parking enforcement. The Wrangler Sahara was no longer offered.

All Wranglers except the SE were available with a hard top with full steel doors, roll-up windows and tinted glass. Also offered for the Sport and Rubicon models was the dual top option that provided the hard and soft tops in matching colors.

The success of Camp Jeep New York in 2004 ecouraged the Chrysler Group to undertake an even more ambitious project for the February 2005 Chicago Auto Show held at McCormick Place. "Camp Jeep at the Jacob K Javits Center was a home run earlier this year, drawing over 20,000 visitors and conducting more than 36,000 test drives over a two-week period," said George Murphy, Senior Vice president Global marketing. "Based on this overwhelming success, we decided to expand the concept to include the Chrysler and Dodge brands in Chicago."

Jeep said the 2005 Wrangler Rocky Mountain Edition gave its drivers the "freedom to ROCK OUT". (DaimlerChrysler Media Services)

The result was a 156,000ft² exhibit that was equivalent to nearly four football fields surrounded by the world's largest indoor auto show test drive track. Although this specially designed half-mile track was neither a Camp Jeep operation or a Jeep 101 activity, the track did include a Jeep Trail Rated course designed to demonstrate the Jeep's off-road capabilities, including traction, articulation, ground clearance, maneuverability and water-fording.

Camp Jeep New York returned to the Jacob K Javits Center in March 2005 for an encore appearance at the New York International Auto Show.

For 2005, the course, now identified as a Trail Rated test track, was upgraded to include a new 20ft hill climb.

"People want to do more than just look at vehicles," said George Murphy. "At the Jeep display, event goers will see the vehicles inside and out, feel their capabilities and get a taste of the lifestyle that goes with them. Chrysler Corporation is the only automotive manufacturer to offer on-site test drives at auto shows."

Chrysler's commitment to this demonstration of Jeep's off-road prowess was based on research indicating it paid big dividends. The Chrysler Group had found that 40 per cent of those attending an auto show change their mind as to what they wish to purchase because of their auto show experience. Furthermore, 60 per cent of show goers planned to purchase a new vehicle within the next six months. Eight per cent purchased a new vehicle within four weeks. Twenty-two per cent made a new vehicle purchase within six months and forty per cent did likewise within one year.

A mid-model year addition to the Wrangler's 2005 model range was the Rocky Mountain Edition. Technically a $2635 Rocky Mountain Edition Group option for the Wrangler X, it consisted of 15 x 8in Ravine style aluminum wheels, 30 x 9.50R15 TB OWL All-Terrain tires, 3.73:1

A bit of photographic wizardry and the Rocky Mountain Edition became a 2005 Wrangler Sport for markets outside North America. (DaimlerChrysler Media Services)

Making it to the big screen. In the film Sahara, master explorer Dirk Pitt (Matthew McConaughey), in his Jeep Wrangler Unlimited, takes on the adventure of a lifetime as he embarks on a treasure hunt through dangerous regions of West Africa. (DaimlerChrysler Media Services)

axle ratio, premium two tone seats in a unique cloth with embroidered Jeep logo, fog lamps, heavy-duty Dana rear axle, high pressure gas charged shock absorbers, Black instrument panel bezel, premium fender flares, the seven-speaker option (including seven speakers: center console-mounted sub woofer, two midrange speakers and two tweeters in the instrument panel and two full-range speakers mounted in overhead speaker pods), and Rocky Mountain Edition decal.

Equipped with a manual transmission, the MSRP was $23,025, with the automatic transmission it was $23,850.

When it announced the limited production Rocky Mountain Wrangler, along with versions based on the Grand Cherokee and Liberty Jeeps, on March 7, 2005, the Chrysler Group said it was "kicking winter to the curb".

"One of the things that makes Jeep vehicle owners unique," added Jeff Bell, "is their desire to stand out from the crowd, whether on road or off road. The Jeep Rocky Mountain editions give consumers three unique ways to declare their independence from less capable SUVs."

Dan Tardella, Jeep Marketing Senior Manager, who was responsible for an electronic newsletter promoting the Rocky Mountain Editions sent to 240,000 Jeep owners and prospective buyers, added that "we have a loyal group of owners who are typically interested in a new look."

Just over a week later, on March 14, 2005, DaimlerChrysler announced that Jeep, Paramount Pictures and Bristol Bay Productions would participate in an extensive marketing and publicity campaign built around the release of *Sahara*, an adventure film starring Matthew McConaughey as Dirk Pitt. This was the Jeep brand's second foray into the world of embedded content and branded entertainment in a feature film, and like the earlier *Tomb Raider* film, *Sahara* provided Jeep enthusiasts with plenty of scenes showing their favorite vehicle successfully completing daring maneuvers in extremely challenging circumstances.

In *Sahara*, master explorer and adventurer Dirk Pitt relied upon his Wrangler Unlimited to venture into some of the most dangerous regions of the world. Crossing

Another 2005 non-North-American market Wrangler. In many European countries there were active Jeep clubs operated by Jeep owners. DaimlerChrysler nurtured their growth by offering Jeep enthusiasts a wide variety of outdoor, adventure and lifestyle products through Jeep licensed suppliers. (DaimlerChrysler Media Services)

unforgiving sand dunes, dry riverbeds and treacherous borders, in search of what locals called the 'Ship of Death', a long lost Civil War battleship that protected a secret cargo, Dirk tracked down the answer to a 150-year-old mystery by going where only a Jeep could take him.

Clearly enjoying the Wrangler's second 'starring role' in an action-adventure motion picture, Jeff Bell said, "Jeep 4x4s are a natural fit for a bigger-than-life action-adventure. *Sahara* is no exception – the brutal terrain of the world's largest desert is perfect for highlighting the capability, versatility and spirit of the Jeep Wrangler Unlimited."

The Wranglers also participated in a real life 'Only in a Jeep' adventure. Film director Breck Eisner recalled: "While filming in the Tinghrasse Valley in Western Sahara, we were hit by a freak rainstorm. A dry river bed that that hadn't seen water in years suddenly began filling up, threatening to cut off the 200 people in our crew. With the water getting deeper fast, we knew we had to evacuate everyone over the river to safety. We first tried fording the waters with our rented 4x4s, but they couldn't make the crossing. We realized that only the Jeep Wranglers, which were standing by to be featured on camera in the movie, had enough clearance to cross the rushing water and get people to safety on the opposite bank. In a series of river crossings using the 'picture' Jeep vehicles, the entire crew was ferried to safety. The fact that everyone got back to base unharmed that evening was thanks to the Jeep vehicles."

The Wrangler's performance validated the water-fording aspect of of its Trail Rated badge that reportedly originated with a Nevada Auto Test Center test that required splashing through water that was 19 inches deep at five mile per hours. Footage of this rescue was available on www.jeep.com.

As part of the alliance between Jeep and Paramount Pictures, one thousand Limited Edition Wrangler Unlimited Sahara models were produced. Based on the Jeep Unlimited Rubicon, the Limited Edition Sahara featured unique exterior and interior cues, including a chrome grille, accent-colored fender flares, 30in Moab wheels with accent colors, exterior Sahara badges, and premium two tone seats. The Sahara was also fitted with tail lamp guards, a unique khaki-colored spare tire cover and a serialized interior badge. The base MSRP for the Unlimited Sahara was $30,375.

The production of the Rubicon Unlimited made it convenient to separate the 2005 line-up into the short-wheelbase SE, X, Sport and Rubicons, and the long-wheelbase Unlimited and Rubicon Unlimited models.

The feature availability for the short-wheel models was as follows:

A – available *NA – not available* *P – package* *S – standard* **Feature**	**SE**	**X**	**Sport**	**Rubicon**
Exterior				
Body side steps (Black):	NA	NA	A	NA
Front and rear bumpers with end caps and front bumper guards (Black):	S	S	S	S
Full steel doors with roll-up windows:	A	A	S	S
Fender flares[1]				
Medium Gray or Dark Khaki:	S	S	S	NA
Neutral Gray Metallic:	NA	NA	NA	S
Fog lamps:	NA	NA	S	S
Locking fuel cap:	A	A	A	A
Tinted windshield:	S	S	S	S

Deep tinted sunscreen rear quarter and back light windows (paired with hard top):	NA	A	S	S
Rear quarter and lift gate windows:	S	S	NA	NA
Body color grille:	S	S	S	S
Diamond plate sill guards:	NA	NA	NA	S
Black vinyl spare tire cover[2]:	NA	NA	A	NA
Top colors				
(Medium Gray or Dark Khaki)[3]:	A	A	A	A
Soft top with soft windows:	S	S	S	S
Hard top with full steel doors, roll-up windows, rear window wiper, washer and defroster:	NA	A	A	A
Interior				
Add-A-Trunk:	NA	NA	A	A
Passenger assist handle;	S	S	S	S
Power outlet (12-volt, auxiliary):	S	S	S	S
Color-keyed carpet (front floor, rear footwell and cargo floor):	S	S	S	S
Cargo tie down loops[4]:	S	S	S	S
Air conditioning:	A	A	S	S
Heater with instrument panel ventilation:	S	S	NA	NA
Mini floor console with dual cup holders:	S	NA	NA	NA
Full-length console with four cup holders:	NA	S	S	S
Color-keyed door trim panels with map pockets and pull handles:	S	S	S	S
Color-keyed front carpeted floor mats:	A	A	A	A
Locking glove compartment:	S	S	S	S
Electrochromatic rearview mirror with reading lamps, compass and temperature display:	NA	NA	P	P4
Radios:				
AM/FM stereo with CD:	S	S	S	S
Four speakers:	S	S	NA	NA
Seven speakers and sub woofer in console:	NA	P5	S	S
Six-disc, in-dash CD changer:	NA	P[5]	A	A

Seat Fabrics				
Vinyl	S	NA	NA	NA
Cloth:	A	S	S	S
Front seats:				
High-back reclining buckets:	S	S	S	S
Driver and passenger tip-and-slide:	S	S	S	S
Rear seats:				
Fold-and-tumble bench:	S	S	S	S
Speed control (with leather-wrapped steering wheel:	NA	A	A	A
Full sport bar padding:	S	S	S	S
Low-pivot tilt steering column:	S	S	S	S
Steering wheels:				
Soft-feel, four-spoke:	S	S	NA	NA
Leather-wrapped, four spoke (with speed control):	NA	P	P	A
Power train and Chassis				
2.4.0-liter Power Tech engine/6-speed manual transmission:	S	NA	NA	NA
4.0-liter Power Tech/6-speed manual transmission:	NA	S	S	S
4.0-liter Power Tech/4-speed automatic transmission:	A	A	A	A
Power front disc and rear drum brakes:	S	S	S	NA
Four-wheel disc brakes (included with Brake and Traction Group):	NA	NA	P	S
Four-wheel anti-lock brakes:	NA	NA	P	S
Trac-Lok differential:	NA	A	P	NA
Tru-Lok differential:	NA	NA	NA	S
Engine block heater:	A	A	A	A
Dana 30 front axle:	S	S	S	NA
Dana 44-3 heavy duty front axle:	NA	NA	NA	S
Dana 35 rear axle:	S	S	S	NA
Dana 44 heavy-duty rear axle (packaged with 30in tires):	NA	NA	P	S
3.73 axle ratio (with automatic transmission):	S	A/ P	A/ P	NA
4.11 axle ratio:	NA	NA	NA	S
Fuel tank and transfer case skid plates:	S	S	S	S
Power steering:	S	S	S	S

Gas-charged shock absorbers:	S	S	S	NA
Digressive shock absorbers (included in 30in Tire and Wheel Group):	NA	NA	P	S
Full-size spare and matching wheel:	S	S	S	S
Tires[6]				
P215/75R15 Goodyear Wrangler RT/S raised black letter AT:	S	S	NA	NA
P225/75R15 Goodyear Wrangler GS-A OWL AT:	NA	A/ P	S	NA
30 x 9.5 R15 LT Goodyear Wrangler OWL AT (packaged with Dana 44 rear axle):	NA	NA	P	NA
LT245/75R16 MTR Goodyear BSW mounted on off-road tires:	NA	NA	NA	S
Tow hooks (two front, one rear):	A	A	S	S
Command-Trac part-time 4WD:	S	S	S	NA
Rock-Trac heavy-duty, part-time 4WD:	NA	NA	NA	S
Full-face steel 15 x 7in wheels:	S	S	S	NA
Ravine 15 x 8in aluminum wheels:	NA	NA	P	NA
Moab 16 x 8in cast-aluminum wheels	NA	NA	NA	S
Next generation front air bags and knee blockers:	S	S	S	S
Child seat tether anchorages:	S	S	S	S
Child Seat Anchor System (LATCH):	S	S	S	S
Front and rear seat belts:	S	S	S	S
Sentry Key theft-deterrent system:	NA	NA	P	P
Equipment Groups				
Brake and Traction Group (four-wheel disc brakes, and Trac-Lok)[7]:	NA	NA	A	S
Convenience Group:	NA	S	S	S
Security Group:	NA	NA	A	A
Smoker's Group (removable ashtray and cigar lighter)	A	A	A	A
Dual Top Group:	NA	NA	A	A
Tire and Wheel Group[8]:	NA	NA	A	NA

Premium Audio Group:	NA	A	NA	NA

[1]The Rubicon's Neutral Gray was new for 2005. The Medium Gray for the SE, X and Sport replaced Black.
[2]Not available with 30in Wheel and Tire Group
[3] Medium Gray replaced Black as a color for the Wrangler's top and fender flares
[4]This Security Group option also contained a Sentry Key. anti-theft system
[5]Premium Audio Group

The Wrangler Unlimited models for 2005 were offered with these items:

A – available *NA – not available* *P – package* *S – standard* **Feature**	Unlimited Base	Unlimited Premium	Rubicon Unlimited
Exterior			
Body side steps (Black):	A	A	NA
Front and rear bumpers with end caps and front bumper guards (Black):	S	S	S
Full steel doors with roll-up windows:	S	S	S
Fender flares			
Medium Gray or Dark Khaki:	S	NA	NA
Body color:	NA	S	NA
Neutral Gray Metallic:	NA	NA	S
Fog lamps:	S	S	S
Locking fuel cap:	A	A	A
Tinted windshield:	S	S	S
Deep tinted sunscreen rear quarter and back light windows	S	S	S
Grille			
Body color:	S	NA	S
Bright:	NA	S	NA
Headlamp bezels (chrome-plated):	S	S	S
Diamond plate sill guards:	NA	NA	S
Top Colors			
Medium Gray:	A	A	A

Dark Khaki:	A	NA	A
Tops			
Sunrider soft top with sunroof:	S	S	S
Hard top with full steel doors, roll-up windows, rear window wiper, washer and defroster:	A	A	A
Interior			
Passenger assist handle:	S	S	S
Power outlet (12-volt, auxiliary):	S	S	S
Carpeting (color-keyed)			
Front floor:	S	S	S
Rear footwell, rear wheelhouse and cargo floor:	S	S	S
Cargo tie down loops (4):	S	S	S
Air conditioning:	S	S	S
Full-length console with four cup holders:	S	S	S
Electric rear window defroster (hard top only):	P	P	P
Molded color-keyed door trim panels with map pockets and pull handles:	S	S	S
Color-keyed front carpeted floor mats:	A	P	A
Locking glove compartment:	S	S	S
Instrument panel bezel with Silver paint treatment:	NA	S	NA
Electrochromatic rearview mirror with reading lamps, compass and temperature display:	P	S	P
Radios			
AM/FM stereo with CD:	S	S	S
Seven speakers and amplified sub woofer in console:	P	S	S
Six-disc, in-dash CD changer	A	A	A
Seat Fabrics			
Cloth:	S	NA	S
Premium Cloth:	NA	S	NA
Front seats:			
High-back reclining buckets:	S	S	S
Driver and passenger tip-and slide:	S	S	S

Rear seats:			
Fold-and-tumble bench:	S	S	S
Speed control (with leather-wrapped steering wheel):	A	P	A
Full sport bar padding:	S	S	S
Low-pivot tilt steering column:	S	S	S
Steering wheels			
Leather-wrapped, four-spoke (with speed control):	P	P	P
Power train and Chassis			
4.0-liter Power Tech/6-speed manual transmission:	S	S	S
4.0-liter Power Tech/4-speed automatic transmission:	A	A	A
Four-wheel disc brakes :	S	S	S
Trac-Lok differential:	S	S	NA
Tru-Lok differential:	NA	NA	S
Engine block heater:	A	A	A
3.73 axle ratio:	S	S	NA
4.11 axle ratio:	NA	NA	S
Dana 30 front axle:	S	S	NA
Dana 44-3 heavy duty front axle:	NA	NA	S
Dana 35 rear axle:	S	S	S
Dana 44 heavy-duty rear axle:	S	S	S
Fuel tank and transfer case skid plates:	S	S	S
Power steering:	S	S	S
Digressive valve gas-charged shock absorbers :	S	S	S
Full-size spare and matching wheel:	S	S	S
Tires			
30 x 9.5 R15 LT Goodyear Wrangler OWL AT:	S	S	NA
LT245/75R16 MTR Goodyear BSW mounted on off-road tires:	NA	NA	S
(Other tire sizes and brands may have been used)			
Tow hooks (two front, one rear):	S	S	S
Command-Trac part-time 4WD:	S	S	NA
Rock-Trac heavy-duty part-time 4WD:	NA	NA	S

Ravine 15 x 8in aluminum wheels:	S	S	NA
Moab 16 x 8in cast-aluminum wheels	NA	NA	S
Next generation front air bags and knee blockers:	S	S	S
Child seat tether anchorages:	S	S	S
Child Seat Anchor System (LATCH):	S	S	S
Front and rear seat belts:	S	S	S
Sentry Key theft-deterrent system:	P	S	P
Equipment Groups			
Convenience Group:	S	S	S
Security Group:	A	P	A
Smoker's Group	A	A	A
Premium Audio Group:	A	NA	NA

With Impact Orange replacing Solar Yellow, and Shale Green giving way to Deep Beryl Green Pearlcoat, the exterior color consisted of those two new colors plus the following carried-over from 2004: Flame Red, Electric Lime Green Pearlcoat, Bright Silver Metallic, Stone White, Patriot Blue Pearlcoat, Khaki Metallic and Black. All of these colors were available for the Wrangler SE, X, Sport and Rubicon models.

The color selection for the Unlimited models was more restricted:

A – available *NA – not available* **Model**	**Unlimited Base**	**Unlimited Premium**	**Rubicon Unlimited**
Color			
Flame Red:	A	NA	A
Electric Lime Green Pearlcoat:	A	NA	A
Impact Orange:	A	NA	A
Light Khaki Pearlcoat:	A	NA	A
Stone White:	A	NA	A
Patriot Blue Pearlcoat:	A	A	A
Deep Beryl Green Pearlcoat:	A	A	A
Bright Silver Metallic:	A	A	A
Black:	A	A	A

Prices of the Wranglers for 2005 and those of their options were as follows:

Model	**MSRP**
Wrangler SE:	$18,070
Wrangler X:	$20,380
Wrangler Sport:	$23,240
Wrangler Rubicon:	$27,465
Wrangler Unlimited:	$23,995
Wrangler Rubicon Unlimited:	$28,465
*add $610 for destination.	
Option	**Price**
Automatic transmission:	$825
Air conditioning:	$895
Dual Top Group:	$1435
Hard top:	
Sport, Rubicon, Unlimited:	$795[a]
X:	$1160[b]
Metal full-size doors with roll-up windows:	$125
Deep Tint Sunscreen windows:	$240
30-inch Canyon Tire and Wheel Group:	$670
Rocky Mountain Edition Group:	$2319
Four-wheel anti-lock brakes:	$600
Brake and Traction Group:	$435
Dana 44/226MM rear axle with 3.73 ratio:	$310
AM/FM radio and six-disc CD:	$300
Premium Audio Group:	$300[c]
Premium Audio Group:	$595[d]
Seven speakers including sub woofer and tweeters:	$295
Leather wrapped steering wheel:	$300[e]
Cloth high-back bucket seats:	$110

Security Group:	$295
Trac-Lok limited slip differential:	$285
Tow hooks:	$60
CMA Charge 1:	$205
Body side steps:	$150
CMA Charge 2:	$125
Add-A-Trunk lockable storage:	$125
Hawaii Destination Charge:	$50
Vinyl spare tire cover:	$50
Engine block heater:	$35
Front floor mats:	$30
Smoker's Group:	$30
Fuel-filler cap:	$15
Tires:	
P225/75R15 OWL Wrangler AT:	$310

[a]Includes hard top, rear window wiper/washer and rear window defroster
[b]Includes hard top, metal full-size doors with roll-up windows, light tinted front windows, dark tinted rear quarter windows, tinted tailgate window, rear window wiper/washer and rear window defroster
[c]Included AM/FM stereo, six-disc CD player and seven speakers including a sub woofer.
[d]Required ordering of the Rocky Mountain Edition Group. Included AM/FM stereo, six-disc CD player and the seven-speaker option consisting of seven speakers, (center console mounted sub woofer, two midrange speakers and two tweeters in instrument panel and two full-range speakers mounted in overhead speaker pods).
[e]Included leather wrapped steering wheel and speed control.

On March 1, 2005, at the 75th Geneva Motor Show, DaimlerChrysler announced "just in time for spring in Europe", the latest Wrangler Extreme Sport special series. It differed from the 2004 version by having Metallic Graphite painted wheels and Black wheel flares. The exterior color selection was reduced to four choices: Bright Silver Metallic, Flame Red, Patriot Red or Black.

Earlier, on January 5, 2005, a limited edition Wrangler Renegade model had been announced for sale in Australia. Its features included cruise control, Ecco-style alloy wheels, the dual top option, automatic dimming rearview mirror with courtesy lamps, overhead compass and temperature gauge, leather-wrapped steering wheel, side steps and Renegade badging. A choice of four exterior colors was offered: Black, Bright Silver, Light Khaki and Patriot Blue. A limited run of 300 Wrangler Renegades was available.

Following the Wrangler Renegade was the Renegade Extreme Sport model, introduced on May 17, 2005. Only

The 2006 Wrangler Rubicon was regarded by DaimlerChrysler as being "the ultimate Jeep for extreme off-roading". (DaimlerChrysler Media Services)

226 were available and, like the Renegade, each example had cruise control, Ecco-style alloy wheels, dual tops, auto dimming rearview mirror with lamps, overhead compass and temperature gauges, and leather-wrapped steering wheel. Also specified for the Extreme Sport were two tone cloth seats with embroidered Jeep logo, seven speakers with sub woofer and 'Extreme Sport' badging. Four exterior colors were offered: Patriot Blue, Bright Silver Metallic, Black and Flame Red.

The Australian market was one of the most rapidly expanding export markets for the Wrangler. For example, in November 2003, Chrysler Jeep Australia reported that sales of the Wrangler for the first eleven months of 2003 totaled 813 units, a thirty-five per cent increase from the respective 2002 figure. By mid-May. 2005, the sale of 578 Wranglers represented a rise of 72 per cent over the same 2004 period. Included in this total was the delivery of over one hundred Wranglers in each of the year's first four months (January – 141, February – 171, March – 154, April – 112).

Chrysler Jeep Australia credited this sales pace to the US free-trade agreement price repositioning and the popularity of specialized limited edition Wrangler models, such as the Wrangler Renegade and the Renegade Extreme Sport.

Citing the Wrangler's growing popularity, Chrysler Jeep Australia Managing Director, Gerry Jenkins, said: "Following last year's Wrangler success, we have taken an ambitious approach and gone to great lengths to secure extra stock and extend our factory target to strive for outright yearly record sales and put us ahead of even the first full year of sales results.

A 2006 Wrangler Unlimited. Its standard equipment included a 4.0-liter engine, 6-speed manual transmission, 4-wheel disc brakes, Sunrider soft top with sun roof feature and 30in tires mounted on 15in aluminum wheels. (DaimlerChrysler Media Services)

"With the affinity the Australian public has with the vehicle, especially the specialized Wranglers like Renegade Extreme Sport, we are confident it can be achieved.

"Jeep Wrangler Renegade Extreme Sport, with its additional features, offers something even more individual and unique. And with more than $4000 of extra value for only $2000 more, it represents outstanding value."

The prices of the 2005 Wranglers for Australia were as follows:

Model	Price (Aus $)
Wrangler Sport 4.0-liter (6-speed manual):	$29,990
Wrangler Sport 4.0-liter (4-speed automatic):	$31,990
Wrangler Renegade (6-speed manual):	$31,990
Wrangler Renegade (4-speed automatic):	$33,990
Wrangler Renegade Extreme Sport (6-speed manual):	$31,990
Wrangler Renegade Extreme Sport (4-speed automatic):	$33,990

For the 2006 model year, the Wrangler was offered in a Golden Eagle Edition. This Jeep's lineage dated back to the 1970s and 1980s when Golden Eagle CJ-5s and CJ-7s were popular with Jeep owners. Features of the 2006 version included Golden Eagle logo and script identification on the hood, fenders and spare tire covers, a Dana 44 heavy-duty rear axle, gold 15in Ravine aluminum wheels, 30in tires, two tone premium seats and a painted center stack bevel.

Replacing Electric Lime Green as an exterior paint color for the Wrangler was Solar Yellow. Similarly, Patriot Blue was replaced by Midnight Blue.